Post-Process Theory

DISCARDED

DISCARDED

PE
1404
P615
1999

Post-Process Theory

Beyond the Writing-Process Paradigm

Edited by Thomas Kent

Southern Illinois University Press

Carbondale and Edwardsville

UNIVERSITY OF WINNIPEG, 515 Portage Ave., Winnipeg, MB. R3B 2E9 Canada

Copyright © 1999 by the Board of Trustees,
Southern Illinois University
All rights reserved
Printed in the United States of America
02 01 00 99   4 3 2 1

"Dedication" from *In Search of Our Mothers' Gardens:
Womanist Prose* copyright © 1983 by Alice Walker. Reprinted
by permission of Harcourt Brace & Company and David
Higham Associates.

Library of Congress Cataloging-in-Publication Data
    Post-process theory : beyond the writing-process
paradigm / edited by Thomas Kent.
        p.   cm.
    Includes bibliographical references and index.
    1. English language—Rhetoric—Study and teaching—
Theory, etc. 2. Report writing—Study and teaching—
Theory, etc. I. Kent, Thomas, 1947– .
    PE1404.P615 1999
    808'.001—dc21
    ISBN 0-8093-2243-9 (alk. paper)   98-44170
    ISBN 0-8093-2244-7 (pbk. : alk. paper)   CIP

The paper used in this publication meets the minimum
requirements of American National Standard for Information Sciences—Permanence of Paper for Printed Library
Materials, ANSI Z39.48-1984. ∞

Contents

Acknowledgments

I would like to thank two editors at Southern Illinois University Press, Carol Burns, who guided this project through the stages of its development, and Tracey J. Sobol, who encouraged me to undertake this project. I would like also to acknowledge Camille Hale for her fine copyediting and the secretarial support provided by Iowa State University.

Introduction

I suspect that the readers of this volume already know the central tenets of the writing-process movement about as well as they know the letters of the English alphabet. In our training as composition teachers, most of us cut our teeth on the claims that writing constitutes a process of some sort and that this process is generalizable, at least to the extent that we know when someone is being "recursive" or to the extent that we know when to intervene in someone's writing process or to the extent that we know the process that experienced or "expert" writers employ as they write. However, the central assumptions that inform what has come to be called "post-process" theory may not be so well understood. Breaking with the still-dominant process tradition in composition studies, post-process theory—or at least the different incarnations of post-process theory discussed by many of the authors represented in this collection— endorses the fundamental idea that no codifiable or *generalizable* writing process exists or could exist. Post-process theorists hold—for all sorts of different reasons—that writing is a practice that cannot be captured by a generalized process or a Big Theory. Yet if writing is not a generalizable process, what do post-process theorists think it is?

Most post-process theorists hold three assumptions about the act of writing: (1) writing is public; (2) writing is interpretive; and (3) writing is situated. The first assumption makes the commonsensical claim that writing constitutes a public interchange. By "public," post-process theorists generally mean that the writing act, as a kind of communicative interaction, automatically includes other language users, as well as the writer. If writing is a public act—if what we write must be accessible to others—then the possibility for a "private" writing evaporates. We are never alone; we write always in a relation with others. In fact, some post-process theorists expand this claim and argue, in a Davidsonian fashion, that we could not write at all if it were not for other language users and a world we share with others. So when post-process theorists claim that writing is a public act, they mean that writing constitutes a specific communicative interaction occurring among individuals at specific historical moments and in specific relations with others and with the world and that because these moments and relations change, no process can capture what writers do during these changing moments and within these changing relations.

Of course, no one would deny that lots of codifiable shortcuts exist—our knowledge of conventions, our ability to manipulate genres, our facility with words—that help us communicate more efficiently during the act of writing. However, knowing these shortcuts does not mean that we hold a Big Theory, nor does it mean that we know a repeatable process that can be employed successfully during every writing situation. To say that we all know shortcuts or that some of us know more shortcuts than others means only that we cannot start from nowhere when we write; everyone starts writing from somewhere, and depending on our communicative situations, we may have more or fewer shortcuts at our disposal. However, an important question remains about what writers actually do during these passing communicative moments and within these shifting relations that characterize the writing act, and the response to this question foregrounds the second claim made by many post-process theorists: writing is a thoroughly interpretative act.

By "interpretive act," post-process theorists in general mean something rather broad, something like "making sense of" and not just exclusively the ability to move from one code to another. To interpret something means more than only to "translate" or to "paraphrase"; to interpret means to enter into a relation of understanding with other language users. So, understood in this way, interpretation enters into both the reception and the production of discourse. When we read, we interpret specific texts or utterances; when we write, we interpret our readers, our situations, our and other people's motivations, the appropriate genres to employ in specific circumstances, and so forth. Therefore, both when we write and when we read, we must possess the ability to enter into this relation of understanding with other language users.

For most post-process theorists, interpretation or this act of making sense of the world never ceases; it goes all the way down. Interpretation does not end someplace or carry us to some specific destination that provides us with a god's-eye view of the world.

Interpretation constitutes the uncodifiable moves we make when we attempt to align our utterances with the utterances of others, and these moves—I have called them "hermeneutic guesswork" (see *Paralogic Rhetoric* 47–48)—do not constitute a process in any useful sense of the concept, except perhaps in retrospect. By "in retrospect," I only mean that when we look back on a communicative situation, we can always map out what we did. We can always distinguish some sort of process that we employed. However, if we try to employ this process again, we can never be sure that it will work the way we want it to work. Of course, we will be better guessers the next time we write something in a similar situation; we will know what went wrong or right, and we will know the process we employed to produce a successful written artifact. Nevertheless, as we all know, even with this knowledge and experience, we still may miscommunicate; we may make wrong guesses about the rhetorical exigence, or we may misunderstand our readers, or we may simply be unlucky and our readers may misunderstand us, or a thousand and one other things might occur that could make our written communications fail. Finally, the point here is a fairly simple one: writing requires interpretation, and interpretation cannot be reduced to a process. When we say that interpretation cannot be reduced to a process or that it goes all the way down, we also must admit that interpretation does not take place in a vacuum, which brings me to the third claim shared by practically all post-process theorists and many process theorists as well: communication—and, therefore, writing—cannot begin nowhere.

Because writing is a public act that requires interpretative interaction with others, writers always write from some position or some place; writers are never nowhere. Again, this claim is a commonplace idea nowadays; no one denies that writers are "situated"—that writers must have something to communicate in order to communicate—and this idea is accepted by process theorists just as much as by post-process theorists. However, most post-process theorists represented in this book want to make more out of this claim; they want to ride it a bit harder than do most process theorists. For example, some post-process theorists suggest that writing as a communicative act is possible only because we hold a cohesive set of beliefs about what other language users know and about how our beliefs cohere with theirs. In other words, we all require beliefs that help us start to "guess" about how others will understand, accept, integrate, and react to our utterances. Following Donald Davidson, let us call these beliefs a "prior" theory—a cohesive set of beliefs from which we start in order to communicate with others.

Yet, with just a little closer inspection, we can see that no two people ever hold precisely the same prior theories. So what really matters is how people employ their prior theories in action, what Davidson calls, in another context, a "passing theory" (see "Nice Derangement"). The passing theory is what we actually use to communicate; it is the guess we actually make. In a sense, then, the prior theory does not really matter. All a prior theory amounts to is the background knowledge with which we begin in order to create passing theories. Our prior theories do not need to match the prior theories of other people; that is, we do not need to come from the same communities, nor do we need to believe the same things about the world or even speak the same language in order to communicate. However, there is no doubt that coming from the same community will help us communicate more efficiently and effectively. For example, most of the people reading this book will know more or less automatically what is meant by the term "writing process," and such shared background knowledge serves as an incredibly helpful communicative shortcut, but, finally, we do not require such shortcuts. Even if readers of this book know nothing about something called the "writing process," they could be brought around, given enough time, to a good enough understanding of the concept so that they could comprehend the essays in this volume.

Of course, this claim is just another way of saying that people cannot communicate from nowhere; in order to communicate, you must be somewhere, and being somewhere—being positioned in relation to other language users—means that you always come with baggage, with beliefs, desires, hopes, and fears about the world. What matters is how we employ these beliefs, desires, hopes, and fears to formulate passing theories in our attempts to interpret one another's utterances and to make sense of the world. And, first, as the term "passing" suggests, a passing theory goes by us; it never "stops" so that we can capture some sort of unitary, complete, or determinate meaning. Second, a passing theory "passes" away; it never endures, never works twice in quite the same way. Most important, generating passing theories— using our prior theories, our situatedness, to create utterances—can never be reduced to a predictable process. When we write, we elaborate passing theories during our acts of writing that represent our best guesses about how other people will understand what we are trying to convey, and this best guess, in turn, will be met by our readers' passing theories that may or may not coincide with ours. This give and take, this hermeneutic dance that moves to the music of our situatedness, cannot be fully choreographed in any meaningful way, for in this dance, our ability to improvise, to react on the spot to our partners, matters most. By way of summarizing, then, post-process theorists hold that the writing act is public, thoroughly hermeneutic, and always situated and therefore cannot be reduced to a generalizable process.

In this very general discussion of post-process theory, I have intentionally employed qualifiers such as *many, most,* or *some* when I refer to post-process theorists as a group, for some of the authors in this book understand and represent post-process theory somewhat differently than the way I frame the notion. Although the authors appearing in these pages may disagree about the nature of the "post" in "post-process" theory, all of them agree that change is in the air. They see the process tradition giving way to something new, perhaps not a new coherent "tradition" in the modernist sense of the term but certainly a new way of talking about writing and about what writers do. In their attempts to work through the different dimensions of post-process theory, the authors of the following essays address questions such as What is post-process theory? How does post-process theory break with the process movement? What are the pedagogical ramifications of post-process theory? and How might post-process theory help us reform both our writing practices and our critical practices?

Consequently, the essays in this volume have been arranged to correspond roughly to these questions. In the first four essays, Gary A. Olson, George Pullman, Barbara Couture, and Joseph Petraglia address issues dealing with the nature and history of post-process theory; in the next three essays, Nancy Blyler, David Russell, and Debra Journet investigate the impact of post-process theory on specific kinds of writing; in the next three essays, Helen Ewald, Sidney I. Dobrin, and David Foster discuss some of the pedagogical implications of post-process theory; and in the concluding three essays, Nancy C. DeJoy, John Clifford and Elizabeth Ervin, and John Schilb discuss some of the possibilities for institutional and critical reform broached by post-process theory. Although the fourteen authors represented in this book certainly do not toe a party line regarding post-process theory—and right-fully so—they nonetheless display a fresh and enthusiastic engagement with crucial issues that have become moribund in a field still domi-nated by a nearly forty-year-old tradition we all know as the process movement. These essays help us to reimagine the act of writing, and, in so doing, they help us to rethink our past and create a new future for composition studies.

1
Toward a Post-Process Composition: Abandoning the Rhetoric of Assertion

Gary A. Olson

The process movement in composition served us well. It emphasized that writing is an "activity," an act that is itself composed of a variety of activities; that the activities involved in the act of writing are typically recursive rather than linear; that writing is first and foremost a social activity; that the act of writing can be a means of learning and discovery; that experienced writers are often intensely aware of audience, purpose, and context; that experienced writers invest considerable amounts of time in invention and revision activities; that effective instruction in composition provides opportunities for students to practice the kinds of activities involved in the act of writing; that such instruction includes ample opportunities to read and comment on the work of peers and to receive the comments of peers about one's own writing; that effective composition instructors grade a student's work not solely on the finished product but also on the efforts the student has invested in the process of crafting the product; and that successful composition instruction entails finding appropriate occasions to intervene in each student's writing process. In these and other ways, the process orientation helped us to theorize writing in more productive ways than previously and to devise pedagogies that familiarize students with the kinds of activities that writers often engage in when they write. As several "post-process" scholars have pointed out recently, however, the process orientation has its own limitations. Key among these limitations is the fact that the process orientation, as we have conceived it, imagines that the writing process can be described in some way; that is, process theorists assume that we can somehow make statements about the process that would apply to all or most writing situations.

When we conceive writing as a "process" that can be codified and then taught, we are engaging in theory building. The post-modern critique of theory as totalizing, essentialist, and a residue of Enlightenment thinking has made clear that any attempt to construct a generalizable explanation of how something works is misguided in that such narratives inevitably deprivilege the local, even though it is precisely the local where useful "knowledge" is generated. As Stephen Toulmin comments, "When people ask about the future role of theory and they're talking about theory with a big *T*, I'm inclined to shake hands with Rorty and say there is probably no legitimate role for theory with a big *T*; we should be prepared to kiss rationalism good-bye and walk off in the opposite direction with joy in our hearts" (216).[1]

The postmodern critique of theory serves as a useful corrective in that it alerts us to the dangers of creating master narratives and then adhering to these explanations as if we have obtained truth. As Toulmin suggests, however, it is important that we not mistake this useful corrective as being equivalent to the more general attack on theory; to do so would be to conflate two very distinct ideological perspectives on theory. This misunderstanding arises from the failure to distinguish between theory building, the attempt to arrive at generalizable explanations of how something works—that is, to arrive at some kind of truth—and the activity of theorizing, the act of engaging in critical, philosophical, hermeneutic speculation about a subject. *Theory*, the noun, is dangerous from a postmodern perspective because it entices us into believing we somehow have captured a truth, grasped the essence of something; *theorizing*, the verb, can be productive (so long as a "theory" is not the objective) because it is a way to explore, challenge, question, reassess, speculate. Theorizing can lead us into lines of inquiry that challenge received notions or entrenched understandings that may no longer be productive; it can create new vocabularies for talking about a subject and thus new ways of perceiving it.[2]

The problem with process theory, then, is not so much that scholars are attempting to theorize various aspects of composing as it is that they are endeavoring (consciously or not) to construct a model of the composing process, thereby constructing a Theory of Writing, a series of generalizations about writing that supposedly hold true all or most of the time. This is what Thomas Kent and other post-process theorists mean when they complain that process scholars—despite whatever other ideological allegiances may inform their work—are attempting to systematize something that simply is not susceptible to systematization. As Kent has demonstrated quite cogently, writing—

indeed all communication—is radically contingent, radically situational. Consequently, efforts to pin down some version of "the writing process" are misguided, unproductive, and misleading.

That the vocabulary of process is no longer useful is not a reason to despair; it is, rather, an invitation to rethink many of our most cherished assumptions about the activity we call "writing." For example, the work of some postmodern theorists can help us challenge some of our process-oriented notions of writing by questioning a time-honored value in composition: what we might call the "rhetoric of assertion." In one way or another, composing (at least the way it is often taught) has always seemed to be associated with asserting something to be true. Students are instructed to write an essay, which has usually meant to take a position on a subject (often stated in a "strong," "clear" thesis statement, which is itself expressed in the form of an assertion), and to construct a piece of discourse that then "supports" the position. Passages in an essay that do not support the position are judged irrelevant, and the essay is evaluated accordingly. And critical-thinking specialists spend considerable time instructing students on how to locate and evaluate assertions in published and student texts and how to handle their own assertions and support in their own texts. The technology of assertion seems ubiquitous in composition studies.

Now, it is true that some compositionists over the years have advocated introducing into the composition class alternative kinds of essays that are less conspicuously thesis driven or argumentative, but even those who recommend that students write "exploratory" essays or purely personal narratives typically expect such essays to make a point or points.[3] In short, despite our attempts to introduce alternative genres, to help students become more dialogic and less monologic, more sophistic and less Aristotelian, more exploratory and less argumentative, more personal and less academic, the Western, rationalist tradition of assertion and support is so entrenched in our epistemology and ways of understanding what "good" writing and "thinking" are that this tradition, along with its concomitant assumptions, defies even our most concerted efforts to subvert it.

The work of numerous theorists from outside of composition, however, suggests that our efforts to subvert such a tradition may well be worth sustaining. The rhetoric of assertion can be critiqued from a variety of standpoints: that it is masculinist, phallogocentric, foundationalist, often essentialist, and, at the very least, limiting. For example, when Sandra Harding and other "feminist standpoint" theorists argue that the rhetoric of science deludes us into conceiving of science as "objective" when really it is far from it, they are talking, at least in part, about the role of the rhetoric of assertion. Modern science, in Harding's view, plays a kind of solipsistic trick: it defines what "objectivity" is and then excludes whatever does not fit its own definition. Because Western science has traditionally been dominated by white, well-educated (that is, middle- or upper-class) males, the values and perspectives of only this small group have dictated the values and perspectives of science—what is worth studying and what not (heart attacks but not breast cancer?), how a subject is to be studied (male research subjects being used to study specifically female maladies?), how the resulting data are interpreted, and so on. As Harding comments, "The problem is that knowledge that has been generated only from the lives of a small portion of the society (and, at that, the most powerful one) is not useful for most people's projects" (209). She posits that it is much better to move toward a "strong objectivity," one that would take into account the standpoints, the social and cultural positionality of those traditionally marginalized by androcentric, Eurocentric science. This sensitivity to multiple standpoints, multiple social and cultural positionings, would afford a "stronger" objectivity in that the very inclusiveness of alternative positionings would enrich rather than impoverish the perspectives on and information about a subject being examined.

What gives masculinist science much of its rhetorical power, its hegemony over other standpoints, is its unquestioned compulsion to assert truth. It is its very assertive power, its closing off of alternative perspectives, its insistence on closure and resolution that makes science appear so unassailable. Standpoint theorists such as Harding prefer to delay answers, postpone closure, avoid assertion, looking instead for more open-ended, dialogic methods of inquiry—a non-assertive rhetoric. Says Harding, "I think it's important not to close questions, if you're thinking of knowledge as a way of closing questions, saying, 'This is knowledge now, so there's no room for further discussion'" (221). Once we believe that all disciplines, including those in the sciences, are in the business of producing narratives—that is, asserting positions in narrative form—it becomes easy to question the traditional notion of objectivity that has distorted our understanding of exactly what science is. The traditional narratives of science—or of any discourse, for that matter—have always been produced from a single standpoint, that of white, typically upper- or middle-class males. Defining this single perspective and the narratives generating from it as "objective" is a political act that silences other voices and perspectives.

Like Sandra Harding, Donna Haraway argues that there are in fact multiple, contesting narratives produced by those who have been excluded from the knowledge-making projects of technoscience: "There are many actors in our world who can and ought to have a say in the design of the apparatus for the production of scientific knowledge" ("Writing" 54). Haraway makes clear that such attempts to retell the stories of technoscience are not cynical efforts to replace the dominant stories with those of women, an effort that would serve only to reinscribe hierarchies and systems of domination. Rather, they are attempts to increase the number and kinds of stories that get told and the actors who tell them. Far from an anything-goes relativism, refusing the technical and the political is an effort to "insist on the story-ladenness of knowledge, the story-ladenness of facts," to subvert the rhetoric of assertion that so saturates our ways of knowing ("Writing" 57).

Haraway takes this emphasis on situatedness and on resistance to closure and assertion further than do most feminist theorists, specifically noting the necessity to reinvent our notions of writing. "Writing," both in its larger postmodern sense and in its more narrow material sense, is central to living in the world and to enacting the numerous freedom projects of resisting systems of domination—whether in the very uses of discourse itself or in the multiple discourse systems that comprise and constitute our social institutions and academic disciplines. Thus, as Haraway says in *Simians, Cyborgs, and Women*, "writing is deadly serious" (175). She characterizes "the injunction to be clear"—an injunction all too frequently articulated in classrooms and academic disciplines and intimately linked to the rhetoric of assertion—as "very strange":

> I have friends for whom the injunction to be clear remains right at the top of their moral, epistemological, and political commitments. It's always struck me that the injunction to be clear is a very strange goal because it assumes a kind of physical transparency, that if you could just clean up your act somehow the materiality of writing would disappear. This is a psychological problem, as opposed to exactly what's interest-

ing about working in that medium. . . . I've become increasingly more certain that this is part of the substance of *our* work collectively in science studies and that it's not some personal indulgence or some inability to "think clearly." ("Writing" 49)

Haraway calls for a conception of writing ("cyborg writing," in her terms) that resists authoritative, assertive, phallogocentric writing practices; that foregrounds the writer's own situatedness in history and in his or her writing practice; and that makes visible the very "apparatus of the production of authority" that all writers tend to submerge in their discourse, an authority deriving in large part from the rhetoric of assertion. This is not to say that writers must reject authority, but that in a truly ethical and postmodern stance they must reveal how authority is implicated in discourse.

In describing her concept of a subversive, cyborg writing, Haraway comments,

> Cyborg writing has inherited the kind of acid consciousness of people like Derrida and others who have made it simply impossible to engage in authoritative writing *as if* the subject who did such a thing weren't implicated in the practice and *as if* the history of writing weren't the history of the differentiation of the world for us with all of the sticky threads to questions of power and to whose way of life is at stake in marking up the world that way rather than some other way. ("Writing" 49)

Haraway's cyborg writing is an attempt to make visible the fact that writing is always already ideological, always already political—always saturated with questions of power and domination. Thus, authority and the social positions from which one is entitled to assert it are centrally important. She writes,

> Many of the myths and narratives are not available to you from what I would call "cyborg positions." You have to take your implication in a fraught world as the starting point. I don't think that's true for authoritative writing practices that try very hard to produce the kind of masterful "I," a particular kind of authority position that makes the viewer forget the apparatus of the production of that authority. I think cyborg writing is resolutely committed to foregrounding the apparatus of the production of its own authority, even while it's doing it. It's not eschewing authority, but it's insisting on a kind of double move, a foregrounding of the apparatus of the production of bodies, powers, meanings. ("Writing" 50)

Haraway's concept of a situated, multiplicitous, nonassertive writing practice is similar to that of Jean-François Lyotard, who sees writing (in the expanded contemporary sense of the term) as central to postmodern "openness" and resistance to certainty. For Lyotard, true writing is the attempt to "resist the network of exchanges in which cultural objects are commodities," to resist "the simple and naive exchangeability of things in our world" ("Resisting" 173). His conception of writing is in contradistinction to the traditional notion of writing as an activity whose objective is to "master" a subject, to possess it, to pin it down through a discourse of assertion. It is precisely this phallocratic preoccupation with mastery, says Lyotard, that has impelled philosophy as a mode of discourse into its present state of "extreme crisis." The compulsion to master by erecting huge systems of answers, the "search for a constituting order that gives meaning to the world," makes the philosopher "a secret accomplice of the phallocrat" ("One Thing" 118).

In *Peregrinations,* Lyotard says that the idea that writing "pretends to be complete," that it presumes to "build a system of total knowledge" about something, "constitutes *par excellence* the sin, the arrogance of the mind" (6–7). Typical discourse, especially academic discourse, entails what Lacan called "the discourse of the master," and Lyotard refuses to set himself up as a master, preferring instead to be a "perpetual student." Instead, he claims, what is needed in philosophy, in the sciences, in life is "perpetual displacement of questions" so that "answering is never achieved" ("Resisting" 185). Since questions always already carry within them their own answers, are always "interested," it is the act itself of questioning, of remaining open, that is most useful to Lyotard. An "answer," then, is only interesting insofar as it is a new question, not in that it allows someone to assert a solution and thereby close off inquiry. What is needed, he suggests, is to move away from a discourse of mastery and abstract cognition toward a way of being that recognizes affect, the body, and openness—a posture he defines as "feminine." In fact, Lyotard perceives a strong relationship between this nonassertive writing and "femininity," in that he perceives femininity as associated with an openness to something unknown without any compulsion to master it or to assert a position on it. For Lyotard, the opposite of a discourse of mastery is "passivity," the ability to *wait* patiently, not for answers or solutions, but simply to wait—to remain in a state of perpetual receptiveness. This very "refusal of the temptation to grasp, to master," is "real femininity" ("Resisting" 184). His redefinition of writing, whether or not we agree that it is "feminine," seems a sensible stance in the postmodern world, a stance that we may well want to carry into the post-process composition class.

In fact, Lyotard challenges the very notion of composition as it is generally conceived, suggesting, as does Haraway, that we reinvent writing:

> In composition there is a sort of mastering, of putting things together so as to order them. It seems to me that the opposite is the ability to be weak, a good weakness, so-called passivity. I don't mind this term, though I tried to propose the term *passibility*. In this certain representation we can have the way of thinking in Zen Buddhism or certain Eastern philosophies or religions: the ability to wait for, not to look at, but to wait for—for what, precisely, we don't know. That's my ideological representation of the necessary attitude for writing. . . . It's an event not to know. It's good; there's no prejudice. ("Resisting" 183–84)

Thus, the work of Lyotard, Haraway, Harding, and many other theorists suggests that it is incumbent upon us all—especially, it would seem, those of us in rhetoric and composition—to challenge received notions of writing, of composition itself, to move away from a discourse of mastery and assertion toward a more dialogic, dynamic, open-ended, receptive, nonassertive stance. Of course, none of these theorists has "proven" anything about writing, none has provided an unassailable truth, and none has posited a "theory" of writing in the strict sense of a generalizable, universally applicable explanation; what they *have* done, however, is to speculate productively about how writing is deeply implicated in structures of power and domination, how writing can never be disconnected from ideology, how writing as traditionally conceived is driven by a discourse of mastery and a rhetoric of assertion.

Critiques of the discourse of mastery, the rhetoric of assertion, arise from numerous sites, not just the few mentioned here. The theorists who propose them often have divergent, even opposing agendas and would not agree with one another on a multitude of points; however, the fact that they all in one way or another are theorizing about writing in similar ways and are proposing a rethinking or reinventing of writing suggests that collectively they may have something significant to contribute to our own understandings, our own speculations. Such theorizing can have a profound effect on composition as a field, especially as we continue to grapple with questions of disciplinary identity. And, of course, if such speculations truly make sense, if they help us conceive of writing in new and potentially more useful and productive ways, then it is also incumbent upon us to adjust our pedagogies accordingly so as not to reinscribe naive or less useful conceptions of what it means to "compose." Thus, such work can potentially have significant implications not only for our own scholarly understandings of the workings of discourse but also for how we enact those understandings in the post-process classroom. And, undoubtedly, such theorizing is likely to be much more useful than process-oriented efforts to "master" the writing process, to define it, to systematize it.

Notes

An earlier version of this chapter with a very different focus appeared as "Theory and the Rhetoric of Assertion," *Composition Forum* 6 (1995): 53–61.

1. This is not to suggest that Toulmin should be considered a postmodernist. In fact, he half jokingly has referred to himself as a "neo-premodernist." His take on the role of theory, however, is consistent with that of many postmodernist thinkers.

2. Instructive is Richard Rorty's discussion of how, on a much grander scale, a new vocabulary can serve as a tool for "doing something which could not have been envisaged prior to the development of a particular set of descriptions, those which it itself helps to provide" (*Contingency* 13).

3. For one of the many arguments in favor of having students write exploratory essays, see Winterowd; for various discussions about using nontraditional, dialogic genres in composition instruction, see Covino.

2
Stepping Yet Again into the Same Current

George Pullman

The purpose of this essay is to argue by means of illustration that the history of the writing-process movement is not so much a history as a rhetorical narrative. I define a rhetorical narrative as a motivated selection and sequencing of events that sacrifices one truth in order to more clearly represent another. True histories, of course, also involve selection and are therefore to some extent rhetorical, but they are less profoundly motivated by political (or juridical) agendas. The method of arrangement for this essay is first to rehearse the history of the writing-process movement, with as much integrity as the space permitted allows, and then to point out a number of oversimplifications and obfuscations within that history in order to suggest that the process movement first constructed and then dismissed current-traditional rhetoric in order to valorize itself, much as Plato first constructed and then dismissed rhetoric (Schiappa) in order to justify and promote the work of his Academy. My ultimate point is that as long as we persist in believing that some epistemic system eventually will analyze writing so thoroughly that it will become possible for nearly anyone to teach anyone how to write and as long as we maintain the dream of the theory that will underwrite the handbook to end all handbooks, we will continue to sacrifice our understanding of the past for the sake of promoting our current disciplinary needs.

It is certainly possible to argue convincingly that the history of the writing-process movement was a triumph of compassion and empiricism over tradition and prejudice. From 1885, when Harvard University first required "English A" as a temporary solution to the perceived illiteracy of its incoming students (Connors, "The Abolition Debate"), until 1968, when the writing-process movement is said to have changed everything (Young; see *contra* Crowley), composition instruction consisted of weekly themes, which were almost never revised. Occasionally, a student might be required to rewrite a piece, but that was only if the original effort was egregiously substandard and the teacher was in a generous mood. Otherwise, the method of composition was strictly linear: outline, write, edit, submit. The modes of discourse were taught as genres rather than as strategies to be employed differently within different contexts. Arrangement consisted of introduction, body, conclusion. All introductions started out general and became specific, regardless of context. Invention was separate from composition. The truth of the subject took precedence over the needs of the audience or the writer. There were two styles. One was clear, brief, coherent, unified, and active, even vigorous. The other was awkward, vague, redundant, cliché, incoherent, disunified, and passive, even effeminate (see Brody on "manly" writing). A passing paper was a grammatically accurate, linear expression of a monological opinion or a fully developed, fully exposed description of some clearly defined thing. The subjects for these weekly themes were typically commonplaces such as "the religious life is preferable to the commercial life," which descended directly from traditional declamatory exercises (Russell). These commonplaces required no specific knowledge because they relied entirely on what the ancient (Aristotelian) tradition called "artistic proofs," probability and informal reasoning— what every properly prepped young man would have heard at dinner and in church.

In addition to being highly routinized, writing was also highly undervalued. Because writing played no part in the construction or acquisition of knowledge, its function within the academy was limited to the transmission of facts discovered by other means. In other words, it was merely instrumental, a means to more important ends. Writing was something one simply learned to do. It was a skill, and a universally applicable skill at that. The plain style and correct grammar were all one needed to know about writing, regardless of what or where one was going to write, or who one was, for that matter. Once a person learned how to write, there was no need for further study or practice. Because of this, composition was not considered a subject of inquiry. Great texts might be objects worthy of study in and of themselves, but they were fictional rather than factual. The act of creating such texts held no academic interest because the academy was largely engrossed in gathering and disseminating facts. Moreover, it was assumed that an entering freshman ought to be able to write. If he or she could not, then weekly theme writing would provide the practice he or she lacked. A passive style, like a slack body, could be properly hardened given a few weeks of intense training and discipline. If practice alone was not enough, then the student probably lacked the intelligence requisite for a university education. Because the ability to write academic prose on demand was an expected entrance requirement, students could "test out" of Freshman Composition; therefore students perceived writing instruction as an embarrassing misery, a form of punishment. Similarly, because writing instruction was considered remedial instruction, providing that instruction was considered menial labor. Indeed, established scholars usually could avoid teaching Freshman Composition. Thus both the teachers and the students were stigmatized.

This debased and debasing linear model of writing instruction was labeled "current traditional rhetoric" by Daniel Fogarty in 1959. He coined the expression to contrast his vision of a new Freshman Composition course with the course as it was then typically taught. Whereas the handbooks of his day offered advice based solely on a cursory reading of Aristotle's *Rhetoric,* Fogarty wanted to base his "new rhetoric" on the theories of language offered by I. A. Richards, Kenneth Burke, and S. I. Hayakawa. It may have been enough for Aristotle's ephoebes to concentrate on clarity, brevity, and vigor, but now, with the onset of the cold war and rapidly changing technologies, young North Americans needed something different, something founded on scientific principles and therefore reliably suited to modern communication challenges. Thus Fogarty felt a new urgency for Freshman Composition, one that did not blame the course on the students' illiteracy but championed it as a critical moment in the fight for culture and democracy.

During the political upheavals of the sixties and well into the seventies, Fogarty's renewed commitment found support with some of the more politically minded teachers of Freshman Composition who did not see their students as ill-prepared young people, but rather as victims of disparate educational opportunities. For these teachers, access to higher education was a basic right because literacy and democracy were inseparable. If a student could find his or her way through the open door of the university, then he or she could, with enough patience and diligence on everyone's part, be taught to write. Moreover, because a proper democracy depends on a properly informed electorate, and therefore a literate electorate, illiteracy was a social problem rather than an individual failing. Thus the prejudice against those in the composition classrooms slowly abated, and slowly their work became valued as writing, or at least as writing in process. Their struggle toward coherence was seen as a struggle toward liberty. With coherent expression came an articulate "voice" and therefore a fully articulated self; thus writing instruction became identified with self-discovery and authentication, something all people needed regardless of social or educational background. It was still possible to "test out" of Freshman Composition, but failing to do so was no longer disgraceful. All students in progressive classrooms were encouraged to revise their papers before they were graded, to seek peer council, and to get feedback from the professor before and during revisions. The single preparatory outline was replaced by multiple heuristic drafts. Topics no longer were assigned by the teacher, and relevance replaced tradition. Students were encouraged to write about personal experiences and political issues. Style was now a matter of personal "voice." Arrangement was organic rather than regimented, and the five-paragraph theme was replaced by various genres. Spelling, punctuation, and grammar were taught, but only incidentally. Invention became the primary focus of instruction, and composition was explained as a legitimate method of knowledge creation (as epistemic, in the jargon of the time). Composition teachers were no longer editors and judges. Now they were coaches and fellow writers. In 1968, Richard Young took stock of all the changes in composition and declared that the composition paradigm had shifted. Current-traditional rhetoric, the linear, debased, and debasing model of prose composition, had gone the way of Newtonian physics. The writing process had arrived. Freshman Composition students no longer were despised. However, their teachers were not so well respected, although conditions were improving. Most of the people who taught composition zealously did so because of their political convictions rather than their strictly academic interests.

During the seventies and into the eighties there was a shortage of work for literary scholars, and many of the most determined to work in academe took what they hoped were (and what were advertised as) temporary jobs, nontenured but renewable positions teaching multiple sections of Freshman Composition. Many of these teachers just graded themes in a current-traditional manner and worked hard on their literary scholarship or resigned themselves to grumbling drudgery, but others saw Freshman Composition as a problem to be solved, and they began to regard their students as subjects of study rather than as objects of pity or misery. The guiding principle of this research was the belief that if they could just unlock the mystery of what good writers do, then they could teach others how to do it also. Among the pioneers, Janet Emig studied twelfth graders via what was later developed into the case-study method of ethnography. She discovered that the students who got high grades tended to revise their work and spend more time on it than those who got poorer grades. She backed this up with research into the composing processes of professional writers based on interviews published in the *Paris Review* and with biographies of poets and novelists who acknowledged that they revised their work numerous times before submitting it for judgment. Roughly a decade later, Linda Flower and John Hayes took this form of ethnographic study and anecdotal evidence and combined it with cognitive psychology and a technique called "think-aloud protocols," where the subject announced what she was doing as she composed. Thus the importance of planning and problem solving was discovered, as was the fact that writing is "recursive" or iterative rather than linear. Of course, there were many more and many different advances in composition research. Britton, for example, and the expressivists, Macrorie and those who studied what "real" writers do, Odell and those who studied what real workers write, Bruffee who added social construction to the mix, and Elbow who brought in peer-centered instruction. I am hitting only a few of the high points for the sake of illustrating how it is possible to argue that through the careful research of many people, empirical reasoning began to reveal how writing really happens. The result was a research agenda that continued to underwrite the writing-process theory of composition and the model of Freshman Composition that it informed.

Along the way, because a research agenda had been created, Ph.D.-granting programs and decent working conditions for composition teachers were fought for and won. Many of the people teaching Freshman Composition were now also teaching composition at upper levels and graduate seminars on composition theory and the history of rhetoric, and while many of their literary colleagues saw this as creeping incompetence, illiteracy infiltrating the upper divisions, these teachers saw themselves as specialists whose research could be valuably disseminated at any level. During the eighties and into the nineties, tenure-track jobs were relatively plentiful for composition scholars. There were more and more journals dedicated to composition and rhetoric, more conferences, more societies, and therefore more opportunities for publication. Thus one could say that Emig and others made it possible for composition teachers to transform themselves into composition theorists whose careful research led to knowledge that improved the academic status of writing instructors, while at the same time improving writing instruction itself as well as college students' writing abilities. Eventually, even the writing of entering students was improved by the writing-process movement because all language arts teachers were informed by the writing-process theory of composition. Traditional rhetorical instruction based largely on a single dusty textbook (and one largely ignored until this century) was completely replaced by a pedagogy that was based on original research into an actual phenomenon, what good writers do, and thus not only was composition a legitimate field of study, but its classes were no longer for the disadvantaged.

One can tell this story of the triumph of compassion and empiricism over tradition and prejudice with conviction, acknowledging the dissenting voices along the way, those who argued that think-aloud was seriously unreliable, for example (Cooper and Holzman; Voss), or those who have argued that despite all the noise about process, Freshman Composition remains unchanged and that the textbook trade has merely current-traditionalized the writing process (Crowley). Yet even taking these and other critiques into account, one cannot completely dismiss the changes that have happened under the banner of the writing-process movement. There is something undeniably convincing about the triumph of observation story as it is told because it justifies composition's existence in the academy. And yet, as with any history, when looked at from a rhetorical perspective, its opposite can also be told with equal conviction, which is not the same thing as saying that there is an antithesis that once brought to light will show the way to synthesis, a brilliant illumination of the right way to teach composition based on a better understanding of its history. Rather the opposite story merely points out the prejudices inherent in the writing process, which in turn suggests that rather than being a real history, the triumph-of-reason-over-prejudice story, the great paradigm shift, is in fact a rhetorical narrative. Rhetorical narrative is not bad historiography; it is the inevitable result of the search for coherence and unity among disparate texts and practices—the inevitable oversimplification that language always performs on experience, like using "Emig and others" to signify the thousands of different compositionists who have taught and written in this country for the last two decades, or presuming that "the writing process" refers to a single set of invariant acts the way a manufacturing process might. Even the generic label *Freshman Composition* belies vast circumstantial and pedagogical differences.

Along these lines it is important to remember that the apparently technical term *current-traditional rhetoric* is a nominalization and reification of Fogarty's unhyphenated expression *current traditional rhetoric*. We tend to think that *current-traditional* has a clearly denotative linguistic function, that it refers to a historical phenomenon with clearly recognizable boundaries and properties which can be differentiated from all other things, and that there were no other rhetorics at the time, no other traditions, no other practices. We tend, in other words, to think of *current-traditional* as a label, which is what I called it a few pages ago. We forget that Fogarty's expression did not refer to a theory but was instead a shorthand and off-the-cuff way of alluding to the way the tradition of rhetoric was currently being purveyed in the Freshman Composition textbooks of his day. Because we forget this, we tend to think that current-traditional rhetoric was a bogus theory based on prejudice and misunderstanding, a kind of mindless application of traditional folklore or naive interpretations of Aristotle's *Rhetoric* when in fact it did not exist as a theory except to the extent one could extrapolate a theory from the textbooks current at the time. The situation here is analogous to what Plato did to the Sophists, or rather what the tradition of Platonism did to a group of individuals who led different lives, pursued different interests, and had no professional association with each other. It is naive to use the expression *Sophistic rhetoric* because there is no one such thing and never was except as Plato constructed it for the sake of kicking it down. The same is true with what people have done with Fogarty's expression *current traditional rhetoric*, which is relative and changes with changes in rhetoric, so that now the current traditional rhetoric is different from the current traditional rhetoric that was current fifty years ago. The expression refers to how traditional rhetoric influences our current understanding of composition, which means that current traditional rhetoric is today concerned with understanding how the tradition is written, with the work of people such as Richard Enos, and Jarrat and Schiappa, while the current traditional rhetoric in Fogarty's time was concerned with how to apply Aristotle's insights to Freshman Composition. In a sense, the reified expression *current-traditional rhetoric* does little more than create a daemon for the sake of expelling it. Unless we keep this sophisticated reading of the expression in mind, we will overestimate the novelty and veracity of the writing process, and thus we will mistake a rhetorical construction for an actual historical fact.

The idea that the writing-process theory was entirely new and based entirely on empirical observation, that it was a kind of scientific revolution, masks the fact that one can find previous instances of process within composition theory and practice. Fifteen years before the paradigm shift is said to have occurred, Barriss Mills described writing in terms of a process (Crowley, *The Methodical Memory* 66). There is in fact evidence suggesting that process theory had an early champion in Barret Wendal, a nineteenth-century American (Newkirk) and an even earlier precursor in George Jardine, an eighteenth-century Scott (Gaillet). The talk of paradigms also masks the fact that the process theory of composition was very much consistent with changes that had happened and were happening around it. Because the process approach is a student-centered pedagogy, for example, it has clear connections to nineteenth-century educational reforms, to Dewey in particular (Marshall, "Of What" 53). It also arose simultaneously with reader-response criticism in literature departments and with the advent of creative writing as a workshop-based discipline that had its own identity separate from literary scholarship. The writing process was not, in other words, so much discovered as created and not so much created as imported. So thinking that the writing-process theory was derived solely from empirical observation obscures the influence of broader educational, social, and technological changes. In order to describe the writing-process movement solely as a triumph of empirical observation over tradition, it is necessary to construct a context for the empirical research which not only slights the history of composition but also fails to acknowledge the ideological implications and motivations of that research.

The writing process is generally justified as a distillation of the practices in which all "good" writers engage. It is what "real" writers do. However, if "the writing process" were really the way all successful writers write regardless of context, then unless all writing is somehow supportive of a single ideological system, there would be no obfuscatory ideological baggage attending the process. Such baggage does exist, however. The idea that what "good" writers know is what all would-be writers need to know, the principal upon which the writing process movement was based, rests on a number of constitutive prejudices. The writing-process movement largely assumed that good writers were those who one found interviewed in *Paris Review*, "creative" writers, people who made a living writing the kind of thing that literature scholars analyzed. This prejudice was left largely unchallenged because most of the people teaching composition started out writing essays about literature and got interested in that because they either wanted to write literature or were crazy about reading it. Thus the literary essay became the unexamined paradigm for all nonfiction prose. People teaching composition from within technical writing, of course, have had suspicions about the paradigmatic value of the humanistic essay, but the people who read *College English* do not always read *Technical Communication*.

Since Britton, of course, many people have begun composition classes with the personal narrative rather than with the argumentative essay, believing that the process of writing about a personal event could clarify the meaning of that event for the writers and thus improve their understanding of themselves, which in turn would improve their ability to write. It is therefore not immediately obvious how the essay generically controls our understanding of writing. But if we consider the origin of the essay as Montaigne's work, then we can see how the personal narrative turned into a public display of insight is very much embedded in the essayist's goals as a writer. In the Western tradition of philosophy there is a long-standing presumption that self-awareness is a requisite for clear thinking, at least when it comes to nonfiction prose construction, that a well-ordered mind produces well-ordered prose, and that disordered prose signifies a disordered mind (see Crowley, *Methodical Memory*). The "creative" writer might be able to compose in some somnambular haze, but automatic writing has never been held out as an option for the ungifted, "uncreative" prose nonfiction writer. Even free writing is seen as a heuristic, a place to start writing rather than as a way of producing finished prose. If one's prose is a reflection of one's mind, then a person who can write clearly is a better person than one who cannot, and a person who writes regularly, searching always for clarity, is pursuing a superior way of life. The valorization of "the author," the idea of writing as a way of life, the idea that the self is a text to be constantly revised, amplified, polished, and presented for critique and praise is very much embedded in the writing-process movement. Ken Macrorie began a recent article on process by first asserting, "As I look back on my experience as a teacher of writing . . ." and then immediately revised himself, saying, "Stop right there! . . . I should have said, 'when I look back on the experience of my students as writers' " (Macrorie 69). The revision of "teacher of writing" to "students as writers" underscores the entire movements' transformation of writing as an instrumental skill into an ontological category, a way of being. Thus rather than simply being a better way to teach people how to write better, the writing-process movement teaches a set of values and attitudes about life and how to live it, the self-reflective, contemplative life that Plato held out to Phaedrus as an alternative to the life of political power that the young man thought he wanted.

The idea that writing is a way of life, which attends such slogans as writing is rewriting and vision is revision, and that (essay) writers are somehow better than non(essay)writers because they have keener insight and more polished self-reflecting mirrors is a humanistic prejudice that narrows the perspective on writing to the point where much of the canonical advice is useless outside the Freshman Composition class and the literature classes for which it prepares people. Many writing teachers, for example, still believe that the active voice is easier to interpret than the passive voice and that all good writing is active. Many teach their students to write always in the present tense, without realizing what ideological baggage of the "eternal living tradition" variety comes with it or the fact that the history paper that the student writes next quarter will be absurd, the biology report anthropomorphized to the point of hilarity. It is often very difficult to convince people that what they call "better prose" is simply more squarely in line with the conventions they are used to, that passive constructions are not necessarily less easily interpreted. The very idea that a "good" piece of writing is what any educated person can read without benefit of local knowledge or contextual assumptions—the hermeneutic principle upon which essay prose (and humanistic hermeneutics) rests—is completely absurd in most writing situations. The highly elaborated code which is often misleadingly called the "written register," as though any less elaborated code is something less than writing, is relevant only in humanistic circumstances. Very often in business one cannot afford to spend the time creating fully elaborated code, and even if one could, there is no incentive to create business documents that just anybody can read. Similarly, in scientific writing, one must judiciously exclude shared information and rely on a collective understanding of procedures and materials. Over-elaboration is disruptive for the intended reader and is potentially insulting. In some cases, it could even be dangerous from a security standpoint. We tend to talk about readability as a universal goal and a quality that all good writing has when in fact it is a local strategy. A perfectly good piece of writing might well be unreadable to people who lack the requisite knowledge of facts, procedures, and practices.

The wealth in time and resources that makes possible the isolation necessary for the humanistic essay is a key component of the self-reflection such writing requires. Unless one can afford to spend hours tinkering with words, to let one's clothes mildew in the hamper, one's dishes crystallize in the sink, one's lawn grow wildly, and one's relationships wither, then one cannot afford to write a polished essay. It just requires too great an investment in time and energy, even for expert writers, but especially for novices. Leisure and reflection are not bad things, of course, but they are not always possible; therefore, any writing process that builds numerous revision loops into the production of any piece of prose and leaves the impression that such loops are necessarily a part of all good writing obscures the fact that rapid production can sometimes be a virtue as well as a necessity. Thus, because it carries ideological baggage with it, calling the writing-process movement a paradigm and seeing it as a triumph of reason over prejudice obfuscates the ideological components of the movement, which is not to say that the writing-process movement is bad, only that the theory on which it depends and the model for Freshman Composition that it underwrites are rhetorical narratives rather than empirical facts.

All consideration of ideological baggage aside, if "the writing process" were an adequate theoretical description of writing, then all writers, regardless of what kind of texts they produce, from novelists to webmasters, would write in essentially the same way, using the same iterative sequences of brainstorm-draft-revise-peer review, and so forth, and each of these steps would be essentially similar. However, the process of document creation is not context invariant. The genre, the circumstances, the subject, and the whole dynamic of the rhetorical situation influence what process will lead to what document. Additionally, several different processes might lead to essentially the same document. It is even possible that circumstances might require a process that directly obstructs the production of the most useful document. The process of writing a software manual, for example, is controlled by the process of writing the code, so that the people writing the manual often have to revise as the code changes, and, because the code is more important from a business standpoint, once the code is set, the pressure to bring the product to market compresses the time that the documenters have for revisions—to say nothing of revisionings. The process of writing an examination that requires discursive answers without the opportunity for revision is another example of a context in which the belief in the existence of a single writing process is potentially detrimental. If the writing process as it is taught can actually obstruct the production of an adequate document in certain circumstances, then it cannot be considered universally applicable; therefore, it cannot be considered a universally valid description of how to write.

The reason that the great paradigm shift never took place is that the paradigm is really a metaphor for a rhetorical situation, and both current-traditional rhetoric and the process theory of writing have an identical rhetorical situation: the classroom. The perceived exigence is ill-literacy, an ignorance of important conventions with the result that those who have been granted the opportunity for an education apparently cannot obtain that education, which conflicts with our educational systems' fundamental belief in the democratic necessity of an educated public. The scene of this situation is the Freshman Composition classroom, a safe space in which to practice new conventions that have been abstracted from real practices and universalized for the sake of simplicity. The proposed solution is to analyze writing into its constitutive acts or parts with such accuracy that anyone who can learn to follow the procedures will be able to produce a good piece of prose. And the fundamental belief upon which the solution rests is that it is actually possible to analyze writing so thoroughly that some step-by-step procedure with universal application will emerge, which is where the rhetorical problem becomes an insurmountable problem.

Writing, whether the acts or the products of the acts, cannot be usefully theorized. We have absorbed the academy's notion that knowledge produces insight without fully recognizing that the object we are looking at is only an object in a trivial sense. The product of writing (a text) is an unstable entity, the diaphanous effect of multiple interpretative efforts by people who may or may not share contexts or inter-pretative practices, who may or may not occupy the same context at the moment of the text, who may in fact have the text in common only as a site of combat over other issues such as control over a circumstance of which the text is merely a sign or even an epiphenomenon. In other words, a text cannot be evaluated once and for all because every time it is read its effects are at least slightly different, and we cannot know a text apart from its effects except in the trivial sense of word counts and fog indexes and physical properties. Because the product is un-stable, the process that produces the product cannot be described fully, except perhaps in particular instances. Using a word processor scripted to save a file into a new sequentially numbered file every ten seconds or so, one might be able to observe the production of a text, but to as-sume that such an example or even a huge data base of such examples would yield a description of the process of writing is to assume a uni-formity that does not exist. Writing is not epistemic in the sense that no one true system of explanation can be constructed out of analysis and codified in a textbook in such a way that anyone can teach any-body else how to write in fifteen weeks.

Because we have listened to the history of rhetoric uncritically, we still hear Plato's complaint that Sophistic education was based on a knack for flattery while his philosophy was based on metaphysics; so, while we change the "philosophy" as philosophies change, replacing them eventually with science and now soon with technology, the fact remains that we can teach writing but we cannot be sure who will learn it or who will become good at it, or even that the ones who learned it learned it from us or that they could not have learned it if they had not met us. We tend to think of teaching and learning as correlative terms. If you can teach writing, then others can learn it, and if others are learning it, then they are being taught. However, I suspect that the connection between writing instruction and writing production is far less succinct.

As long as we continue to search for the theory that will enable a universally applicable rhetoric, we will continue to step back into the same river of rhetorical history, where the textbooks that were written previously are used as proof that rhetoric was improperly grounded, despite the fact that textbooks are always pale reflections of the insights from which they were derived because they have been modified by the rhetorical situation of the classroom, just as removing the dramatistic pentad from the corpus of Burke's work and turning it into a three-page heuristic eviscerates its explanatory power, just as Cicero looked at *On Invention* as a jejune piece of parrotry when he was many years from school and had practiced law and politics long enough to know that rhetoric is so complex that it cannot be fully codified, that the codes that can be written must serve only an introductory purpose and must never be mistaken for (or reconstructed as) real rhetoric as it is lived and practiced.

3
Modeling and Emulating: Rethinking Agency in the Writing Process

Barbara Couture

The process movement, in at least one reading of it, was a bold move to claim agency for authors whose words and deeds had little significance within the context they were produced, namely school classrooms. In his introduction to the anthology *Taking Stock: The Writing Process Movement in the '90s,* Lad Tobin says that the movement is a rebellion against pedantic obsession with textual correctness, formulaic display of rhetorical form, and the mechanistic drafting procedure of "outline, write, proofread, hand in" (3), a regimen that was drilled into every grade school child and yet summarily was ignored by many students as a viable procedure for getting the job done. (You must remember, as do I, routinely drafting essays and producing the required outline to match them afterwards.) Yet once articulated as a pedagogy, our attention to the "writing process" placed an equally stubborn grip on students' composing efforts. I recall in my early years as a "composition specialist" being invited to speak to a group of Detroit public school teachers and being told by many of them that they knew all about the writing process: I learned from them that on Monday morning, in each of their English classes, their students must do "prewriting"; on Wednesday they must "draft" their papers; and on Friday, without fail, they must "revise" them. Pedantry clearly is one paradigm the process movement had failed to subvert. How did the emphasis upon process, like so many ideas about writing that are derived from scholarship and research, lose so much when applied en masse in our classrooms? At least one reason can be traced back to how we traditionally have approached composition instruction, teaching students to model technique rather than to emulate expression.

To master a technique we employ a device, we model what our teachers or other masters do or have done; to master expression we strive to emulate others, to be like them, worthy of them, perhaps even better than them. Certainly the process movement was "interested," if we can say that, in expression, or at least in expressiveness, yet this attention in itself has yielded little to help teachers get at the root of the expressiveness which its founders purportedly had hoped to unleash in our students. Attention to process *per se* does not help writers develop expression, that is, writing that conveys not a "persona," but rather one's "person" as a living agent who makes a difference in a community of others striving to do the same. At the same time, however, we are now in a far better position to achieve this aim, having the process movement as our legacy, and we are also, perhaps, in a far better position to understand its importance.

In the few pages granted me here, I shall sketch briefly a vision of how process pedagogy took hold in composition studies and subsequently became translated as the technique of modeling a product or a procedure. Then I shall suggest a different route for its future. In my view, if we reduce writing to either a product or a procedure, we must teach it as a device or tool for doing something that is distinct from the doer, the human agent who gives it design, whose being writing expresses. We need to move both composition theory and pedagogy beyond the dualistic device paradigm that separates our acts from ourselves and begin to understand and teach writing as design. To move from device to design, we must study writing as it expresses the integration of human will and action, of thinking and expression; this entails giving up the notion that these functions are separate or, more to the point, that the first is abstract and interior, whereas the second is concrete and exterior. Writing is both will and action, internal agency and external product. As I hope to show by citing the work of two prominent scholars, the intention to address writing as it both develops and expresses the subjective agent behind it underlies "process" pedagogy and defines the scholars who founded the movement. I offer some speculation as to why this intention has failed to take root in the writing classroom. In concluding, I cite new developments in rhetorical theory that I believe now provide us with better resources to help students understand writing as personal agency than we had available when the process movement first came on the scene, resources that may lead teachers to fulfill the movement's original promise.

From Product as Model to Process as Model

The movement from product to process in writing instruction paralleled a number of developments in other fields, including critical theory and educational research, as well as changes in our postsecondary student populations. This latter influence introduced a new problem to colleges and universities during the sixties and seventies: how to teach students who were not as prepared as their predecessors to handle college writing. Finding our old teaching methods to fail, some writing instructors, most notably for our profession Mina Shaughnessy, took a scholarly approach to the problem, studying what their students did when they wrote, what procedures they used to produce the writing that their teachers found so lacking, inappropriate, and undisciplined. The shift from product to process was blessed in a way, too, by the shift in textual studies from the New Criticism to structuralist and cultural critique, approaches that "approved" of looking at the context in which writers produce writing as an appropriate source to look for explanations of its meaning. Add to this the popular dispersal of scholarship on the processes of reading, notably the work of Norman Holland and Wolfgang Iser, and the translations of scholarship on the social contexts of reading in the pedagogy of David Bleich and, later, Stanley Fish, and we have a scene ripe for the full development of a paradigm change—a shift from the task of modeling ideal written products to developing the agency of the individual writer.

In the field of composition studies itself, the shift from concern with the written product to the processes of the writer was both jump-started and championed by teacher-scholars such as Donald Murray, Ken Macrorie, and Peter Elbow, who examined their own approaches to producing text, found them to differ greatly from current prescribed practices, and promoted self-examination and collaboration as methods of developing a personalized process for composing texts themselves, a process that liberated the writer's individual "voice" by freeing him or her from constraining procedures that "blocked" the production of text. Also, pedagogical emphasis on the writing process grew out of the emergence of composition as a research area, inheriting the research methods of science and the social sciences, methods that focus their studies not on texts, but on the real-world contexts of people and things reported in them. Composition research also responded to studies in child development and educational psychology, which attended to the stages of cognitive and educational functioning, a tradition influenced heavily by the work of Jean Piaget. Paralleling these developments were the outcomes of the Anglo-American Conference at Dartmouth College in 1966, where scholars from the United States and Britain began to speak about how writing figures in the growth process, how it develops thinking and learning (see Smagorinsky 65–67). This developmental model was applied most notably in American school curricula by James Moffett as a theory of teaching the rhetorical modes in a sequence from narrative to argument. The explosion of interest in the psychological and social contexts for writing, in the processes of interpretation, and in the development of cognition as it is reflected in language skills all contributed to an elaborated writing-process pedagogy, yet, to my mind, the depth and breadth of scholarship this pedagogical theory represents has not been reflected in interpretations of the writing process in the writing classroom. The writing process, like the stultified procedure of outline, draft, revise that preceded it, has been interpreted in the main as a structure to be modeled and not as the full development of the writer's agency, a much more complex phenomenon.

Teaching the writing process as the modeling of technique certainly is consistent with a tradition of composition pedagogy extending from the practice of imitating good writing by good writers; through the practice of perfecting the argumentative strategies of deduction, induction, comparing, contrasting, and defining; to following the basic pattern of the five-paragraph theme, mastered by most of us in high school English and freshman composition classes. And, too, emphasis on process as model has reflected an overt desire of many composition instructors to identify methods for improving writing instruction so as to "right" their students' writing (see Sirc's discussion of this trend in the seventies). In short, it is not such a wonder that many of us who have been freed from the constraints of the rigid pedagogy of correctness by Moffett, Elbow, and the like nevertheless have interpreted the writing process as yet another method for getting writing done "right." Yet with even a surface glance at the professional development of some of the scholars behind this movement, advocacy of process emerges as much more than attention to the procedure by which writing gets done. Emphasis on the process of writing renewed—or was intended to renew—our concern not only with helping students write better but also with helping them *be* better, that is, develop into better persons through achieving agency, the capacity to act and to make a difference among other persons for having done so. This goal is reflected in the publication trail of at least two prominent founders of process pedagogy: James Moffett and Peter Elbow.

Both Moffett and Elbow were personally invested in a study of writing processes as they might lead both to better writing and more developed personal agency. Moffett reinterpreted the rhetorical modes as they parallel processes in our personal development as thinkers and speakers, first conducting interior dialogue, and eventually moving through conversation, correspondence, and public narrative to public inference. This interior development represents a progression from less complex narrative discourse to sophisticated argument, all of which can be described in terms of the process of thinking about and interacting with our environment: we begin by "recording . . . the drama of what is happening" in real time;then we develop a true narrative of "what happened"; then we generalize about observed events; finally, we theorize about what "may happen" based upon one's observations (Moffett, *Teaching the Universe of Discourse* 47). Moffett's articulated sequence was developed as a curriculum for the writing classroom, and in the early seventies, there were a plethora of curriculum plans at all levels, grade school through Freshman Composition, which pushed students from narrative to argument within the course of a semester or year. In the ubiquitous application of Moffett's developmental process, little heed was given to the fact that some students had suffered through the "narrative-to-argument" progression in every writing class from junior high to freshman English. The sequence was employed to help students develop techniques for writing, a task easily separated from the complex process of developing a *person* who is writing, not just in this class, but all of his or her life.

Teachers generally missed, in their application of Moffett's popular curriculum, how concerns about personal development infused the work of the man behind the method, James Moffett himself, a consummate scholar and teacher who believed—and still does—in the role of the public schools in preparing students to become vital participants in society, to work together on our common problems, to divert their will toward words in action that enable both these processes. And, perhaps more to the point, writing classrooms *per se* took little notice of Moffett's continuing personal development as a someone who was

trying to discover the relationship between interior reflective thinking and exterior social action as well as to express that discovery to
others. *Coming on Center*, published nearly fifteen years after *Teaching
the Universe of Discourse*, revealed Moffett's commitment to linking language functions to reflective living; here he describes prewriting activities as a kind of absorptive meditation enabling the writer not only
to focus more intently and to see more clearly what he or she observes
through "regarding writing as revised inner speech" (179) but also to
develop a more spiritual outlook toward life (148–70).

Moffett's desire to link writing, spirituality, and personal agency has
continued throughout his career. In *Storm in the Mountains*, his stun-
ning case study of a book-burning controversy in Appalachia that was
inspired in part by his language arts curriculum, he defines the difference between religion and spirituality, finding the former to be culturally based and the latter an essential human need and condition.
The battle over censorship on religious grounds, he concludes, is
largely a symptom of a lack of faith in ourselves, a failure of spiritual
development, rather than the fallout of exposing students to information that contradicts a particular religious view: "If you have enough
faith in yourself you know you can risk to know [something that you
do not wish to believe] and not lose yourself" (Moffett, *Storm* 223). His
practical implementation plan for encouraging such spiritual self-
reliance is to encourage truly individualized learning in the schools,
giving students the choice to read several different texts simultaneously. This strategy avoids the imperative of choosing one text over
another for all students or requiring all students to read all alternative texts at the same time, and it has the side benefit of involving the
community in selecting books to add to—rather than take away from—
the classroom library. Moffett's model of gathering students in the same
place to read different things builds a context that allows differences
to sit side-by-side in the same classroom, where the eventual "mixing"
will result in "influencing" by mere association rather than by forced
indoctrination (*Storm* 212–14). The process of learning, Moffett concludes, is one of negotiating identity, of being able to drop one's
"guards" in order to "enter another's point of view" (*Storm* 222): it is
a process of developing the self through engaging or "mixing it up"
with others.

In a recent essay appearing in *Taking Stock*, Moffett has re-
emphasized his vision of the integral relationship of the processes of

writing and personal development. He reiterates the importance of narrative as it leads to personal growth and development as a writer and as a person, and he contextualizes his vision of writing within new pedagogies projected for our classrooms of the future, such as the "project" approach, which encourages students to work together to address contemporary problems. Projects simulate "what practitioners do in real life" in making connections between people and sites to solve our common problems ("Coming Out Right" 28). But for Moffett this effort does and always has meant something more than getting things done, than progressing through a skill sequence or mastering a set of discourse types; beyond this, it has led to our becoming better persons, more effective agents who are able to address social ills through attending to our own personal development and our spiritual well-being. People want to get "better" Moffett insists, not just at their writing but at everything writing and speaking allows them to do as persons. He insists, very aptly, that "we don't just want our *writing* to come out right, *we* want to come out right" ("Coming Out Right" 29); our classrooms, he admits, have not been the most comfortable sites to address this very human and intimately personal need.

A deep concern with the development of writers as persons courses through Peter Elbow's publications about the writing process as well, a concern that has not translated to the writing classroom as easily as his techniques for generating ideas and getting over writer's block. *Writing Without Teachers*, Elbow's "self-help" composition text, which virtually took college composition programs by storm, ostensibly was about empowering writers as agents, freeing them from writer's block through directing them to concentrate on generating writing rather than on analyzing "descriptions of good and bad constructions" (vii). In his preface, Elbow opens with a statement about our common desire for agency, to feel the master of oneself, both personally and socially: "Many people are now trying to become less helpless, both personally and politically: trying to claim more control over their own lives" (vii). Getting control over "words," Elbow offers, is one way to get control of our lives. His book is filled with self-help techniques to achieve this aim, from ways to generate writing without "blocking" (free writing), to working with a group of other students to talk about how your writing affects you and them. Near the end of *Writing Without Teachers*, Elbow tells how he came to this approach, through responding to the writing of his own students, "trying to transmit my experience of [their] words," in order to give students a "wider range of reactions" than the single, often obtuse comment offered in the margins of a student paper (121). The methods he advocates stem from his personal experience in "encounter" and "therapy" groups where he learned the value of "people telling what . . . words had made happen in them" (121). In short, Elbow translated experiences that had allowed him to achieve control and power in his own life and classroom into a series of techniques that the struggling student writers with whom he so empathized might use to do the same. But his pedagogy, elaborated over his life career, is much more than a collection of these techniques.

In subsequent essays and books, Elbow continued to explore the processes, first, of generating writing though "growing," letting one's writing expand, mature, and change into something else and "cooking," or letting one's words and ideas percolate, bubble, or ferment and mix, so that one can draw relationships between them and, second, of "doubting" and "believing," the processes of adopting a critical stance, on the one hand, and accepting a view carte blanche, on the other hand. In *Embracing Contraries,* he applied these concepts to the processes of learning and teaching and suggested that we learn through viewing the developing of ideas as the interaction of "contraries," such as alternately accepting a stance as true or valid and critiquing its truth or validity. These oppositional processes are as essential for teachers as they are for learners, for teachers must be willing not only to critique their students' judgments but also to accept them as valid in order to give them the space to challenge or defend these positions themselves. Elbow clearly intended his metaphors of cooking, growing, doubting, and believing to stand not only as techniques for doing the processes of writing, teaching, and learning but also for being a writer, being a learner, being a teacher and being recognized by others as such. They are formulative of these roles in persons.

The relationship between writing and becoming is treated explicitly in "The Uses of Binary Thinking," appearing in the *Taking Stock* collection. Here Elbow shows how seven human activities that comprise the educational experience—among them, reading, writing, learning, teaching, and doing research—involve the experience of negotiating conflicts and of embracing contraries, such as balancing the aims of generating and criticizing when trying to write or balancing the teaching roles of facilitator and examiner when interacting with students. In order to decide effectively how to act, we cannot make black-and-white choices that absolutely support one belief over another, nor can we compromise to eliminate completely the differences we perceive; rather we must see "binary oppositions" as the "uniquely valuable occasions for balance, irresolution, nonclosure, nonconsensus, nonwinning" (Elbow, "The Uses" 182) that form the experience of conscious knowing. Seeing such oppositions is not a process that can be codified, but rather a complex phenomenon of being. What we may have forgotten—or never understood—about the process movement as it was conceived by its founders in the early seventies, Elbow tells us, was that it reflected "a burgeoning interest in the *experience* of writing," in writing as a human phenomenon of knowing and learning ("The Uses" 195). He sees a connection between a scholarly interest in the complexity of experience and one's "willingness to articulate contrasts and leave them unresolved" ("The Uses" 195), an openness to the reality of personal experience that has not always meshed well with the goals of academic scholarship. This willingness to leave conflicts brewing in our minds, to engage constantly in an internal dialectic, also leads to a willingness to engage in dialectical thinking in conversation, that is, to engage in a process by which we "internalize," at the same time, opposing views and so "enlarge" our minds and "assumptions" (Elbow, "The Uses" 199). Because we learn by embracing contraries, Elbow tells us, we should welcome the "eternal warfare between concepts in [our] individual minds" which we experience in trying to enact the processes of writing, teaching, and learning. He also notes that if we each make a personal effort to negotiate our internal conflicts, this effort may result "in more cooperation and less zero-sum warfare between people" ("The Uses" 199).

Elbow's utopian dream that the process of "embracing contraries" may lead to social harmony echoes Moffett's vision of a learning environment in which we learn together to "get better" together, as individuals and as a society. Yet, like Moffett's work, the adaptation of Elbow's philosophy in the writing classroom has been—and perhaps is—more comfortably made as the application of pedagogical devices to structure the process of writing and its contexts. We set up discussion groups to explore contraries, encourage students to monitor their writing processes to see if they allow for "growing" and "cooking," replay the "doubting" and "believing" games in class discussions of student papers. I would wager that not much serious consideration is given in our classrooms to these activities as they frame a way of being, as they emulate the person of someone, such as Elbow or Moffett, who is trying to show others how they themselves are developing their personal agency, trying to get better as persons among persons.

I could wax encyclopedic about the reasons why our writing pedagogy has focussed on modeling techniques rather than on the process of becoming better persons: the reasons why it has are far more easy to number than the reasons why it should not. Most obvious is the fact that writing and its counterpart, reading, are regarded as language *skills*; to develop a facility in these skills, we believe, has little to do with personal worthiness or betterment. Values-clarification exercises, of course, have had a prominent place in school writing curricula as have discussions of the importance of personal virtue. But becoming a better person has not had much cachet as a requirement for becoming a better writer, and, indeed, Why should it? many of us might ask. Concern with becoming a better person is presumed to underlie all studies in the humanities, and, as such, it is nothing we need "trot out" every day in each of its specific disciplines. It certainly is not requisite to their mastery. And, of course, becoming a better person is, we might argue, an individual matter. Teachers and scholars now are acutely aware of diversity in knowledge structures and the values that accompany them. It is not within the purview of any one of us to declare for another what it means to become a better person, and, even if we could, we believe that such judgments of moral worthiness are more rightly addressed in families, churches, and religious schools than in the classrooms of public high schools, colleges, and universities. Plus—we might reasonably conclude—we really do not have the time in the writing classroom to discuss such matters. Given the obvious need that our students have to acquire the skills of writing, we do them the best service by providing them with written products and composing processes to model so that their writing—if not the students themselves—will "come out right."

We pay a price, however, by reducing those acts that make us uniquely human—speaking and writing—to a device or technology to be mastered, ignoring their more central role in shaping the way we are and live. Albert Borgmann, in a philosophical inquiry into the character of contemporary life, has suggested that the "device paradigm" now pervades every aspect of human activity, reducing our interactions with the world to a technical interface with reality rather than elaborating them as a social engagement with implication for the development of our personal lives. As an example, he compares the task of building a fire in a stove to warm one's home to warming the house by forced air heating or radiated electric heat, the latter both supplied by a switch or control. The latter technical devices make available heat without the user's investment in physical skill or the building of social relations to reach that goal. With the wood-burning stove comes the effort of chopping wood, involving oneself and others in keeping the wood box filled and fire tended, learning the skill of starting and maintaining fires, and incorporating these activities into the fabric of a shared family or community life. Devices make things available to us without requiring any investment from us; they reduce human activity to the mere process of acquiring a commodity (Borgmann, *Technology* 40–48).

Within the commodified structure of education in high school and college classrooms, it is not surprising that we have treated writing more as a device than anything else. Writing is a tool to be used by our students to produce papers that show what they know and have learned, to write reports that back up recommendations with accessible facts, to articulate procedures that show how they have made judgments that follow practices accepted by engineers or social workers or other professionals. To help students produce these products, we teach them the rhetorical modes; the five-paragraph theme; the processes of prewriting, writing, and drafting; and perhaps even the techniques of tagmemic analysis, problem solving, brainstorming, or cooking and growing. These devices have all made the teaching and mastery of writing available to us, in much the way air ducts and temperature controls have put heat in our homes. To think of getting better at what we do, whether it be building a fire or writing an academic article, as fully integral with how we live, as deeply enmeshed in our development of self, we need to deconstruct the powerful hold this "device paradigm" has on our processes of teaching and learning. But not only this; we also must replace this paradigm with an equally powerful and concrete conceptualization of the writer as a personal agent. We need to transform our narrow conception of writing as a device, a tool whose construction and use can be modeled, and begin to view writing as design, a creative act of a unique human agent who is driven not only to model others but also, as I shall argue in the next section, to emulate them, to be like them and perhaps better than them.

From Modeling to Emulating

Two very important developments in rhetorical and critical theory since the process movement took hold have set the scene for conceptualizing writing as something more than modeling. First, textual theory has deconstructed the foundational belief that truthful writing corresponds to a single concrete reality and that facts are disassociated from beliefs. Research in women's ways of knowing, cultural studies, critical theory, and rhetoric have disabused us of the notion that linguistic expression corresponds to an objective reality "out there" and, consequently, has led us to question whether favored forms of presenting arguments and "real" evidence lead to more truthful conclusions than marginalized forms. A single model for generating ideas, conducting research, and writing and revising a draft does not capture all the effective ways that human beings solve the problem of acquiring knowledge and communicating it to one another. The telling experiences of women in school recorded by Mary Field Belenky and her colleagues in *Women's Ways of Knowing* alone have influenced the development of whole curricula to acknowledge differences in the ways men and women approach learning and writing. The list of new scholarship on the discourse types and cognitive patterns that are favored by women is increasing steadily, with studies exploring contexts ranging from school playgrounds to corporate offices and university research labs (see, for instance, Code, Kirsch, and Rose). And, of course, the wide-ranging theory and empirical research under the broad umbrella of cultural studies has led us to rethink assumptions about the neutrality of certain discourse forms favored in the academy or in the business world; we now overtly acknowledge that discourse modes and styles establish power relationships, exclude some groups, and mask underlying ideologies and assumptions about the way social groups do and should work. Research in the culture of academic disciplines, for instance, has led us to question whether the scientific method, modeled as an ideal process for conducting and reporting research, disguises how research is actually done, conclusions reached, and evidence supported (see Latour and Woolgar, for one well-known example). We question, now, how much of scientific writing reflects "science" and how much reflects "rhetoric" and whether emphasis on the latter has gotten in the way of exploring solutions to our social and physical problems more deeply and openly.

A second development, which I believe has countered interpretations of writing as modeling, is a radical change in our characterizations of textual genre. In critical and rhetorical theory, genre is now treated as something far more complex than a designation of a rhetorical or poetic mode or form. Genre refers to the entire context of textual production and reception, a process that is never static (see Berkenkotter and Huckin; Swales). In fact, textual theory suggests that we are mistaken in viewing genre either as a product or a process that has a conventional form. An example is the work of this collection's editor, Thomas Kent, who has argued in *Paralogic Rhetoric* and several other publications that the writing process is not about modeling generic conventions (indeed, whether such conventions exist and carry stable meaning is doubtful), but rather about developing theories about what others mean, how their texts work to convey these meanings, and continually adjusting how we speak and write to others so that our texts communicate to them on the same ground.

In short, our current scholarship on diverse ways of knowing, meaning, and communicating strongly suggests that modeling specific conventions and procedures will not ensure that writers learn all they need to know in order to communicate effectively to others. At the same time, it does suggest that writers need to know quite a bit about what it is that others *do* when they communicate in writing so that they can act like them and, perhaps equally important, *be* like them in order to occupy a common field within which each other's communications are heard and understood. Writers need to know how and why to choose a strategy, have confidence in its projected result, and implement it successfully. In other words, writers need to become subjective agents, making willful judgments effected in concrete actions that convey them successfully to others. This takes more than learning how to be better writers; it involves learning to become better persons. It is a task learned not through modeling but rather through emulating, trying to be like those who we want to "be with," so to speak, whose lives give shape to the way we value our own. This is a very broad claim for writing instruction and one that is as difficult to articulate as it is to translate into an effective pedagogy for the writing classroom. But we have some powerful resources to address both of these tasks in new philosophical approaches to critical and rhetorical theory.

Several philosophers and critics—among them Alasdair MacIntyre, Charles Taylor, Stanley Cavell, Wendy Farley, and James Kellenberger —are now exploring the relationships among ethical expression, personal agency, and our conception of societal progress. Throughout much of this work runs a common theme: our knowledge systems and belief in societal progress are dependent upon our recognizing human life and its achievements as a thing of common value, one that is not relative to our cultural differences but rather represents our common aspirations to be knowledgeable, productive, and caring and to get better at doing so. Furthermore, these scholars find the ground for truthful expression to lie not in scientific proof, legal accuracy, or rhetorical skill but rather in an acknowledgment that we are dependent upon others to secure our own safety and happiness; hence, our task is to become more attuned to others and more open to them in order to work and communicate with them, developing a common truth. To accomplish this, we need to become better persons among persons. I wish to spend a few paragraphs here exploring some of these themes as articulated by Charles Altieri, one critic who I believe to have translated quite concretely the philosophical goals of becoming better persons into rhetorical terms. In doing so, I shall indicate the implications of some of Altieri's claims for my proposal that we treat writing as design and that writing skills are developed through emulation.

To treat writing as design is to interpret expression (writing) as it reflects the will of the subjective agent, the writer. To develop writing skill through emulation is to interpret the writing process as the process of becoming a better person. In *Subjective Agency*, Altieri supplies a philosophical foundation for interpreting expression as a willful act and the process of developing expression as one of emulation or striving for personal worthiness among others. His objective in this work is to develop an "expressivist version" of subjective agency, locating the enactment of personal identity in the processes and products of verbal expression. Altieri defines willful acts as those that invest us in certain identities and that make us effective in the world through aligning us with recognized discourse practices:

> Where wishing is a matter of imagination, will is a matter of how an agent orients itself towards its practices. Consequently will is not a matter of inner life. The closest we can come to describing it is to treat it as

> simply the aligning of conative energies with the world so that they seem continuous with it and effective within it. (50)

The process of achieving alignment with certain recognized practices, for instance, discourse styles and ways of knowing, involves choosing what to value on the basis of some personal formula for one's own happiness, idealizing that choice, and then negotiating that choice with others in order to see it realized within our lives. In order to understand thoroughly that practice of negotiation, we must dismiss broad assumptions about how cultural practices differ and break these practices down "into units small enough that we can talk about degrees of sharing or can come to recognize how contrasting paths intersect and diverge" (14). In other words, if we wish to describe how we go about expressing our identity to others, we cannot speak of modeling discrete practices that exist "in toto" somewhere. Achieving personal agency is a constant process of matching available expressive resources with our design for our own lives, of adjusting to those resources, and of noting how they coincide with or differ from our intended expression; in this way, we try to give our lives meaning in the terms of existing "cultural grammars," as Altieri calls them (167). In my view, this process also underlies the function of embracing contraries as Elbow has described it. We allow ourselves to believe those ideas that others believe and to value them because others do, while at the same time we articulate our own beliefs as they both incorporate others' beliefs and values and as they stand against them. Altieri explains the context in which the process of valuing and negotiating differences has meaning in our lives: it is the means through which we develop our personal identity.

But development of personal identity has no effect and gives no satisfaction if it is not recognized by others. Altieri argues that personal expression as an enactment of identity is recognized by others when others interpret individuals as caring about the identities in which they engage. In Elbow's terms, this sincerity might be conveyed by projecting a personal voice in writing. But it is more than this: in order to be recognized as personally invested, says Altieri, expression must project a consistent identity over time. Agency or social power is achieved when one's actions have an effect upon others who begin to recognize an agent as making a difference in this world. Expression that works in this way, Altieri posits, carries "the force of a promise" (75). Not only does a promise recognize "historical antecedents" or values that precede an agent and have influenced his or her convictions, but also it "offers the agent's work upon those antecedents as its claim to make a difference for others" (75). Certainly, our review of the life work of James Moffett and Peter Elbow suggests in each case an agency that has been developed with the force of a promise. With each succeeding publication, both scholars have continued to elaborate and follow through on the convictions that sustained them in the past. This consistency of approach has much to do with how their views have been accepted and valued within the community of teachers who read their work and follow their practices. Expression that has a lasting effect upon others, Altieri tells us, has personal style, which is more than the distinctive voice of sincere conviction, as it has so often been portrayed in process pedagogy. Personal "style dramatizes agency as it negotiates the boundaries between knowing and willing" (Altieri 77). It seems to me that Peter Elbow's prose style conveys quite directly this negotiation; it is prose that displays the exuberance of having been written freely and without constraint as well as the consideration that develops from testing ideas over time through multiple iterations and readings with others. Elbow's style reveals him to live the act of writing as he has enjoined us to practice it. His style reflects a life with design, with commitment to an overriding goal or value, which his readers recognize to have guided his expression with some consistency.

The reasons that Elbow and Moffett have given to ground their pedagogical practices reveal their commitment to a way of living and to continually get better at it. But to realize that kind of commitment as subjective agents, Altieri tells us, our expression must make demands not only upon ourselves but also upon others who help us realize how our actions might be configured to better realize the kind of persons we strive to become: "Agents need not only to see themselves in the eyes of internalized others within their communities but also to be able to imagine making demands on those communities to stretch themselves to see how deeds and reasons might be configured" (179–80). Our reasons for acting not only must be consistent with our own life design, but also they must be valued by others. We may be forced at times to reconcile the desire to act in ways that are valued by others (as a "condition" to be recognized by them) with the desire to act in ways that not only make life more enjoyable for us but also establish our own singular identity: "Any adequate account of 'what I am' will have to take up the affective and practical implications of [the] gulf between identity conditions and a life worth living" (Altieri 176). As a subjective agent, Altieri tells us, the "I" wants more than to find itself mirrored in others and they in us; the "I" wants "to be understood in its intentional orientations, which include efforts both to modify the self and to modify the grammars that one inherits" (208). We want to be recognized by others as singular persons with unique identities. And while yielding to the cultural conditions that constrain our words and actions, we also act to change these conditions. But in order to be recognized for having made these adjustments, we must establish caring relationships with others. In order to project our identity and commitments, Altieri concludes, we must maintain a caring attitude "not because we have any specific image of ourselves, but because we have ideals of relatedness that require and reward such states" (207).

Some of the care we extend toward others does involve copying and modeling what we believe to be valued by them. We use models to understand others' particular perspectives or "tilts" upon the world: "Copies bind us to a shared world; models indicate our capacities to give distinctive emphasis to certain aspects of that world" (43). But eventually, we shape our own intentions as they differ from these various perspectives, being better able to do so for having shared the views of others. The entire process of expressing ourselves, Altieri suggests, is dependent upon our ability to regard what we will to do "as a mode of relationship by which [we as] agents indicate, and at times make explicit, [our] consent to or investment in certain passions and paths of action" (210–11). That relation involves investing in the identities and values of others as well as in our own. We seek to agree with others not because we believe in some abstract ideal of the superiority of agreement but because through making this effort we "[foster] aspects of identities that others can appreciate and respond to" (Altieri 212). In short, we seek to reach common understanding so that we can be perceived as people who have values that are "shareable" with others. Furthermore, Altieri suggests that the whole point of deciding what to say or how to act in a world of others is not bound up with some abstract moral code about telling or seeking the truth and an assessment of the consequences of doing so; rather it is bound up with "who the person can become by virtue of exercising that virtue [e.g., truth telling] in [a given] situation" (183). We define ourselves as moral agents by speaking and acting in certain ways that "make explicit for various others what is implicit in the complex of decisions, actions, and interpretive contexts relative to which certain judgments about worthiness are sought" (Altieri 187). In other words, we aim to act like worthy persons, realizing that goal through showing overtly how we relate to contexts in which qualities of worthiness are expected by others.

Then subjective expression is the complex task of discovering who we are through articulating our values within the history of values and identities developed by others, thus showing how our presence on this earth makes a difference, a contribution to that history. We become better at this, better at being subjective agents among other agents— better persons among other persons—through relating to others with caring attitudes. Writing as the expression of our agency reflects a purposeful design for living, realized through emulating others whose actions represent the persons we would like to be and whom we wish to recognize that identity in us.

We are in the midst of an era of expanding interest in the ways that persons realize their identity through words and actions that solidify personal relationships and define their interests within a variety of cultural groups. Scholars have begun to articulate verbal expression as the desire to emulate others so that we might be recognized as making a difference among them. I wish to close this essay by suggesting just a few ways that this elaboration of how we achieve verbal agency through emulating others might play itself out in the college classroom. I anticipate, for instance, that in teaching students about audience analysis we might expect them to consider not only the usual demographic data—including educational background, knowledge of topic, interests or prejudices relative to our purposes—but also how they as persons speaking to other persons might be seen to have merit or worth in the eyes of their chosen audience. When we assign a series of composing tasks and evaluate them, we might consider not only whether a student's procedures and products show growth in inventiveness and mastery of mechanical skill, rhetorical form, and argumentative sophistication but also whether they reflect a student's intention to articulate his or her life as having purpose in a world of others, as expressing the care and attention for others that will ensure reciprocal care and attention to his or her own singular needs. Finally, when grading student papers—whether they be lab reports, summaries of outside readings, research papers, personal essays, scholarly articles, or grant proposals—we might expect to judge whether these writings in all their varieties carry the "force of a promise." Do they build on historical precedents whether they be established procedures, past research, or reflections on personal experience? Do they show how arguments or convictions have emerged from the writer's judgment of these precedents? And do they show how the writer has acted and developed within these traditions as a person who makes a difference among others?

If we begin to address these concerns about personal agency overtly in the writing classroom, I believe we also will begin to teach writing more effectively as personal expression, as the willful action of a person among persons who are articulating together our common aspirations while distinguishing within them our singular selves. Through such attention we can situate the mechanical device paradigm of modeling written products and procedures within the broader task of teaching writing as design, as the enactment of our effort to emulate others, to honor our shared traditions, and through that sensitivity point to our shared future. In short, we can carry on the work of the process movement but this time with the force of a promise.

4
Is There Life after Process? The Role of Social Scientism in a Changing Discipline

Joseph Petraglia

Social scientism and the process movement in writing are intimately related. And, of course, process and the "composition-centered" structure of the writing field are also closely bound. In this chapter, I consider the nature of the interconnectedness of process, method, and the professional shape of the writing field, for we now find ourselves at something of a crossroads—a crossroads both in the sense that the discipline is confronted with a choice of direction and in the sense that paths that had steadily converged prior to process now appear to be growing apart once more. This is due not only to the generally anti-empirical cast of much *post*-process writing theory (ironically, a situation that empirical work has been instrumental in bringing about) but because empirical approaches to research have been evolving as well and the interventionist agenda of the old social scientism that undergirded process has been replaced with a trend toward description. But complicating the situation further, neither post-process theories of writing nor a "new" social scientism have done much to alter the professional profile of the writing field, which remains entrenched in the pedagogical enterprise I have characterized elsewhere as "general writing skills instruction." This threatens to put contemporary social scientism in a double bind—an unsuitable ally of post-process theories that reject empirical study and out of synch with the profession that has traditionally provided the site for investigation into writing. The latter section of this chapter briefly sketches our options for averting the threat to social scientism, as I understand it, and for developing a post-process profession.

It is on an occasion such as this that the desire to present an argument hypertextually seems especially compelling to me, for the linearity of print suggests a series of simple cause-and-effect relationships and strategic "moves" that I neither see nor wish to convey. Nevertheless, I hope that even a tidy narrative may have its uses, and in this spirit I wish to consider briefly what the implications of being "post-process" may be for empirical writing research and, ultimately, for the future of the writing profession. I should begin by defining the senses in which I use the terms *process* and *post-process* and *old* and *new social scientism*.

Process and Method

The reader undoubtedly has a richer understanding of "process" and the "process movement" than can be provided in a few paragraphs. This is partly due to the sheer longevity of the movement and its institutionalization within the field. Like many colleagues, perhaps, process is all I have ever known—my own freshman writing course began with my teaching assistant's explanation that we were going to freewrite, keep journals, have our peers review our drafts, revise globally, and so forth because (as we would be reminded repeatedly) *writing is a process.* Professionally too, I came of age at a time and place (Carnegie Mellon in the late eighties) where process was in full bloom and so much a part of the conventional wisdom that the cognitive models of writing to which we were introduced were easily understood as the fulfillment of the movement's Manifest Destiny.

In a nutshell, the process movement was a amalgam of theories, models, and pedagogies that were devised as an antidote to the current-traditional paradigm in writing that focused on the written product rather than on the means by which the product was produced. Though John Warnock (561) suggests that current-traditionalism's focus on product reflected the New Critical approach to literary study, methodologically, it may have more in common with the behaviorist model in psychology. Current-traditionalism treated writing behavior as a sort of stimulus-response: teachers provided instruction, and students produced texts as a result of that instruction. Little reference was made to exactly how or why that happened—it just did, and composition theory in the early half of this century (to the extent that it could be called such) speculated on what kind of instruction permitted the student *qua* black box to produce the best writing. Just as many psychologists grew dissatisfied with behaviorism's obscurance of mind and sought to uncover the mental processes by which complex behaviors were produced, a small group of writing theorists began to reject the mystery in which current-traditionalism had enveloped writing. Instead, they argued, writing was less a single behavior than a series of procedures and strategic choices that formed a complex system of text production: in short, a process.

Understanding writing as a process gave the field a new understanding of rhetoric as a practical art, a variety of *techne*, and it provided an entry into the worlds of both research and teaching that, perhaps more than any other "event" in the field, disciplined writing in every sense of the word. It imposed a coherence on an inchoate collection of what Steven North has called teacherly "lore" and provided a catechistic structure through which writing could attain a distinct academic identity. At the same time, process opened the door to new methodological possibilities. While one may, of course, simply theorize about systems, the more rational, predictable, and communicable one requires a system to be, the more likely it is that the system will lend itself to scientific analysis. In the case of writing, it is clear that the system had to be highly specified, for it had to serve a composition field dedicated to the *production* of rhetorical skills. For writing specialists, the process movement could not stop at the level of speculation; it had to offer a regime. Thus, a faith in both the describability and the manipulability of the processes by which writers produce texts allowed teachers to do their job in a more academically legitimated manner. Although Lester Faigley, in *Fragments of Rationality*, emphasizes the important contribution of expressivist theorists such as Donald Murray in bringing process to the fore, it was research such as Janet Emig's *The Composing Processes of Twelfth Graders* that had the greatest impact on the field, generally, and it was through such early empirical efforts that the process paradigm in writing attained a genuinely academic profile and, I would argue, shaped the field as we know it.

It is not difficult to understand the allure of social scientism for the writing field, as science had exerted enormous influence in practically every corner of human experience for hundreds of years and several other fields with a historic relationship to rhetoric and writing, such as psychology and education, had given themselves over almost completely to scientific method over the course of the last century. Of course, the most paradigmatic science was Newtonian physics, which provided the seventeenth-century model that late nineteenth-century social science sought to emulate (Gardner). Newtonian materialism set out the mechanistic world view that held that objects, including organisms, were machines—fabulously complex machines in the case of humans, but ultimately reducible to a system of wheels and pulleys or cogs within an elaborate clockwork. Physics was a model of certainty, methodological and theoretical clarity, and what appeared to be an undeniable force for positive change. It is little wonder, then, that writing theorists would want to follow in the footsteps of social science just as the social sciences had followed in those of physics.

A distinctive characteristic of social science throughout most of this century has been its interventionist mission: social scientism has been valued chiefly for its potential to engage and remediate social ills. Just as the *telos* of the physical sciences was bound up in the production of practical methods and objects, so did it seem clear to newly white-coated social scientists that any truly worthwhile study of human behavior would have as its objective the discovery of the means by which behavior could be predicted and directed toward useful ends (Baars; Danziger). Within this framework it was considered only natural that scientific research should, as in physics or chemistry, intervene in the world and extend human control over it. And, of course, such a mission would be seen as appealing by educators in most disciplines, as the profession of teaching is inextricably linked to intervention in the lives of students. In writing, social scientism permitted specialists to make the very important claim that an individual's writing process not only could be understood but also could be fixed. The social scientification of the writing process induced a kind of construct-stability that permitted writing teachers to view the purpose of writing research as the discovery of optimal processing irrespective of situational variables, much as the "information-processing" paradigm that displaced behaviorism in psychology constructed an image of the learner as an optimal problem solver (Gergen; Sack, Soloway, and Weingrad). Sacrificing a growing awareness of the situatedness and complexity of writing to the greater gods of process enabled theorists, researchers, and teachers to do something they very much wanted to do: develop strategies and heuristics that were applicable to general writing-skills instruction.

In short, a program of empirical research that could provide prescriptions for how to write dovetailed neatly into the longstanding tradition of rhetoric-as-*techne* generally and especially into its nineteenth-century avatar, composition. Uniquely among disciplines, perhaps, the purpose of research in writing was tied to the furtherance of pedagogy; an improved understanding of the composing process was worthless if it could not bring with it recommendations for how to improve students' writing. The objectification of the writing process permitted by empirical method provided a "thing" that could be intact, and thus worthy of emulation, or broken, and thus in need of repair. Rhetoric's roots in *techne* made the notion of a scientifically "treatable" writing process immediately intelligible; after all, the thrust of rhetorical theory for two millennia had centered on dissecting and redissecting the whole of rhetoric into manageable parts.

Post-Process and the New Social Scientism

Though one might quickly stipulate a definition of "process," the same cannot be done as easily for "post-process." The field "after" process has become more hybridized and complex, which only seems natural given the qualitative and quantitative increase in scholarly attention writing has received over the last two decades. And as in so many other "post" enterprises (e.g., post-modernism, post-colonialism, and post-feminism) the meaning of the prefix is often contested (Bahri). As I understand it, "post-process" signifies a rejection of the generally formulaic framework for understanding writing that process suggested. Of course, the fundamental observation that an individual produces text by means of a writing process has not been discarded. Instead, it has dissolved and shifted from figure to ground. It infuses our awareness of writing, it tinctures our thoughts about writing instruction, and trace elements of it can be found in practically every professional conversation. Ironically, however, I take this as a sign that our increasing disciplinarity has led us *past* process. In other words, we now have the theoretical and empirical sophistication to consider the mantra "writing is a process" as the right answer to a really boring question. We have better questions now, and the notion of process no longer counts as much of an insight.

Though reductive, it nonetheless may be possible to characterize the field after process as one that is attempting to animate two complementary observations: first, that writing genres, audiences, and writers themselves are socially and culturally constructed and, second, that the ways in which writing gets produced are characterized by an almost impenetrable web of cultural practices, social interactions, power differentials, and discursive conventions governing the production of text, making writing more of a phenomenon than a behavior. The idea that human perceptions of reality are socially constructed is an old one, though it has only perhaps become common currency in the writing field with Kenneth Bruffee's essay, which linked Vygotskian socio-historicism and Rortian pragmatism with traditional classroom concerns such as collaboration. Such theories emphasize the intersubjective nature of knowledge and learning and (as they harken back to the epistemological skepticism of the early Sophists) find an easy resonance with both classical and contemporary theories of rhetoric. Since Bruffee, James Berlin has called a social constructionist approach to the writing field a variety of "social-epistemicism," and even among those writing professionals who might decline to take on some of the baggage that label carries with it, the idea that writing is a culturally and socially mediated behavior is, like the idea that text is the outcome of a process, uncontroversial.

In tandem with the widespread acknowledgment of writing's "socialness," the systematicity that a notion of a writing process implies has been critiqued in the rhetoric and writing field as theoretically inadequate from political, social, philosophical, linguistic, and socio-cognitive perspectives, to name but a few. Thomas Kent, for instance, concludes his essay on the rhetoric of paralogy with the quintessentially post-process observation, "Our current conceptions of rhetoric, drenched as they are in the Platonic/Aristotelian formulations of logic, process, and system, cannot account for the hermeneutic dimension intrinsic to both discourse production and discourse analysis" ("Beyond System" 505). Such an appreciation of the context dependence of writing behavior, heavy with situational variables and interpretative screens, makes the notion of an easily identifiable writing system or process suspect. Certainly, the assumptions that permitted early social scientists of writing to develop process theories and models of writing behavior are much more difficult to uphold if we acknowledge the centrality of interpretation to communication.

But in the same way we have moved past process, social scientism in writing also has evolved to meet the challenges the hermeneutic turn has presented. A vast literature in fields ranging from education (e.g., Lincoln and Guba) and the philosophy of science (e.g., Laudan), to social psychology (e.g., Smith, Harré, and Van Langenhove) and elsewhere has grown up around what Reason and Rowan have dubbed the "New Paradigm": a sometimes radical theorization of empirical methodology that seeks to accommodate our postmodern skepticism toward foundations while retaining its scientific essence. Variously cast as an alternative empiricism or as an alternative to empiricism, the New Paradigm is not a paradigm at all, but a shorthand for an eclectic assortment of frameworks devised for the study of human activity. Without attempting to account for all of this New Paradigm's permutations, my argument requires that I at least characterize the shift as the writing field has experienced it.

Although writing researcher Carol Berkenkotter (following Guba) has labeled the shift as one between positivism and yet another "post" (post-positivism), it is perhaps less problematic in the present context to simply differentiate "old" from "new" social scientism.[1] Morgan and Smircich note that "the choice and adequacy of a method embodies a variety of assumptions regarding the nature of knowledge and the methods through which that knowledge can be obtained, as well as a set of root assumptions about the nature of the phenomena to be investigated" (492). In the following table, I follow Morgan and Smircich's lead and attempt to encapsulate the difference between the old social scientism that gave process its impetus and the new social scientism that now encourages us to move on.

	Old Social Scientism	New Social Scientism
Ontological Status of Writing	writing as a compendium of discrete, general skills used by individuals	writing as a socio-cognitive phenomenon dependent upon historical and cultural context
Purpose of Writing Research	discovery of the processes by which effective writing can be produced or taught	generation of deeper and more complex understanding of writing and its contexts
Product of Writing Research	heuristics to assist teachers and students of composition	"thick" description of writing behavior and patterns of writing behavior
Disciplinary/ Professional Orientation	practice and pedagogy-centered	theory-centered (though not exclusively)

To distinguish the old from the new social scientism, one might first note that most contemporary empirical research on writing rejects the assumption—central to the process movement's "success"—that writing is largely a body of discrete writing skills and procedures that transcend context. Although the early cognitivism-in-writing tradition in which the process movement culminated always maintained that writing was a complex and recursive behavior, for both methodological and pedagogical reasons, it was rarely treated as such. In both teaching and research, the process approach did not deal with the gestalt of writing, only its subprocesses and only one at a time. I think Alan France is correct in his assertion that

> cognition introduced a research method that furthered decontextualized writing by translating it into a record of internal mental processing. Composing-aloud protocols—student writing without the student—provided generalizable data, objects that could be subjected to the rigors of cognitive science. . . . This led away from the interface between individuals and culture, from discourse as social dialogue, and from writing as an intertextual and cultural process. (92–93)

I would argue that the separation of individual from context was not so much a problem with cognitivist method, however, as it was part of the old social scientism that so appealed to the process movement's internal logic.

The new social scientism, in contrast, is rooted in an interest in situating writing in physical and metaphysical spaces of time, place, culture, and identity. What is maybe even more significant than the ontological shift between old and new is that the purpose of new social scientific research has evolved from that of understanding processes in order to teach them to producing more and more comprehensive accounts of what it means to be a writer and to write. In contrast, the old social science abetted the process urge to produce both heuristics that would lead students to produce better writing as well as frameworks that assisted teachers in the diagnostic procedures they applied to student writing. For this reason, a final major difference between the two forms of social scientism is that while the old social scientism was well-suited to the creation of a discipline rooted in the profession of teaching students to produce writing, new social scientism has strayed from that purely pedagogical function. Instead, social scientism in writing has grown closer to other disciplines that study human activity such as anthropology, sociology, and psychology, disciplines that, though their contents are, of course, taught, are not constructed with their teachability in mind.

But in becoming post-process and postmodern, we might wonder along with Gregory Cizek if we are also becoming post-scientific. Certainly, the "new social scientism" as presented in the table above appears rather anemic; practically any sort of research, empirical or otherwise, seems to slot neatly under such a rubric. So to highlight the essentially scientific flavor of the new social scientism let me note the ways in which old and new social scientisms in writing share some common assumptions. Both, for instance, subscribe to the beliefs that (1) rhetorical behaviors such as writing and speech lend themselves to empirical investigation that must be held accountable to a priori standards of validity, that (2) theories of rhetorical behavior should be tested empirically where possible, and that (3) empirical claims are always left open to contestation by other empirical evidence. Empirical verification or falsification of any claim is never the last word, and findings are perhaps best thought of as a heuristic for thinking in careful and structured ways. The goal in both the old and the new social sciences is to improve on earlier accounts of the phenomenon under study. In this sense, then, the new social scientism remains a progressive enterprise (in the sense that it lays claim to an increasingly better account of the data) even as it has abandoned any positivistic pretensions of arriving at Truth (McGuire and Melia; Bereiter).

One might say that the label "social scientism" now identifies not so much a difference between speculation (i.e., "pure" theory) and number-crunching as it does a researcher's attitude toward issues of *accountability*. Although the new social scientism has grown more impressionistic in some respects, several approaches to writing research remain outside the realm of social science. For instance, neo-expressivist and many social-epistemic varieties of writing theory lay no claim to empirical status and set no standards for validity (although they do not foreclose on claims to correspondence with the "real-world" in some sense). Conversely, other theoretical and research frameworks that do, in fact, claim social scientific status (i.e., including some of the frameworks which Reason and Rowan subsume in their New Paradigm) may not conform to social scientism's minimal requirements as I have set them out. For instance, studies may attempt an "objective" description of the context, justify their selection of "subjects," and use data such as quotes, frequency counts, and coding systems that are checked for interrater reliability, even though they demonstrate little concern for issues of triangulation (via member-checks or other confirmatory processes) or falsification. This pseudo-empiricism is seen in some case studies, ethnographic or otherwise naturalistic studies that believe a thick description of a writing situation to be an end in itself rather than a hypothesis-generating step that lends itself to more systematic investigation (Lincoln and Guba). At this end of the methodological spectrum, Boland has argued that such research relies on the hope that its claims will resonate with sympathetic readers who share its values and objectives. In contrast, what I see as the new social scientism in writing, like the old, does not rely primarily on hope and insists on the integrity of the evidence that it gathers to argue its claims. New social scientists of writing would want to argue with Kevin Davis's contention that writing phenomena "exist because researchers made them exist through their research" (125) not because they reject the idea that research creates many of the constructs it purports to study but because they believe there is a real world of writing activity to which their research must be held accountable, even if issues surrounding the realness of that world and criteria for accountability are subject to rational dispute.

Thus, the shift from older to newer models of social scientific inquiry does not necessarily entail a wholesale rejection of the former; witness the fact that reports of cognitivism-in-writing's death (cf. France) have been greatly exaggerated. Cognitivism (now more appropriately called "sociocognitivism," perhaps) continues to be a dynamic lens through which to view learning, as revealed in the widespread interest in Vygotsky, Dewey, and constructivism in practically every education-related discipline. In the writing field, David Russell elaborates a sociocognitive perspective when he argues that writing entails participation in "some historically situated human activity" that calls for particular kinds of writing that "cannot be learned apart from the problems, the habits, the activities—the subject matter—of some group that found the need to write in that way to solve a problem or carry on its activities" (194).

Lauren Resnick nicely summarizes the questions the new social scientific perspective on literacy seeks to address:

> *Who* are the actors—both writers and readers—in these [literate] situations? How do they define themselves in relation to the texts they engage with, to each other, to other people who may also engage with those

texts? *Why* are they reading and writing? What are they attempting to do with the written word? What kinds of institutional or broadly social invitations, permissions, and constraints influence their activities? *How* do people read and write? What are the processes, cognitive and social, that define literate practices? Finally, *what* do people read and write? What are the texts themselves like, and how do their characteristics facilitate particular forms of literate practice? (171)

By any measure this is an ambitious inventory of questions as well as a fairly representative list of the concerns evinced by the new social scientism. Because the new social scientism is more epistemologically aware than the old, it is sometimes more self-conscious and more aware of its own limitations. Nevertheless, this newfound reflexivity is perhaps social scientism's most appealing strength: in Bonnie Nardi's words, "There is a new kind of post-postmodern voice struggling to speak clearly here; it is polyvocal and dialogical, to be sure, but also committed to social and scientific engagement" (15).

In Search of a Post-Process Profession

To recap, the process movement was ideally suited to the old social scientism of its time, and although critics of empirical method were vocal even then, I have argued that the logic of "process" made the social scientification of the field almost inevitable. Research, both empirical and theoretical, throughout the seventies and much of the eighties could be counted on to define the process of writing, articulate specific parts of the process, or assist students through the process or through a part of the process. Perhaps historians of the field will look back on these decades as a rare time when theory, research, pedagogy, and profession were largely in synch: theories of process were furthered by empirical models of writing behavior, and teachers of writing could happily draw from both to support their claims to a hard-won space for composition in the academy. Together, the old social scientism and process accomplished a great deal; their marriage professionalized the writing field, established composition as a legitimate area of inquiry, and, what is most significant in my view, incidentally provided rhetorical theory an entree into the academy that speech, communications, and classics departments cannot match, at least in terms of size and resources.

But to finally return to the question that titles this chapter, "Is there life after process?" I suppose the answer depends on what you call living. As I have noted, contemporary social science research on writing moves away from the old social scientific assumption that the purpose of research is to intervene and to manipulate. For the writing field, so bound up in *techne* and pedagogy, this might come as distressing news, for social scientism no longer fills the rather narrow niche the writing profession has carved out for it. The new social scientism in writing seems divorced from these concerns, indeed, divorced from immediate classroom exigencies generally. Instead, sociocognitive and other strands of post-process research are more likely to suggest the ways in which the enterprise of composition is misguided and why the explicit teaching of writing—as rhetorical *production*—is a losing proposition.

In an introduction to a recent anthology on the shaky relationship of writing theory and research to pedagogy, I noted that journal articles and conference presentations on writing seem to be growing both in theoretical sophistication and in irrelevance to the composition classroom. This is because while we may be theoretically post-process and while we may be methodologically attuned to the new social scientism, professionally, the dominance of the general writing-skills classroom reminds us that we continue to inhabit a process-centric universe. If the demands of *techne* continue to leave the composition classroom our disciplinary *raison d'être*, I suspect that the current gulf between research and theory on one side and the profession of composition on the other can only widen. A number of scenarios this disjuncture could engender come to mind. In the worst-case scenario (which practically all writing professionals would certainly wish to avert), the writing field hunkers down into the general writing-skills trenches and reverts to the purely service status it has struggled to overcome. Overwhelmed by its traditional English department rival (i.e., literature) but now also playing a distant second fiddle to cultural studies, writing is relegated once again to the realm of scribal skills, and the profession is reduced to the job of conveying how-tos, reciting rules-of-thumb, passing out essay assignments, and correcting exercises (and even this diminished job will lend itself very well to performance by increasingly intelligent computer tutoring systems).

Another, more likely, scenario may be simply a retreat from empirical research that nonetheless maintains writing's theoretical integrity. Here writing is cast as another site of cultural studies lending itself to theorizations of power, ideology, and the construction of identity, and so forth, that seek little validation from empirical research. Though post-process theory, like the new social scientism, can direct our attention away from the general writing-skills classroom, its purely speculative nature more readily allows for business as usual by permitting "radical" pedagogists to present composition as a means of ideological engagement and social activism (a supreme irony, in my view, but another topic for another paper). This second scenario may not be entirely unappealing to many, of course.[2] Yet I would like to propose a third scenario and speculate on what I see as a more positive future for both social scientism in writing and for the discipline, bearing in mind that writing, as a profession, will continue to emphasize pedagogy over the generation of new content and that while scientism's missionary zeal has been curbed, social scientific research will continue to be most highly prized for its ability to address classroom concerns. Actually, this third scenario has two dimensions—one which we have already begun to explore, but another that, in the long run, may better ensure rhetoric and writing's vitality in the academy.

This first dimension is one that currently engages much of the writing field's best efforts: it is the study of how members of discursive communities learn to write within specialized domains outside the composition classroom. There is a great deal we have learned about writing conventions and techniques in various disciplines as well as in the workplace, and one can comfortably assume that WAC, technical writing, and professional writing will, if anything, grow increasingly important to the profession. Such growth ensures social scientism a role in the writing field as, once again, researchers are seeking systems, or, now, patterns of interaction between situational variables and text production—both of which lend themselves to qualitative and quantitative investigation. A bit further afield and of less immediate pedagogical relevance, the burgeoning rhetoric of inquiry movement is also one that lends itself to empirical as well as theoretical study, and social scientism in this area can be counted on to inform writing theory elsewhere.

Although social scientism's existence in writing might be assured by these agendas, it is not necessarily a comfortable existence, for writing in the disciplines, however important, does not offer social scientism the security or prominence that process afforded it. This can come only with a reconceptualization of what it means to "teach writing." This reconceptualization requires that the discipline let go of its current pedagogical shape (i.e., its focus on supplying students with productive rhetorical skills that can be exercised through writing) and instead deploy its efforts to inculcate *receptive* skills. If my assertion that writing research (and theory) can no longer support a generic writing *techne* is correct, a turn away from developing rhetorical skills and toward development of rhetorical sensibilities seems a reasonable one. I see such a turn as critical not only to social scientism's future in the writing field but also to the continued health of post-process theory as well.

A model for this might be found in the speech communications work of the early seventies, which identified "rhetorical sensitivity" as a worthwhile outcome of rhetorical instruction. Roderick Hart and Don Burks argue that in the development of rhetorical sensitivity in students lies our greatest hope of "facilitating human understanding and to effect social cohesion" (75), which we might take as the ultimate goal of any communications education. Rhetorical education, according to Hart and Burks, should direct a student toward the selection of those aspects of his or her self that could, and perhaps should, be rhetorically transformed when confronted with particular social conditions and situations. In their view, the ideal rhetorical training will have at its core the development of a *sensitivity* to the rhetorical possibilities available to students and will provide some guidance as to how they may determine to select among those possibilities.[3] They suggest that

> when we are being rhetorically sensitive, we are well aware that a rhetorical situation rarely presents a choice of saying or not saying, of telling it like it is or not telling it at all; rather, rhetorical sensitivity demands that we consider verbal alternatives, that we attempt to process and to choose among all possible verbal strategies *before* giving utterance to an idea. (89)

Instilling rhetorical sensitivity therefore contrasts sharply with the traditional speech or writing-skills classroom that emphasizes students' abilities to produce rhetorical texts.

Although Hart and his subsequent collaborators never really provided concrete curricular recommendations for advancing receptive rhetorical skills, David Kaufer and Patricia Dunmire seem to do so with their metaphor of writing as knowledge design, which generates a pedagogy whereby writing students take apart and analyze the situated rhetorical performances of others. They argue that the importance of a reflective pedagogy based on the concept of knowledge design arises from the need for students to recognize the material effects brought to bear by some texts and the inability of other texts to realize similar effects. We hope that, in the end, students will internalize the reflective sensitivities they have learned . . . [and] apply the same sensitivities to their own text. (230)

Similarly, in addition to WAC classes, Russell has called for introductory and interdisciplinary courses that "directly raise the awareness of students, teachers, and the public *about* writing, its uses and its power—for good or ill—in the cultures and activity systems that employ it" (71). The object of such courses would not be to improve students' writing skills but to make students informed consumers of written discourse in the hope that they may become better producers of it as well. In these and other articulations of the "receptive skills" writing classroom, the content's grist is provided by theory, of course, but also by empirical research into rhetorical behavior. In this way, social scientism can play a role in the writing field similar to the role it plays in other disciplines.

In conclusion, we have become much more interested in the ecology in which writing takes place than in the mere fact that writing is the outcome of a variety of steps and stages. And as we move into the post-process phase of our discipline's evolution, research cannot be counted upon to serve as *techne*'s handmaiden in the same way it did in process's halcyon days. What this means for social scientism in writing, I believe, depends on the ability and willingness of writing professionals to evolve not only post-process, but post-composition. But this begs many questions, not least of which is our collective ability to imagine professional and pedagogical frameworks that do not have the explicit teaching of students to write at their heart. And even if we do muster such resolve, a tougher question will be whether university administrators and taxpayers can be convinced to subsidize a writing field that declines making promises its research and theory suggest cannot be kept. Another field, which some are already calling "writing studies," may be growing up alongside and within composition and may one day be in a position to challenge the status of composition as the main site of professional identity. Within a writing studies framework, both post-process theory and the new social scientism can be put in the service of pedagogy, but this can be done only if serious thought is put toward revisioning writing, not only as a content but also as a profession.

Notes

1. In suggesting an "old/new" distinction, I am not merely signaling the difference between quantitative and qualitative research, nor the shift from controlled experimental research to quasi-experimental and more "naturalistic" studies, though these other distinctions hint at a general progression in social scientism's recent evolution.

2. This chapter has focused largely on the tensions between social scientism and writing's professional status, though as Charney reminds us, the alleged incompatibility of postmodern theory and empirical method, to which I have only alluded, presents a set of equally contentious issues.

3. A later assessment instrument (RHETSEN) was developed and tested for reliability and validity (Hart, Carlson, and Eadie). The recognition that a pedagogical objective centering on receptive rather than productive skills would have to at least make a stab at assessment criteria, seems very prescient given many of our current debates over evaluation.

5
Research in Professional Communication: A Post-Process Perspective

Nancy Blyler

Currently, research in professional communication focuses, at least in part, on describing and explaining the writing process as it occurs in workplace and organizational settings. Carl Herndl, for example, claims that the dominant research strategy in professional communication is "descriptive and exploratory" (349), where scholars attempt to discover how the "production of meaning" occurs (351). Along the same lines, Rachel Spilka asserts that

> most reported research has been descriptive, with investigators observing how a workplace culture influences composing process behavior and decisions and how such workplace practices are deemed acceptable or unacceptable by particular workplace cultures. (209)

Fueling this concern with describing composing-process behavior has been not only the desire to understand workplace writing but also the desire to amass a body of information that can be used to guarantee effective pedagogy. With such information, scholars assert, intervention in students' writing processes can be enhanced. Spilka, for example, discusses the need to find "a set of reliable pedagogical tools"— a need so great that "future research in professional writing" has to "respond more strongly" to pedagogy by making methodological changes. These changes will allow us to discern "reliable patterns" despite "disparate research designs" (Spilka 215), thus enabling us to identify effective and ineffective workplace writing practices and to improve the instruction our students receive.

While Spilka addresses our general desire to use research as a guarantee of effective pedagogy, other scholars are more specific in their remarks. For example, Marion Larson claims that because "research in organizational socialization" indicates the influence of "organizational roles"—both "actual and perceived"—on writing decisions, instructors ought to "[design] courses with this knowledge" (364).

Instructors should, in other words, introduce students to the constraints organizational roles place on composing in workplace settings.

Similarly, James Reither notes research indicating the importance of collaboration in the context of on-the-job writing. Given this finding, asserts Reither, some scholars "reason that if team writing is common practice in certain kinds of workplaces, and if students are being prepared to take roles in those workplaces, then teachers should give students team writing and revising assignments" (195). In this way, scholars obviously expect, the writing processes these students engage in will more closely resemble the processes they will use on the job.

Now, I do not want to suggest that there is anything wrong with this desire to help professional communication students learn how to write. Nor do I want to suggest that research results about workplace writing are useless or uninteresting. What I do want to suggest is that, from a post-process perspective, the kind of thinking I describe above is deeply flawed. In the next section, I explain this assertion.

A Post-Process Perspective
and Research on Workplace Writing

According to post-process scholars, the goal of describing and explaining the writing process as it occurs in workplace settings and the use of research results about that process as a guarantee of effective pedagogy are both flawed because they depend on two incorrect assumptions about the writing act: first, that composing is a systematic, codifiable entity we can isolate and examine; second, that understanding and mastering this codifiable entity are necessary prerequisites to learning how to write. From a post-process perspective, assumptions such as these are inaccurate, examples of a belief in what Donald Davidson terms a "conceptual scheme": a means for "organizing experience" ("On the Very Idea" 183) that mediates between communicators and the world (see Dasenbrock 9–12 and Kent, "On the Very Idea" 425–26 for a discussion of Davidson's notion of a conceptual scheme). Briefly put, in professional communication research, scholars assume that they can study a codifiable process called "workplace composing," while in professional communication pedagogy, they assume that students must learn about—even internalize—this process if they are to write well on the job. According to this view, then, the process of workplace composing must mediate between students and those with whom they communicate, in order for effective writing to occur.

However, post-process scholars contend that mediation of the kind promised by an entity called the "composing process"—mediation that makes "knowledge of the world" (Kent, "On the Very Idea" 426) or, in this case, knowledge of workplace writing dependent on a conceptual scheme—is unnecessary because, in fact, no separation or Cartesian split that must be mediated exists between individuals and the world (Kent, "On the Very Idea" 426; Thralls and Blyler 23). Rather, according to post-process scholars, knowledge of the world and hence knowledge of writing result directly from interpretation (Dasenbrock 12–13), as this occurs in communicative or "public interactions with other language users and with the world" (Kent, "On the Very Idea" 430).

In such interaction, claim post-process scholars, writers engage in a hermeneutic guessing game, attempting to suit their interpretations and their writing to the interpretations of those with whom they wish to communicate (Kent, "Paralogic" 26–27). Writers develop, then, what Davidson terms a "passing theory"—a modification of the "prior theory" ("Nice Derangement" 442) or "set of assumptions" that writers hold "about the dispositions, beliefs, and language-use" of their communicants (Dasenbrock 13; see also Kent, "On the Very Idea" 432–34 for a discussion of prior and passing theories). In doing so, writers "shift ground continually until [they] find a close enough fit between [their] hermeneutic strategy and another's strategy" (Kent, "Paralogic" 31), as they attempt to reach a common understanding with others in the world.

Because hermeneutic guessing of this kind is "paralogic," post-process scholars assert that it can never be "codified" or "reduced to a formal method or technique" (Kent, "Paralogic" 30). It can never be reduced, then, to a systematic entity called the "composing process," to be examined through research or taught to students as a guarantee that they will be able to write well. Rather, say post-process scholars, students must engage in and, by doing so, become proficient at this uncodifiable, paralogic guessing (Kent, "Paralogic" 37), since it is fundamental to writing effectively in any situation—including those situations students will encounter in the workplace.

This contention of post-process scholars concerning the hermeneutic, paralogic nature of writing undermines both the goal of professional communication research—to describe and explain the writing process as it occurs in workplace settings—and the desire to use research results about that process as a pedagogical guarantee. Concerning professional communication's research goal, for example, post-process scholars assert that although examining the act of writing may well produce interesting stories (Kent, *Paralogic Rhetoric* 70; Thralls and Blyler 26), such research can tell us nothing "determinate, immutable, or generalizable" about how writers in the workplace or elsewhere go about communicating (Kent, *Paralogic Rhetoric* 55; Kent is discussing ethnographic research, a form currently on the rise in professional communication [Debs 239; Doheny-Farina 253]). Such research therefore can never be used to draw generalizable conclusions about writing that would hold across "acts of discourse production or discourse reception" (Kent, *Paralogic Rhetoric* 55), can never be used, in other words, to codify composing process behavior as it occurs on the job.

Further, concerning the desire to use research results about this process as a guarantee of effective pedagogy, post-process scholars contend that since the composing act is uncodifiable a writer can never know in advance, "in some predictable way, what it is she wants to say and how to say it" (Kent, "Paralogic" 36). Given this unpredictability, a body of knowledge that has been gathered about writing in one situation cannot be used to ensure that students will be able to write effectively in another (Kent, *Paralogic Rhetoric* 55; see also Thralls and Blyler 24–25), cannot be used, in other words, to devise a pedagogy that will guarantee results across multiple communicative interactions. Rather, say post-process scholars, such research can only provide useful "background knowledge" (Kent, "Paralogic" 39; Thralls and Blyler 25) about workplace writing, knowledge that can suggest possible hermeneutic guesses but can never predict in advance of a communicative interaction which guesses will be successful and which will not.

Given this post-process critique, scholars in professional communication who are interested in a post-process perspective may want to rethink their goal for research and, along with it, the use to which research results are put. In the next section, I discuss the critical approach as one direction such rethinking might take.

The Critical Approach: Rethinking Research in Professional Communication

The critical approach, I contend, is useful when rethinking professional communication research because rather than focusing on generalizable descriptions and explanations of entities as they exist in the world (e.g., composing process behavior on the job) the critical approach is "hermeneutic" (Mumby, "Critical" 18) in orientation. That is, critical researchers are concerned not with describing or explaining entities in the world but instead with interpretation and meaning (Mumby, "Critical" 18; Putnam 32), a concern that they combine with an abiding interest in domination and power, as a necessary prelude to critique and social change (Anderson and Irvine 82).

The critical approach is remarkably varied, including under its rubric work called by different names—for example, participatory action research (e.g., Fals-Borda and Rahman), critical interpretive research (e.g., Putnam), and feminist research (e.g., Klein, "How to Do"; Mascia-Lees, Sharpe, and Cohen)—and extending across disciplinary boundaries and theoretical formulations. Critical research has been undertaken by scholars in, for example, organizational communication (e.g., Deetz and Kersten; Mumby, "Critical" and *Communication*); education (e.g., Anderson and Irvine; McLaren, "Field Relations"; McLaren and Lankshear); journalism and mass communication (e.g., Grossberg, "Critical Theory"); and sociology (e.g., Fals-Borda and Rahman; Whyte, *Participatory*; Whyte, Greenwood, and Lazes)—and has been shaped by a variety of theoretical influences, including feminism (e.g., Mascia-Lees, Sharpe, and Cohen); Freirian radical pedagogy (e.g., McLaren and Leonard); liberation theology (e.g., Fals-Borda and Rahman); post-structuralism (e.g., McLaren, "Collision"; McLaren and Lankshear); European phenomenology, hermeneutics, and critical theory (e.g., Mumby, *Communication*); and neo-Marxism (e.g., Grossberg, "Critical Theory").

Because research done under the rubric of the critical approach varies greatly in terms of disciplinary roots and theoretical influences, an exhaustive description is beyond the scope of this chapter. However, I want to further discuss the key principles I mentioned earlier, principles that, regardless of discipline or theoretical orientation, critical researchers hold in common: a rejection of descriptive, explanatory research of the kind I detail here; a focus on interpretation and meaning; and a concern with domination and power, as a precursor to critique and social change.

DESCRIPTIVE, EXPLANATORY RESEARCH

Given their hermeneutic orientation, critical researchers overwhelmingly reject descriptive, explanatory research that aims at generalizable information about entities in the world, claiming such research relies on the belief that through "more powerful methods and concepts" we can come to "more and more accurate representations" (Mumby, "Critical" 18–19; in professional communication, Sullivan and Porter describe this view as the reliance on "a tried-and-true method, and the actual observation of behavior" [229]). However, critical researchers contend that more powerful methods and accuracy of representation are not appropriate concerns, since regardless of methodology we can never approach closer to the truth (Mumby, "Critical" 18).That is, we can never approach closer to the ideal of an objective world existing outside of human subjectivity (Putnam 34, 40, 44; Putnam labels this view "positivist" [31], in a discussion similar to Kent's of the impossibility of a world existing outside of language [*Paralogic Rhetoric* 62–67]). Rather than concerning themselves with this ideal of a world free from subjectivity, critical researchers focus on interpretation and meaning.

INTERPRETATION AND MEANING

In common with other interpretivists (see Putnam for a discussion of various interpretive schools of thought), critical researchers believe not in a world outside of subjectivity but rather in the "centrality" of subjectivity and meaning (Putnam 32). That is, far from focusing on description and explanation of a world separate from the self, critical researchers wish to examine the "subjective and consensual meanings that constitute social reality" (Putnam 32). In doing so, critical researchers assert that social structures and practices, which "originate in human interactions" (Putnam 35), are "created through ongoing actions and intersubjective meanings attributed to these actions" (Putnam 44). In other words, social structures and practices are constituted from the actions and discourses "we have at our disposal through which we make sense of our day-to-day politics of living" (McLaren and Lankshear 386).

To critical researchers therefore communication is not merely a "process of information exchange." Rather, critical researchers view communication as formative, as involved in "the creation and maintenance of symbolic meaning systems" (Mumby, *Communication* 5). It is these meaning systems—these structures and practices shaped by discourse (McLaren and Lankshear 381) and imbued with meaning—and not a reality free from subjectivity that critical researchers feel warrant their attention.

Critical researchers also believe that merely attempting to understand these intersubjective meaning systems is insufficient (Putnam 53; Putnam calls research that aims only at understanding "interpretive naturalistic" while Mumby terms it "descriptive hermeneutic" ["Critical" 19]). Driven by the desire to question "what [reality] could or should become" (Putnam 53), critical researchers wish to interrogate existing social structures and practices (Deetz and Kersten 148, Putnam 53), viewing them as "the product of unequal social relations and conflicts of interest" (Anderson and Irvine 82) where the more powerful dominate at the expense of those with less power. Critical researchers thus are committed to uncovering sources of domination and the workings of power, thereby furthering critique and social change (Anderson and Irvine 82; Deetz and Kersten 148, 154; Putnam 53).

CRITIQUE AND SOCIAL CHANGE

In this commitment to critique and social change, critical researchers again take a "discursive" stance (Mumby, "Critical" 19), asserting that communication is implicated in—indeed, is "fundamentally constitutive of"—power and arguing that "one of the most important areas in which power is exercised is in the struggle over meaning" (Deetz and Mumby 32; see McLaren and Lankshear 381 for a discussion of this struggle as it pertains to research). In the struggle over meaning—which critical researchers stress is central to their conception of social reality (McLaren and Lankshear 385)—the interests of those who have power dominate, their "privileged forms of representing experience" becoming naturalized as "regimes of truth" (McLaren and Lankshear 392) that are taken for granted and hence rarely, if ever, examined (McLaren and Lankshear 386).

Concerned about the workings of privilege and regimes of truth, critical researchers attempt to lay bare circumstances where such domination occurs—where, in other words, "an individual or group has the ability to frame discursive and nondiscursive practices within a system of meaning that is commensurate with that individual's or group's own interests" (Deetz and Mumby 32; see also McLaren and Lankshear 405). In doing so, critical researchers focus on "the 'why' of this reality construction," with the expectation that inequities of power—inequities, that is, in terms of the ability of groups or individuals to realize their interests—can be laid bare and the status quo changed (Deetz and Kersten 160; Fals-Borda, "Some Basic" 3–4; McLaren and Lankshear 405).

With this focus on interpretation and meaning as these relate to critique and social change, critical research obviously differs greatly from its descriptive, explanatory counterpart (see Charney, however, for a discussion of the interpretive, socially constructed nature of "empiricism" and for a defense of this research against charges that it is "implicated in injustice" [571]). I contend, however, that—unlike descriptive, explanatory research—critical research is appropriate for scholars in professional communication interested in a post-process perspective. In the next section, I discuss the reasons why.

Critical Research and a Post-Process Perspective

Critical research is appropriate for scholars in professional communication who are interested in a post-process perspective because whereas descriptive, explanatory research involves theoretical assumptions that post-process scholars contend are deeply flawed, critical research and a post-process perspective are theoretically compatible. More specifically—though the language might differ at times—critical researchers would agree with post-process scholars that no Cartesian split needing mediation exists between individuals and the world. Hence, critical researchers also would reject the notion of conceptual schemes, while affirming the hermeneutic, paralogic nature of communicative interaction. Below I examine these important theoretical intersections.

NO CARTESIAN SPLIT

Post-process scholars affirm their belief that no split exists between "an 'in here'—usually thought of as *mind* or *subjectivity*—and an 'out there'—usually thought of as *world* or *objectivity*" (Kent, "On the Very Idea" 426; italics in original). Hence, "the old Cartesian dualisms of subject and object, mind and world, or language and reality," to post-process scholars, are no longer valid (Kent, *Paralogic Rhetoric* 55).

In the context of discussing their research approach, critical researchers advance a similar claim. Asserting, for example, that no division should exist between the subject and object of research—between, in other words, researcher and participants (Fals-Borda, "Remaking" 152; see also Anderson and Irvine 90; Gaventa 121)—Orlando Fals-Borda uses "Cartesian" ("Remaking" 151) for knowledge generated within a "subject/object [research] binomial" ("Remaking" 152). Rejecting this type of subject/object relationship between researcher and participants—which William Foote Whyte, Davydd Greenwood, and Peter Lazes term an "elitist model" (20)—critical researchers opt instead for a subject/subject relationship (Fals-Borda, "Remaking" 151; "Some Basic" 4–5), where researchers attempt to "break down the bifurcation" between themselves and those they study (Mumby, "Critical" 20). In rejecting any division between researcher and participants, critical researchers recognize "the negotiated, intersubjective nature of the representational process"—that is, the centrality of interpretation—as it pertains to research (Mumby, "Critical" 20). Critical researchers therefore believe that researcher and participants generate knowledge together, as they engage in a "hermeneutical journey of self-discovery" (McLaren, "Field Relations" 158).

In this hermeneutic journey, say critical researchers, researcher and participants "interact, collaborate, discuss, reflect and report in collectivities on an equal footing" (Fals-Borda, "Remaking" 152). Critical research, in other words, is not like descriptive, explanatory—or subject/object—research, where information is sought "by the researcher" under the guise of the scientific method and then "passed on to the group" (Gaventa 124). Instead, critical research "involves" participants in the research "from the initial design of the project through data gathering and analysis to final conclusions and actions arising from the research" (Whyte, Introduction 7; see also Whyte, Greenwood, and Lazes 20). Indeed, in a research situation that John Gaventa terms a "knowledge democracy" (121), "those who are directly affected by a problem have the right to acquire information about it themselves" (123). Peter McLaren says that the other has the hermeneutical privilege in naming the issues before it and in developing an analysis of its situation appropriate to its context. . . . The marginalized have the first right to name reality, to articulate how social reality functions, and to decide how issues are to be organized and defined. ("Field Relations" 161; see also Anderson and Irvine 92)

Given their focus on a subject/subject research relationship, critical researchers would agree with post-process scholars that no Cartesian split exists between individuals and the world. Critical researchers therefore also would reject the notion of mediating conceptual schemes, made necessary by that split.

NO CONCEPTUAL SCHEMES

Post-process scholars clearly reject the notion of conceptual schemes that mediate between individuals and the world. Regarding the composing process, for example, post-process scholars claim that since writing demands "hermeneutic skills" (Kent, "Paralogic" 25) it cannot be reduced to a systematic process designed to bridge a Cartesian split between communicants. Further, regarding the scientific method, post-process scholars deride as false the "myth" that by use of this method as a conceptual scheme, scientists can "discover the essential 'out there'" (Kent, *Paralogic Rhetoric* 61), thus "distinguish[ing] between objective truth and subjective belief" (Kent, *Paralogic Rhetoric* 63). To post-process scholars, rather, the "acquisition of knowledge" is "interpretive and subjective," requiring no codification by the scientific method as a conceptual scheme.

Like post-process scholars, critical researchers also reject the notion of the scientific method as a means for systematically arriving at truth (Fals-Borda, "Remaking" 146–50; "Some Basic" 7). Because they see no distance between themselves and the world (Whyte, Greenwood, and Lazes 21), critical researchers turn their attention from traditional science and the scientific method as a conceptual scheme to what Fals-Borda terms "common people's" or "popular" science ("Remaking" 151): an "experiential" activity ("Remaking" 149; "Some Basic" 4) impossible to codify, where researcher and participants work together in the search for "collective knowledge" ("Remaking" 151; see also Fals-Borda's discussion of the union of academic and popular knowledge ["Some Basic" 4] and Mumby's discussion of "dialogical" research ["Critical" 21]).

In such an uncodifiable, experiential activity, the scientific method as a conceptual scheme has no privileged place (Fals-Borda, "Remaking" 146, 150–53). That is, although critical researchers and their participants might use the techniques of science—for example, a variety of quantitative and qualitative methodologies (Fals-Borda, "Some Basic" 10; McLaren and Lankshear 382), the "careful handling of data" (Fals-Borda, "Remaking" 148), or "rigor" in checking facts (Whyte, Greenwood, and Lazes 41)—these techniques are situated within a research activity that recognizes—as post-process scholars do—that communicative interaction is hermeneutic and paralogic in nature.

HERMENEUTIC, PARALOGIC NATURE OF COMMUNICATIVE INTERACTION

Post-process scholars embrace a theory of communicative interaction as hermeneutic and paralogic, where meaning making—by, for example, conducting research or writing—is viewed as a "collaborative, dialogic, and thoroughly public activity" (Kent, *Parologic Rhetoric* 68) but not a systematic process with guaranteed results.

Popular science of the kind critical researchers advocate is similarly hermeneutic and paralogic. Therefore, it is highly interpretive, situational, and nongeneralizable. For example, in what Whyte, Greenwood, and Lazes term the "continuous mutual learning" (as opposed to the "standard" scientific) model, "the researcher is constantly challenged by events and by ideas, information, and arguments posed by the project participants," thus following "previously unfamiliar pathways" where researcher and participants can "think in new ways" and "generat[e] provocative new ideas" (42). As Fals-Borda says, then, "imitation or replication of techniques is not recommended, even when they have proved successful." Instead, it is "preferable to undertake new actions every time, depending on the specific conditions and circumstances of each experience." "Freedom to explore and to recreate in these conditions," says Fals-Borda, is an "essential characteristic" of critical research activity ("Remaking" 149)

This freedom to explore—this paralogic approach to research—occurs because of the "dialogic" and "thoroughly public" nature of popular science. Gaventa, for example, cites citizens collaborating to investigate their community power structures, such as housing codes and mineral and land ownership, or banding together to engage in right-to-know movements concerning toxic chemicals or waste as forms of this dialogic and public research (123–24). In these situations, critical researchers claim, the participants develop "popular and indigenous ways of gaining information" (Gaventa 125), thus regaining "what had previously been the property of the expert" (Gaventa 124). Using "community-based approaches and information sources" (Gaventa 126), participants contribute their "specific local knowledge and know-how" and act as "critics" who "adapt the research to their own reality." What results, says Fals-Borda, is "an enriched overall knowledge" ("Remaking" 152) that the participants themselves appropriate ("Some Basic" 9), where they are empowered to produce their own "more humane" and "liberating" view of the world (Gaventa 131).

As my discussion illustrates, a post-process perspective and the critical approach are theoretically compatible. Granted, the focus of critical researchers on critique and social change—their interest in "grappling with the complex relationship between power and knowledge and how this works to affirm the interests of certain privileged groups against others" (McLaren and Lankshear 405)—may seem somewhat foreign to post-process scholars. However, I contend that a research approach where, with the collaboration of the researcher, the participants define the research problem and search for and appropriate knowledge is fully compatible with a perspective where the teacher is viewed as "a collaborator . . . simply another voice in the dialogic interactions inherent in discourse production and analysis" (Kent, "Paralogic" 37). Given, therefore, the theoretical intersections between a post-process perspective and the critical approach, researchers in professional communication who find themselves in tune with post-process theory should consider adopting critical research. However, doing so has a number of very important and very practical implications.

Implications of Adopting the Critical Approach

If researchers in professional communication wish to adopt the critical approach, they must consider both disciplinary and institutional implications.

DISCIPLINARY IMPLICATIONS

The most pressing disciplinary implication of adopting the critical approach is the necessity for rethinking the goal of research and its connection to professional communication pedagogy. No longer, for example, would the goal of describing and explaining the writing process as it occurs in workplace settings or the aim of amassing information as a guarantee of effective pedagogy direct the discipline's research choices. Rather, in keeping with critical research's emancipatory thrust, the goal of the researcher would be—in concert with participants—to interrogate existing social structures and practices, with the aim of uncovering the workings of domination and power and thus fostering critique and social change.

Along with the necessity for rethinking the goal of research, researchers in professional communication also would have to rethink the kinds of research sites they select and the types of funding they seek. Regarding sites, critical researchers in professional communication would no longer base their choices on the data a given site might generate about the process of workplace composing. Rather, their primary criterion would be whether or not potential workplace or academic co-participants had the freedom and motivation to engage in a critical research project that—together with the researcher—*they* would select, devise, and carry out. For example, McLaren decided to conduct his research at a Catholic school rather than in the Toronto public schools because he had been "recognized as someone who had written a controversial book." The school board and administrators of the Toronto schools therefore deemed his presence to be "too risky," a constraint that would have severely compromised his critical research goal ("Field Relations" 154–55). Critical researchers in professional communication also would have to be flexible in this way, willing to recognize that the critical approach is not suitable for all research sites (Mumby, *Communication* 155; Whyte, Introduction 8; Whyte, Greenwood, and Lazes 19) and willing to select a different site if the appropriate conditions for critical research did not exist.

Finally, regarding the types of funding, critical researchers in professional communication would have to rely less on business and industrial sources—whose major interest in funding research is not critique and social change but rather "timely solutions" to business problems (Suchan 476; see also Whyte, Introduction 8–9 for his discussion of the "professional expert model")—and rely more on sources amenable to the emancipatory thrust of critical research. Primary among such sources would appear to be foundations. To cite one possibility, the Kellogg Foundation has funded a number of projects designed to foster critique and social change, both at Iowa State University and in Iowa. One such project, Shared Visions, is intended to support grassroots movements engaged in furthering sustainable (that is, smaller-scale and environmentally sensitive) agriculture. With funding and research support from this project, for example, farmers and townspeople interested in what is termed "community-supported agriculture" have collaborated to set up an alternate delivery system, whereby the farmers market organically grown produce directly to their customers, often bringing weekly "market baskets" right to the participating townspeople's doors. Certainly, a funding source such as the Kellogg Foundation could well be interested in critical research projects involving professional communication. Additional sources of funding might include the federal government or granting sources within specific institutions. For example, Iowa State University sponsors one grant program designed to improve undergraduate education and another for research concerning science, technology, and the humanities. Either of these sources might prove amenable to a critical research project.

In addition to these disciplinary implications, critical researchers in professional communication would have to consider institutional implications as well.

INSTITUTIONAL IMPLICATIONS

Regarding institutional implications, critical researchers in professional communication would have to recognize that administrators at their colleges and universities might not understand or value critical research in the same way that descriptive, explanatory research is valued. For example, Fals-Borda emphasizes the conflict between "lessons learned in the academic halls" and critical research ("Remaking" 148), as well as the status accorded to traditional scientific research ("Remaking" 150; "Some Basic" 7).

This devaluing of critical research could have a direct impact on the careers of researchers within specific institutional settings. In order to be tenured or promoted, for example, researchers must please department chairs, members of tenure and promotion committees, and deans, all of whom can either recommend or deny tenure or promotion. If any of these important institutional audiences rejects the critical perspective as a valid approach, the results for the individual researcher might be disastrous.

Under such conditions, educating these audiences becomes crucial. In doing so, critical researchers in professional communication would have to consider effective packaging of their work, drawing on interdisciplinary sources such as those I discuss to document its legitimacy. Critical researchers in professional communication also would have to link their work to initiatives—for example, external funding—that their particular institutions value (see Blyler, Graham, and Thralls 79–83 for a discussion of these linkages and of the need for effective packaging). The fact that numerous critical researchers, such as many of those cited here, have had successful academic careers indicates that institutional acceptance of critical research is indeed possible.

Conclusion

Although research done under the rubric of the critical approach is a radical departure from descriptive, explanatory research, I believe that critical research is a valid option for those interested in a post-process perspective. In common with that perspective, critical researchers reject the notion of a Cartesian split between individuals and the world, making reliance on a conceptual scheme such as the scientific method unnecessary. Similarly, as do post-process scholars, critical researchers view communicative interaction as hermeneutic and paralogic, where communicants—be they the post-process teacher and students or the critical researcher and participants—engage in a "hermeneutical journey of self-discovery."

It is true that the political thrust of critical research—its focus on critique and social change—may not have formed a large part of the post-process agenda. However, this political thrust is fully compatible with post-process work. Researchers in professional communication therefore—who might find themselves drawn to a post-process perspective—should consider the critical approach as a potential research alternative.

6

Activity Theory and Process Approaches: Writing (Power) in School and Society

David Russell

More years ago than I care to remember, when my daughter Madeleine was in third grade at Roosevelt Elementary School, I went to the Parents' Night Open House. When I walked into Madeleine's room, the first things that caught my eye were four large yellow posters mounted high on one wall. Each of the posters—obviously commercially produced—contained in large black type one word. PREWRITE. WRITE. REVISE. EDIT.

A few years ago, like many others, I was trying to get the National Council of Teachers of English to change certain things about their curriculum standards document (NCTE/IRA). The thing I argued most passionately to change was the phrase "*the* writing process." I held out for the plural, "writing processes," but the change was not made.

The process movement began with psychological or at least psychologizing approaches. In the work of Janet Emig, Sondra Perl, Nancy Sommers, and others, the individual writer is the focus, not the text. This was a very important shift. It was a revolt against a particularly limiting "current-traditional rhetoric," "desiccated rhetorical principles devised by second-rate rhetorical theorists," as Kitzhaber termed it thirty-five years ago (372). The work of the process pioneers revalorized the student as an object of our activities. But their work remained with *the* individual, an attempt to describe psychological processes that might be generalized across students in different settings. The goal was to make students like "real" writers, I think. And that is a worthy goal. But real to whom and for whom? Early on, researchers such as Applebee ("Problems") pointed to problems with notions of *the* writing process, as a unitary psychological process that would be somehow more "real"—less school-bound—than previous ways of learning and teaching writing.

After all, Emig's book is not titled *The Composing Process* but *The*

Composing Process of Twelfth Graders, middle-class, white, American, Eastern, suburban twelfth graders in English class. She and the other process pioneers did their work on *school* writing (processes), leaving the study of noncomposition-class and nonschool writing processes to others and leaving the primary composition classroom genre of the essay unchallenged.

In the last decade some research strands in our profession have made great strides in understanding the composing processes of writers outside of composition classes and outside of schools. In this exploratory essay, I want to ask how we can understand the relation between school writing (processes) and the writing processes beyond school and perhaps the relations between them. After all, we have schools, in part, to select and prepare people to enter and transform the processes (writing among them) beyond school. So the relation between school and society, as Dewey put it, is an important one for those who study and teach (the) writing process(es).

Plural Processes and Activity Networks

The great shift in composition studies of the last decade has been from psychology toward sociology and anthropology, where have been marvelous insights. We have learned above all that *organizations as well as individuals have writing processes* and that analyzing the various writing processes of different networks of human activity—variously theorized as social or discursive practices, communities of practice, or discourse communities—can help us understand how writing works and people work with writing, individually and collectively. Drawing on Vygotskian activity theory, I have used the term *activity system* to mean collectives (often organizations) of people who, over an indefinite period of time, share common purposes (objects and motives) and certain tools used in certain ways—among these tools-in-use certain kinds of writing done in certain ways or processes. These kinds of writing used in certain ways for certain recurring purposes I have called *genres* (Russell, "Activity Theory" and "Rethinking Genre"; Berkenkotter and Huckin, *Genre Knowledge*).

Notice that this definition goes beyond our ordinary sense of genre as a static category of texts that share certain formal features. It includes also processes—uses—of that kind of text. In this sense, a genre enacts social processes, including composing processes. For example, a list of food items might be a grocery list for a family, a tool for reducing temptation for a weight-loss group, an order form for buyers employed by supermarkets, or an invoice for the supplier (Witte). Each of these genres operationalizes routine interactions—processes—with and within supermarkets. But each does so differently for a different activity system, according to the object and motive of the activity system, its history and current conditions—constraints and affordances on action, including those actions of writing (processes). Genres and the social (writing) processes they enact are dynamic, always capable of changing, though always capable of being (temporarily) stabilized as their conditions of use are stabilized. An activity system is a unit of analysis of social *and* individual behavior, something like a discourse community, but it allows us to think about tools without confining ourselves to discourse and about people who interact purposefully without confining ourselves to the warm and fuzzy notion of community (see Harris, "The Idea").

When we view the research literature on writing in organizations through this theoretical lens, it turns out that there is a glorious diversity of genres, of writing processes, which can be analyzed in terms of their socio*logics,* to borrow sociologist Bruno Latour's term, as well as in terms of the individual psychology of *the* writer. Within an organization (an activity system) and among organizations (activity systems) there are a range of genres that form a complex system of genres, mediating the interactions of people and facilitating their collaborative (and competitive) work (Bazerman, "Systems of Genres").

To take only one example, Jone Rymer has shown that the writing processes of internationally known scientists differ a great deal not only according to the personality of the scientist, his or her individual routines (habits, processes) of writing, but also according to the organization of the laboratory and its relation to other organizations (activity systems), such as other laboratories, granting agencies, universities, and so on. It is highly collaborative, structured by the hierarchical division of labor in the lab. For example, the subgenres of data charts and methods sections (within the genre of the experimental article) are roughed out by those who collected the data. One main writer, the senior scientist, does the title, introduction, discussion, and abstract (other parts or subgenres) (223). The processes she describes are not much like the conventional writing-process sequence that we compositionists describe for writing in schools. There are a number of genres (oral, written, visual, manual) that work together in a complex system to produce a research article in such laboratories.

Plural writing processes (genre systems) mediate work within many activity systems. In most activity systems of business and government, revision is accomplished by means of "document cycling," a sequence of revisions—sometimes highly formalized—that allows a document to be developed and negotiated among different people and departments within an organization. Again there are great differences according to the division of labor in what is sometimes called the "discourse community" (Harris, "The Idea"; Kent, "On the Very Idea"). Susan Kleimann, for example, describes two work groups within the U.S. Government Accounting Office (GAO) who use, respectively, highly collaborative and highly hierarchical document cycling, with complex effects on the writing processes of members of the two groups.

The complex negotiations within organizations using various genres (and writing processes) involve the flows of power, extending to the most minute decisions about texts and their processes of composition. For example, Smart describes the way bank managers interact with their research staffs, who prepare written reports that are used by the managers, through oral genres of discussion, to make policy decisions. The expectations of managers condition the writing processes of their research staffs in powerful ways, as the writing of research staffs conditions the oral genres of policy decision making of managers.

Moreover, we have found that there are plural (and interacting) writing processes—and genre systems—not only within organizations (or, more broadly, activity systems) but among them. As one activity system interacts with others, genres mediate those interactions and the writing processes of participants. As complex organizations (activity systems) interact with other organizations and individuals (consumers, clients, patients, citizens), systems of genres and writing processes evolve, as in Devitt's study of accountants ("Intertextuality"), Bazerman's study of patent approvals ("Systems of Genres"), or Van Nostrand's study of scientific granting agencies. Paré's (1993) study of social workers writing the genre of the Predisposition Report to guide judges in sentencing juvenile offenders shows how their typical writing process is conditioned by legal, professional, and family activity systems on the boundary of activity systems of social work.

Writing processes (and genre systems) are not only plural but changing. As social practices (activity systems) change over time, historically, so also their writing processes (and genre systems) change, sometimes in a gradual evolution and sometimes in a rapid revolution. The growing number of synchronic case studies of plural writing processes are being complemented by a growing number of diachronic studies of changing writing processes. For example, Yates (1990) has shown how writing in organizations evolved in the nineteenth and early twentieth centuries with changes in technology (e.g., vertical files, typewriters, printing presses) and social organization (large corporate and governmental networks organized hierarchically and controlled through new genres). Bazerman (*Shaping Written Knowledge*) chronicled the genre and activity of the scientific article, in its change from letters exchanged among seventeenth-century amateurs to a complex intertextual network of experimental articles characterized by complex cycles of review, revision, and credit in the twentieth century. The work of Haas (*Technology*) and others on writing and computers is yielding similar insights into the ways activity systems change their writing processes with the introduction of that family of tools we call "computers."

We have learned that answering the following questions matters a great deal: What kind of writing does the writer process, for whom and for what purposes? We cannot know the writer apart from the genres in use, any more than we know the dancer from the dance, to paraphrase W. B. Yates.

The Writing Processes (Genre Systems) of Formal Schooling: Commodification

To understand students' writing, we need to trace its comings and goings, its circulation in social networks (activity systems), in and out of, around and through schools. We need to examine the sociologics of *the* process approach and the ways in which (and reasons why) its formulation of writing has come to be treated as *the* writing process—in many activity systems of U.S. formal schooling, of textbook publishing, and of composition studies.

The work on writing processes in organizations suggests that the discipline of U.S. composition studies, like other activity systems, also has genre systems, systems that interact with the wider activity systems of formal schooling in complex ways, through composition courses, writing centers, WAC programs (though composition studies is also influencing nonschool activity systems of business, government, and nonprofit organizations, through communications consulting, the Society for Technical Communications, IEEE, community literacy projects, etc.).

Over the last twenty years, the pioneering research on the composing process came to be treated as *the* writing process through a process of *commodification*, long studied in other disciplines but little noticed or studied in composition (Myers; Fahnestock). The discipline of composition studies, like other disciplines, *commodifies* the products of its research and theory to make them useful to practitioners, clients, customers, students. In a process described first by sociologists of science, the genres of core researchers in a discipline (e.g., research articles) are translated into other genres for practitioners (e.g., research reviews, instructions, teachers' manuals, etc.) and for consumers of various kinds, such as customers (trade book popularizations, warning labels, advertising), clients (intake forms, brochures), and beginning students (teaching materials, Cliff's Notes, and—most predominately—textbooks).

By deploying different discursive tools in various (temporarily) stabilized genres, researchers mediate different boundary interactions among activity systems, those of core researchers with other core researchers, certainly, but also core researchers with practitioners, such as teachers, and of practitioners with students. Though textbooks have been criticized for presenting a discipline as a seamless structure of unchallenged facts, it is important to understand that while the textual commodification of disciplinary practice may reify and bury important social actions, commodification in some form or another grows out of the differences in interactions and is therefore necessary for different people in different though linked activity systems, each with different objectives and motives, to make use of the statements of core researchers. Given the specialization of labor, it would be impossible for students—or even most teachers (practitioners)—to have had a history of interactions sufficient to understand research articles, to follow the network far enough to make sense of a highly specialized activity system's genres. And it would be extremely inefficient for core researchers to write journal articles so that introductory students could read them. Articles would be as long as textbooks, and textbooks would be as long as encyclopedias. Textbooks and teachers' manuals and research reviews could not give a full account of writing processes any more than a company could package a tube of toothpaste in such a way as to allow consumers to know the history of that product's development and the complex issues relating to its testing and uses.

This is not to say that textbooks and other genres that commodify researcher knowledge cannot give students useful insight into the social workings of a discipline—and through sidebar vignettes, for example, some textbooks explicitly do. But even such accounts are commodified versions of the work that core researchers have done. The solution is not to shorten the network of disciplinary influence but to provide more useful tools ("knowledge" about writing processes) for more consumers of composition studies' intellectual products, even if those tools are, for beginners just making contact with the discipline, four yellow posters of one word each or the kinds of highly commodified summaries found in teachers' manuals.

Discursive tools of the types found in textbooks (or wall posters) represent the sort of interaction that is sometimes called the "material" or "content" of introductory/general/liberal education. As these metaphors of physical objects suggest, the tools tend to be commodified, stripped of the process of their construction within the activity system, which over a long period of time has gradually made these "facts"—from the past participle of *facare*, "to act, or do" hence: "what has been done."

This kind of reification/commodification is inevitable if there are to be long networks of interaction, and those long networks are essential for power. Like other disciplines, composition has reified the complexity of research and theory that constitutes its core activity, cooled and hardened the white-hot debates of specialists into useful genres: textbook summaries, instructions, precepts. As the National Assessment of Educational Progress (NAEP) research has shown, *the* process approach has been disseminated rather widely even in elementary and secondary schools in the last decade. Textbooks and classroom practice increasingly include this "content," and there is evidence to suggest that it is being usefully employed to improve students' writing (*the* process approach is highly correlated with success on the NAEP, at least at grade eight) (Applebee, et al.).

One danger here, as with all learning, is overgeneralizing some processes until they are useless or counterproductive. But there is

nothing inherently wrong with conceptualizing, categorizing, com-
modifying some production process, some "content." The task for any
discipline or profession is to make (*facere*, "to factualize") the most useful tools, discursive and otherwise, and deploy them to make them
more widely useful—lengthen its network of influence, its power.
What kind of disciplinary network can keep teachers and their students
from holding onto a pedagogy/content, a process/product, when it
is no longer useful, as many relics of the past are enshrined in the curriculum (and in cardboard reliquaries tacked to classroom walls)?

I would suggest that the answer to the danger does not lie in throw-
ing out the old content wholesale for some post-old process/content.
Such slash-and-burn scholarship, fad-and-fix reform, depletes the en-
ergies of all involved without enriching and developing teachers as
professionals, as Applebee points out in his superb discussion of the
effects of tradition on curriculum remaking. Indeed, rapid change is
impossible because in large and complex activity systems such as
schools, the new "content" (tools) exists with the old in an eclectic
bricolage until eventually it gains hegemony—if it ever does.

In my view, the answer lies in patiently creating a longer and wider
network of disciplinary influence (power) through assembling and disseminating useful discursive tools based on research. Composition
studies has the potential to help (or impede) students and other writers at all ages, in many disciplines, and in many walks of life—activity systems. But we can realize our potential—broaden our network
of influence—only if we know more about (involve ourselves as a discipline with) writing processes in many social practices, many systems
of activity, many genres. And we must effectively commodify and dis-
seminate that knowledge, that history of involvement.

In an attempt to overthrow the old order (of schooling), the process
pioneers invented a new order of schooling. But in both orders the
focus remained on rather traditional humanities schoolroom genres:
the personal essay or theme, primarily (Connors, "Personal Writing").
In this regard, sociological /anthropological approaches have given us
a fresh way of looking at writing, this time writing in a wider range
of genres. Process pedagogy based on individual psychology got us
thinking about writing in new ways (and about schooling, as it turns
out). And it allowed teachers and students to have a new object: student composition-class writing processes. After Emig and the process
pioneers, it was difficult for researchers to look at the old modes in

the same way. Sociological/anthropological approaches have given us a fresh way of looking at writing, as a potentially powerful tool mediating a vast range of human social practices.

This approach too will be commodified into textbooks (and perhaps, somehow, even in elementary school wall posters), if it is successful enough to endure. Like the "facts" promulgated in textbooks and classroom materials in other disciplines, the facts of composition, once they make their way out in a system of useful activity, will be translated, simplified, commodified (after all, not everyone who teaches or learns writing can or would want to read essays like the one you are reading). This is already happening with discipline-specific guides to writing and teaching writing, prompted by the expansion of writing-across-the-curriculum programs and writing-intensive courses (e.g., Pechenick). That is good. It shows the usefulness of the approach.

Going "Beyond" Process

What might it mean, as the title of this collection implicitly asks, to go "beyond" process? From the activity-theory perspective I have been developing here, it means to realize that there are many writing processes, study them, (re)classify them, commodify them, and involve students with (teach) them in a curriculum that is sequenced to lead students from the germ cell of insight into writing processes—the PREWRITE/WRITE/REVISE/EDIT my daughter Madeleine was taught—to a progressively wider understanding of writing processes as they are played out in a range of activity systems in our culture(s).

The insights of research into the writing processes (and genres) in place in an activity system (whether corporate, governmental, political advocacy—or school or classroom) can be taught—perhaps very usefully. Such teaching is beginning to occur in technical and business communications, as well as in WAC/WID research and programs, where the insights of core researchers into writing in relevant activity systems are being commodified and used to improve students' uses of writing to enter and transform those activity systems (see for example, Howard; Pechenick). In doing so, the disciplinary network of composition studies is maturing, extending its network of influence (power) by providing useful tools.

Yet research on writing processes in organizations is still in its infancy. There is crucial work to be done. Though there has been important research in the writing processes (genre systems) of nonacademic settings, there has been comparatively little research into the relation between writing processes in activity systems of academic disciplines, professions, families, neighborhoods and activity systems of formal schooling. Most of the research on *the* writing process has focused on *the* classroom. But activity systems of formal schooling form crucial boundaries with other activity systems, those of academic disciplines most directly but also with the professions linked to the disciplines and activity systems of business, industry, government, media, advocacy groups, and so on in which professionals work, as well as the families, neighborhoods, and ethnic communities out of which students come. The dynamic boundary negotiations between school and society, formal schooling and culture, are mediated and (always temporarily) stabilized through systems of written genres (and various writing processes). And, as in nonacademic activity systems, those negotiations within and among activity systems constantly (re)distribute power, constraining and affording writing processes. Here we need research on the broader genre systems (and writing processes) of formal schooling to extend and enrich the usefulness of similar studies in nonacademic activity systems. How is the knowledge in use in these wider activity systems commodified at various levels of schooling, as students learn (or fail to learn) how to write progressively more involving genres within the genre system of a discipline or profession?

Moreover, the complex writing processes and genre systems of classrooms are part of wider genre systems of schools and school systems and national education systems, through which writing (processes) is conditioned in myriad ways institutionally. For example, one crucial but little-studied aspect of the genre systems (and writing processes) of classrooms is their relation to earlier and later classrooms, the movement from K through college—and beyond. The genres of student writing are all reified into a single letter, written on the genre of the report card, which is in turn reified and incorporated intertextually into the genres of transcripts, then diplomas and certificates, then job applications, then school and district and state and national grade reports, then press reports, then other genres of public (political) discourse. School writing (processes) is inevitably conditioned by the need of all industrial societies, whether communist or capitalist, to accomplish the division of labor, to sort students, though that sorting of course can be carried out in different—better and worse—ways (Marshall, "Schooling").

This sorting in response to activity systems beyond *the* classroom and beyond wider activity systems of formal schooling begins early and continues through workplace writing processes. To take one early example, Madeleine's teacher had her students prewrite Monday, write Tuesday, revise Wednesday, edit Thursday, and (I learned) grade Friday to meet a district-imposed requirement for progress reporting—the indirect result of the district's boundary interactions with a school-management company, which was in turn profoundly influenced by certain texts of an activity system known as Total Quality Management.

For Madeleine's teacher to change that pedagogical practice, to broaden the ways she treats *the* writing process, she would not only have to become aware of the range of writing processes to which she could introduce her students, but she would also have to affiliate (network) with other people who could help her change those reporting (sorting) structures (genres) to allow her to restructure the ways writing takes place in *the* classroom in relation to other classrooms. In other words, the genre system (and writing processes) of grade reporting would have to change so that the students could approach writing in different ways. Of course, that is possible—but not for an individual teacher. It would take a network extending to other teachers and, likely, to administrators, parents, PTAs, school boards, state departments of education, and, perhaps, to legislators and their electorates. To fundamentally alter the writing process in that classroom would take a longer (that is, more powerful) professional network, one that can influence school systems and universities and those other activity systems with which activity systems of formal schooling negotiate power.

Ultimately, teachers must participate in the sorting system or leave teaching, even if teachers have primary control of the assessment system. Because finally they must "teach to the test," they need "a test that is worth teaching to," a way of sorting students that allows students to learn about and develop a range of writing processes (and genres) as they expand their involvements with the various activity systems of their culture, to enter and transform those systems. How can our discipline help to restructure the education system to us to help students (and their teachers, families, friends, and future coworkers) do that?

The Future of Process(es) Approach(es)

There is what some might see as an irony in the way a movement that has as its motive encouraging "real" writing—active, dynamic process—has often been commodified into what looks like a static product. However, as I have tried to suggest, I see no irony, only a process of broadening influence. Hence the task is not to toss out "*the* process approach," by demarcating a "post-process" era. For in all organizations that interact usefully with other organizations over time, there must be commodification of their discourse to facilitate that interaction. Whatever discourse might replace "*the* (current) process approach" will also be commodified if it is to have an ongoing usefulness to those outside the core researchers.

The task rather is to extend the activity system of the discipline of composition studies, to offer to teachers and students more and more refined tools for helping people in and entering various activity systems to write and learn to write and transform their activity through writing. Our discipline's motive is to provide tools (commodified knowledge) to other activity systems, so they can better understand and use this marvelous tool called "writing together," to harness for good the variety and power human beings have in this protean technology. And to do so we might do well to understand the (power) relations mediated by the genre systems (writing processes) of school and society.

The most obvious way to see the interaction of activity systems of schooling with boundary activity systems is by studying the ways upper-level students negotiate the boundaries between the genres (and writing processes) of upper-level professional schooling and the genres (and writing processes) of entry-level professional positions. There have been some remarkable recent studies of internships (Winsor; Anson and Forsberg; Dias et al.; Freedman, Adam, and Smart), which describe students/professionals in transition, struggling to make sense of professional networks' writing using the tools they picked up in their schooling. Similarly, studies of the transition from undergraduate to graduate education (Berkenkotter, Huckin, and Ackerman; Prior; Blakeslee) have broadened our understanding of the complex play of power and identity with writing processes in complex hierarchical professional networks.

As one moves to earlier levels of schooling, where the classroom genres and wider institutional genres of sorting are correspondingly diverse and complex, the task of tracing the interactions of school and society through writing (processes) is more difficult. Many studies of writing across the curriculum, including some fascinating longitudinal studies (e.g., Haas, "Learning"; Winsor), emphasize the importance of examining the interplay of activity systems of school, discipline, and work.

When we move to the levels of schooling at which the pioneering research in writing process took place, secondary school and the first year of higher education, there have been relatively few studies that take into account the intertextual genre systems of schooling and the play of power and identity those systems mediate. (The problem is even more pronounced at the elementary and preschool levels [but see Dyson; Green and Dixon].) Part of the difficulty comes from the very persuasiveness of institutional constraints at theses levels. It is hard to see the effects of institutional sorting systems on writing and learning. The recent tendency has been to examine the macrolevel constructions of class, race, and gender without looking at the ways the genre systems of formal schooling mediate those constructions, the microlevel social (writing) processes through which power is constantly (re)negotiated and (re)stabilized. As James Marshall put it fourteen years ago, "To speak of composing processes without reference to the schooling which shapes them may well be to isolate an effect from the cause" ("Schooling" 118).

Yet cross-national studies of writing in schooling are beginning to give researchers some perspective and insight into the different ways genre systems of schooling condition student writing (processes) (Vahapassi). Written assessment systems (and their lack) produce genre systems that mediate students' interactions with other students, teachers, administrators, governments, and employers in myriad ways

In France, for example, Christiane Donahue's comparative research into the genres of student and teacher reading and writing in the transition from secondary education to further schooling suggests that the examination systems (*baccalaureate* and *concours*) explicitly structure the genres of student writing in each discipline, though the genres are still more numerous than in U.S. composition classes, where the genres are relatively few but tacitly and comparatively vaguely structured (*the* essay, *the* research paper). The writing process is based not so much on revision but on repetition, as students write the genres numerous times to prepare for the examination. Through frequent repetition, students learn to write the classroom genres quickly, with more explicit plans, greater syntactical parallelism and repetition, more nuanced comparisons and intertextual reference. The editing process is accomplished through quick editing in the copying from a pencil *brouillon* to an ink examination paper. These school writing processes are conditioned by an education system that is highly structured at the national level, with consistent teacher expectations for students, teacher training using writing, and funding, with greater funds going to designated zones of educational need (Donahue).

In England an examination system of course-work portfolios has grown up over the last twenty years in secondary education, through the influence of James Britton and his colleagues. The portfolios require students to write in a range of generally defined genres. Teachers negotiate the topic and explicit genre of most portfolio pieces with the students and work with them over a two-year course to develop their writing. The students write fewer but much longer pieces than American (or certainly French) students, but the expectations are much higher for the individual pieces. Emphasis is on personal growth without emphasis on process as process, though there is a "hard edge" to the process instruction because the teachers collaboratively grade the student portfolios. Each student's portfolio must be judged by the teachers of that course in the school, then a sample of the portfolios goes to progressively higher levels so that there is consistency in grading at the district and national levels—a process called "moderation."

This examination system has led to widespread and profound change in process-writing pedagogy. There is much less presentational teaching and far more small-group and individual instruction. There is much more professional collaboration among teachers to set and maintain high standards because the reputation of the school staff and the teaching profession as a whole depends on their collaborative handling of assessment. A professional career path for teachers is fostered by the moderation and inspection system—handled by classroom teachers. A system of teachers and university teacher trainers has grown up in many parts of the UK that has spread and refined the pedagogy of personal growth through this "hard-edged" writing-process approach (Russell, "Collaborative"; Russell, Lewis, and Riggs; Freedman and McLeod)

In South Africa the vast transition to an ethnically integrated education system, combined with extraordinarily complex language issues (there are nine official languages), is producing a widespread rethinking of the role of writing (processes) in education. Under apartheid, the separate and vastly unequal schooling produced the most fundamental barriers to any writing process: many students lacked writing materials (even pencils and paper) and books. Now that institutions of secondary and tertiary schooling have been opened, classes are sometimes huge (an introductory college literature course with six hundred students) and the writing that teachers are able to read is greatly limited. Sometimes writing is limited only to timed examination papers, which has the effect of delaying selection—but not changing the eventual outcome of selection.

In response to this crisis, teachers are searching for ways to allow for some effective intervention in students' writing processes and a selection system to facilitate that (as well as greater financial resources). For example, there is now a mobile writing center that tours schools, offering students the kind of writing enrichment that bookmobiles provide for readers. Students can find there the writing and reading materials and the expertise that can give them (and their teachers) a richer sense of the writing necessary to enter more fully into the system of schooling through writing (Moore; Shezi)

The People's Republic of China (Li) is also experiencing a sea change in the role of writing (processes) in schooling. For some two thousand years writing and writing instruction were based on memorization and close imitation of classical (and, in the last fifty years, Maoist) literary models in a relatively few genres. Students learned to write these genres for national examinations, which controlled entrance into further education and leadership positions. As in France, the education system and teacher training are highly centralized. In the last ten years, as part of a drive for modernization, school writing has shifted emphasis from character building to skill training, from literature to communication. For example, in the 1995 examination, for the first time students had to discuss a social issue, medical malpractice. This shift is forcing teachers to rethink the purpose of writing and writing instruction. They may have to develop new pedagogies that will reshape the school writing processes of students in response to new institutional constraints and affordances—and a far wider range of genres (and social practices) that use writing.

These few and preliminary cross-national comparisons of school-based writing processes suggest the importance of stepping back from *the* writing process as taught in one's own activity system of schooling to see, with some perspective, the plural socio*logics* of various networks of people and purposes and tools, including that most protean tool, writing, in the relation between school and society.

The process pioneers began research that reconstructed the object of writing instruction as students, human beings, and not merely texts. That work has been extended to the writing processes (and dynamic genres) of organizations, the sociologics of activity systems, to use the activity-theory formulation. To make lasting changes in writing and learning, composition studies must broaden its study of the microlevel circulation of discursive tools (and power) between school(s) and society(ies) and extend its own tools' usefulness in the activity systems of our culture(s). In doing so, the commodification of writing processes is not an irony to be lamented but a sign of composition's influence to be understood and used, one hopes, for good.

7

Writing Within (and Between) Disciplinary Genres: The "Adaptive Landscape" as a Case Study in Interdisciplinary Rhetoric

Debra Journet

Whatever else we now know about the composing process, we know that it is complex, and we know that it is multiple. Research has helped us see that composing has both cognitive and social dimensions and that composing processes differ according to both individual ability or experience and rhetorical situation or context. Thus, as we study the processes of mature writers composing within knowledge-producing disciplines, such as those of the sciences, we often find a different picture than when we look at the processes of student writers composing within general academic situations, such as first-year composition classrooms.

In this chapter, I echo other researchers in rhetoric and composition (e.g., Bazerman, Berkenkotter and Huckin, Devitt, Freedman and Medway, Miller, Swales) in arguing that it is useful to understand the composing processes of disciplinary writers from the perspective of genre. My discussion proceeds from two assumptions: (1) academic disciplines are not pre-existing categories of discrete subject matters, but groups of participants who share common goals and strategies; (2) genres are not static typological categories of textual forms but are socially constructed categories of rhetorical action and response. Furthermore, the relation between these assumptions is dialectical: the processes through which a disciplinary community negotiates and constructs its knowledge claims mold the generic characteristics of its communicative practices, including its written texts; developments of genres, in turn, shape the discipline that creates and instantiates them.

In the first part of this chapter, I provide an overview of recent genre theory in order to argue that genre offers a productive way to understand many of the questions we have pursued about the composing process—both for novice and for experienced writers, particularly those in scientific disciplines. In the chapter's second part, I illustrate this argument with an example: an analysis of the role of genre in an interdisciplinary scientific argument about evolution. Here I focus on the metaphor of the adaptive landscape, a discursive convention that demonstrates the power of genre in both the creation and communication of disciplinary knowledge.

Genres and the Composing Process

GENRES AND COMPOSITION THEORY

Much recent research into issues of genre—including theoretical, pedagogical, textual, and linguistic studies—has illuminated the complex and pervasive role genres can play in acts of composing. (Most helpful for me has been the work of Bakhtin, whose powerful and flexible theory suggests the ways all acts of communication, both written and oral, function within the ideological and rhetorical framework of what he calls "speech-genres.") A useful overview of this research is offered by Amy Devitt ("Generalizing"; "Genre"), who describes how we have moved from traditional conceptions of genre as a kind of formal "container," to new understanding of genre as a means of action: "a dynamic response to and construction of a recurring situation, one that changes historically and in different social groups, that adapts and grows as the social context changes" ("Generalizing" 580). Particularly significant for those working in rhetoric and composition, as Devitt notes, was Carolyn Miller's germinal article "Genre as Social Action," in which Miller defines genre as "typified rhetorical actions based in recurrent situations" (161), both of which are socially constructed:

> [W]e create recurrence, analogies, similarities. What recurs is not a material situation (a real, objective, factual event), but our construal of a type. The typified situation . . . underlies typification in rhetoric. Successful communication would require that the participants share common types; this is possible only insofar as types are socially created (or biologically innate). (159)

Through the process of constructing situations as recurrent or similar, Miller explains, communities construct generic patterns of discourse that allow speakers and writers to act within those situations in ways that are recognizable and effective. Genres thus represent the cluster of discursive commitments that, as Bakhtin argues, make communication possible: "If speech genres did not exist and we had not mastered them, if we had to originate them during the speech process and construct each utterance at will for the first time, speech communication would be almost impossible" ("Speech Genres" 79). When understood this way, the concept of genre encompasses any act of communication—even everyday examples such as letters and social conversation, as well as more complex cases such as literary texts or scientific reports; in Thomas Kent's terms, no text is ever genre-less, reader-less, culture-less.

One consequence of these new approaches to genre has been to allow us to re-examine a number of significant questions that have been prevalent in composition theory (Devitt, "Generalizing"). This fuller understanding of the power and shaping role of genres in discourse production, especially as they function within academic disciplines, has helped us dismantle the dichotomies often implicit in our questions and better understand the complex and multiple phenomena that can be described as the composing process. Such oversimplified dichotomies can be illustrated in the following typical questions.

Is composing most significantly a cognitive or a social process? Genres function as both cognitive and social categories. They are *cognitive* because they embody the patterns of organization and typification that we use to make sense of and act within the world. That is, most recent genre theory assumes the world does not come to us already organized into categories (of events or situations or knowledge). Rather, we carve up the world according to past experiences, recognizing and constructing particular situations as recurrent—as being, to some degree, similar to (or different from) others we have known.[1] But genres are also *social* because they are ways groups of people have agreed (tacitly or overtly) to organize experience and create knowledge. That is, the typifications we employ and manipulate are not individual or unique. Rather, patterns of understanding and response are situated within our interactions with others. As we learn to typify situations, we also learn to construct typified responses—ways of acting and knowing within recurrent situations.

Although all acts of communication are embedded within genre, the social and cognitive functions of genres are particularly apparent in complex and highly organized academic disciplines such as those of the sciences. Academic disciplines exist within a complex set of commitments, both material and symbolic, that regularize disciplinary knowledge: for example, patterns of training, funding, institutional organization; common problems or representations of reality; preferred methodology; theoretical commitments; and agreements about what constitutes acceptable disciplinary discourse (Foucault; Rorty; Roberts and Good). A discipline recognizes and evaluates a knowledge claim insofar as it relates to prior agreements about what counts as significant problems, as credible evidence, and as convincing solutions. But to construct those agreements, members of a discipline also need to agree on how to represent problems, evidence, and solutions—*both to oneself and to others.* Those agreements constitute a discipline's genres: the acceptable "representational" or "thinking languages" (Berkenkotter, "Theoretical Issues") that allow the production, as well as communication, of disciplinary knowledge.

How are composing "processes" related to composed "products"? We are perhaps more used to thinking of genres in terms of *product*—and thinking about product more in terms of form than content of discourse. In fact, our tendency to consider genre primarily as a formal "product" may be, as Kent has explained, one of the reasons for the decline of genre considerations in our process-oriented pedagogies. When genre is equated solely with textual forms and linguistic conventions, it is easy to see why we have turned away from what can be perceived as an empty category. But increasingly we also understand that discourse communities share not only specialized ways of communicating but also substantive commitments, including a range of values and assumptions that serves to unify social groups. Moreover, many now argue that enculturating students into the canonical knowledge, as well as the conventional forms of academic discourse communities, is a major goal of composition pedagogy.

But it is also important to understand that genres include the *process* by which those products are assimilated, developed, and negotiated. Bakhtin argues that the individual learns to speak, write, and think by learning particular genres; genres thus play an essential role in the development of individual consciousness, or "ideological becoming" ("Discourse" 342). In Vygotskyan terms, genres can be seen as symbolic "tools," or mediational means that facilitate cognitive change. However, learning to use such tools requires more than learning particular applications; it also requires that tools become "internalized," or part of the individual's psychological repertoire (Vygotsky, *Mind* 52–57).

The generic—and interrelated—nature of product and process is particularly important in academic genres, where learning how to write or speak like a biologist, for example, means learning how to think like a biologist. Initiation into generic discourses of particular disciplines entails mastering not only conventional forms but also the epistemological, methodological, and theoretical assumptions that a discipline shares (e.g., Berkenkotter, Huckin, and Ackerman; Geisler; Haas; Prior). Similarly, the process of knowledge production—the research that goes on in lab, field, or library—as well as the ways writing is implicated in that process involve disciplinary conventions and commitments that are generic in nature.

To what degree is composing best understood as the act of communities or of individuals? Because genres represent socially constructed forms of typicality, they are property of *communities,* the patterns of social life operative within particular groups of people. However, genres also are employed by *individuals* within specific situations. They are, in Miller's terms, a way of "mediating private intentions and social exigence" ("Social Action" 163). That is, genres both constrain and enable rhetorical action. They provide the operative rules for behavior within particular social situations. But genres do not simply reproduce social structures; they also provide ways for rhetors to act within those situations. In Berkenkotter and Huckin's terms, genres are "dynamic rhetorical forms" that both "stabilize experience" and "change over time" in response to users' sociocognitive needs (*Genre Knowledge* 4). Although some genres are more flexible and some are more standard than others, every communicative act presents a dialectic between individual intention and socialized convention. The complex relation between the communal and the individual nature of utterances is captured well in Bakhtin's distinction between "centripetal" forces that serve to centralize or unify social groups through normative "official" languages and "centrifugal" forces that decentralize or disperse social groups through what Bakhtin calls "dialogic" language ("Discourse" 272–73).

In scientific writing, the tension between centripetal and centrifugal is most apparent in the dual requirement that a text be both familiar and novel. Scientific work must exist within a context in which it makes sense, but it must also advance some new knowledge. This is particularly apparent in intertextual practices—such as citations, references, summaries, and so on—that demonstrate the complicated relation most scientific texts have to preceding knowledge. More generally, this requirement is seen in the way disciplinary writers have not only to define and solve problems but also to frame those problems in ways that make them relevant to a specific disciplinary community—invoking generic assumptions about what that community finds legitimate, important, or interesting (Griesemer and Wimsatt; Myers).

GENERIC CONVENTION, DISCIPLINARY KNOWLEDGE,
AND THE CHALLENGES OF INTERDISCIPLINARITY

Genres allow disciplinary communities to do their work. They instantiate communal assumptions and values, thus enabling groups of people with shared commitments to create disciplinary knowledge. Genres encode a range of disciplinary norms, including not only discursive forms and vocabulary but also the common problems or representations of reality; the preferred methods and techniques; and the whole range of theoretical, methodological, and epistemological commitments that constitutes a discipline. Research in composition has devoted attention to the challenges writers face as they learn the genres of new discourse communities—including undergraduates who struggle to master "academic discourse" as well as graduate students and professionals as they enter more specialized disciplinary communities. This research reveals how novice writers become enculturated into a discipline by learning to think and write within the context of its current problems and issues, as well as its accepted methodology, conventions, and discourse forms. As Bakhtin has argued, such contextual knowledge is essential for communication.

The cases of novice writers often make explicit what is tacit in more experienced writers: the epistemic and rhetorical, as well as political, power of disciplinary genres. The power of genres is also highlighted, I have found, in cases of interdisciplinary research, where writers try to communicate with diverse groups of readers about phenomena each group can claim as its own and where generic assumptions from more than one community can come into conflict. What a discipline "knows"—what it counts as knowledge—is always formulated within the context of theoretical, methodological, and discursive commitments. But because the construction of a knowledge-claim is inextricably connected to the representation of that claim, the task of interdisciplinary work often requires the negotiation and accommodation of very different generic modes of constructing and communicating knowledge. (On the challenges of interdisciplinary rhetoric, see, for example, Fuller; Journet, "Interdisciplinary Discourse" and "Disciplinary Genres"; Klein; Lyon; Roberts and Good; and the special issue of *Social Epistemology* devoted to "Boundary Rhetorics and the Work of Interdisciplinarity.") Because interdisciplinary projects can illuminate, in particularly interesting ways, the importance of genre in academic discourse, I plan, in the second part of this chapter, to examine the role of a significant generic convention used in the construction and representation of interdisciplinary knowledge in biology.

Bakhtin claims that a "speech-genre" is determined by a "change of speaking subjects" and can thus, as Carolyn Miller suggests, be "as short as a single word or as long as a Dostoyevsky novel" ("Community" 76). Miller herself argues that genres exist at the fairly high level of "complete discourse types based on recurrent situations" ("Social Action" 161). Research into genre at this level includes studies of larger textual forms such as proposals and reports. (See, for example, Myers, *Writing Biology*; Bazerman, *Shaping Written Knowledge*; Berkenkotter and Huckin *Genre Knowledge*; Swales; as well as many of the essays collected in Bazerman and Paradis; Freedman and Medway; Nelson, Megill, and McCloskey; and Simons.) But, as Miller also points out, rhetorical actions exist within hierarchical relations of form, substance, and context that encompass, at a lower level, a broad range of other discursive commitments. Research focusing on genre conventions at these levels has investigated smaller components of academic discourse, such as introductions (Swales and Najjar), citation practices (Bazerman, "Intertextual"; Berkenkotter and Huckin "You Are What You Cite"; Myers, "Stories and Styles"), narrative elements (Geertz; Landau; Myers, *Writing Biology*), graphic features such as diagrams or figures (Griesemer and Wimsatt) and specialized or figurative language (Keller and Lloyd; Halloran and Bradford). (See also many of the essays focusing on specific generic features in Selzer.)

It is on this last category, figurative language, that I will focus in the discussion that follows. I plan to examine the development of a particularly potent convention: the "adaptive landscape," a metaphor that appeared early in what has been called the "Evolutionary Synthesis" of the 1930s and quickly became an accepted part of the generic discourse of evolutionary biology. A metaphor by itself is not, of course, a fully realized genre. But a metaphor that functions in the pervasive way of the adaptive landscape—showing up in conversation, articles, books, and textbooks—is a significant element of the genres of evolutionary biology. Such genre conventions often embed within them the ideological and epistemological assumptions that guide a discipline's discursive practices (Berkenkotter and Huckin, *Genre Knowledge* 60). Further, specific genre conventions, such as particular metaphors or diagrams (Griesemer and Wimsatt), can be easily traced from one site to another.

To explore how the adaptive landscape became a part of the generic "toolkit" of evolutionary biologists, I will focus on textual features of a few key works. I recognize that such a method is inevitably incomplete: the generic features of particular texts, especially those of prominent public texts, are not the only factors involved in how writers negotiate disciplinary consensus. Texts are obviously part of larger traditions of activities, institutions, and organizations (Bazerman, *Constructing Experience*). But while textual features alone do not account for how knowledge is disseminated within a disciplinary community, they do provide a significant perspective on some of the shared assumptions about typicality that allow members of a discipline to make sense of reality and communicate with one another. As Berkenkotter and Huckin have argued, "knowledge production is carried out and codified largely through generic forms of writing" (*Genre Knowledge* 476).

Genres and Interdisciplinary Writing: The Case of the Adaptive Landscape

THE RHETORICAL CONTEXT OF THE ADAPTIVE LANDSCAPE

Current genre studies tend to focus on nonliterary texts and do so by tying "linguistic and substantive similarities to regularities in human spheres of activity" (Freedman and Medway 1). Such analyses are aimed at elucidating "textual dynamics": the dialectical relation between written texts and the contexts and actions that constitute them

(Bazerman and Paradis). These acts of connection between text and context can be accomplished in several ways, including case studies of individual writers, ethnographic studies of the social realm in which the writing is produced, and rhetorical and discourse analysis of specific textual features. In historical studies, where writers and cultures are no longer directly available for investigation, context must be inferred from other sources. In the case of scientific writing, this can be complicated, as context includes specific (and often quite complex) scientific problems as well as a range of cultural preferences and relations, extending from the local commitments of particular groups to larger disciplinary and social ideologies. Thus, textual analysis of historical scientific genres usually depends on studies by philosophers and historians of science, on contemporary and retrospective accounts by participants, on considerations by later scientists, as well as on direct analysis of texts. In the case of the adaptive landscape metaphor, the disciplinary culture and scientific problem are particularly complex, and summarizing them fully would take more space than is available here. Nevertheless, in order to understand the interdisciplinary possibilities opened up by this generic metaphor, it is necessary to sketch briefly the context out of which it arose and functioned. (Much of the research establishing the historical and rhetorical framework of the adaptive landscape is reviewed by Ceccarelli and by Journet, "Synthesizing.")

The image of the adaptive landscape was created by geneticist Sewall Wright, whose work was influential in the Evolutionary Synthesis of the 1930s and the 1940s. The Evolutionary Synthesis brought together Darwinian theory and Mendelian genetics to solve a central problem that had plagued biologists since Darwin: how evolution worked (Bowler). Until the Synthesis, this problem had been approached in different ways by two main groups of scientists; biologist Ernst Mayr has labeled them "naturalists" (those scientists working in fields of natural history such as systematics and paleontology) and "experimental geneticists." In the years after Darwin, naturalists had acquired compelling evidence that evolution had occurred in the history of the earth and they knew a good deal about the evolutionary adaptations of natural populations and species, but they had no generally accepted explanation of how evolutionary change occurred. Experimentally, geneticists were beginning to understand the mechanisms of inheritance, but they tended to concentrate on genetic changes observable in laboratory conditions and were unable to explain the larger scale processes of evolutionary adaptation observable over time in nature.

In the 1930s, this situation changed when three population geneticists—Wright, R. A. Fisher, and J. B. S. Haldane—were able to construct quantitative models, complex mathematical formulae, that demonstrated theoretically what could not be observed directly: that natural selection—when played out in terms of genetic variables such as selection rate, mutation rate, and population size and structure—could result in evolutionary changes of populations (Provine, "Role"). But while the theoretical models of the population geneticists demonstrated that natural selection *could* account for evolutionary change, they did not prove that it *had.* For that remained the further task of the Synthesis: integrating the theoretical models of the geneticists with the knowledge about the temporal and spatial dimensions of natural populations already gathered by naturalists.

Arriving at interdisciplinary consensus, though, was not automatic. One of the most pressing problems facing the authors of the Synthesis was the need to reconcile differences among disciplines with very different research traditions and genres. On the one hand, geneticists operated out of a mathematical or experimental tradition and produced highly quantitative, theoretical discourse with little descriptive data; on the other hand, naturalists worked in the field or museum and produced detailed descriptions and classifications, with little theoretical explanation. Geneticists and naturalists disagreed about theory—the causes, direction, and patterns of evolutionary change; about method—the relative value of experimental vs. descriptive work; and about rhetoric—patterns of discourse and terminology. These disagreements were further exacerbated by the fact that geneticists and naturalists worked in different institutions, read different journals, and attended different conferences. All these disagreements resulted in what Mayr has called "a communications gap" in which geneticists and naturalists "continued to talk different languages, to ask different questions, to adhere to different conceptions (9, 28; see also Cain; Harwood).

The communications gap Mayr describes is at least partly a consequence of the fact that scientists of the synthesis approached questions about evolution with different genre commitments—different sociocognitive assumptions about typicality that allowed them to make sense of experience and communicate among themselves. What was needed were new patterns of typicality: new ways to formulate connections between phenomena that were both familiar and novel. Specifically, in terms of textual commitments, neither the generic discourse of the geneticists (primarily mathematical formulae) nor that of the naturalists (primarily descriptive cataloguing) was adequate to the new knowledge. Instead, biologists' success in synthesizing disciplinary knowledge was connected, at least in part, to their success in synthesizing disciplinary rhetorics. The major writers of the Synthesis formulated what I have called a "boundary rhetoric"—a new set of genre commitments that traversed the space between multiple disciplines and that allowed writers to create and communicate a new interdisciplinary knowledge. Berkenkotter describes this space as a Vygotskyan zone of proximal development: "a combining of intellects and disciplinary resources, tools and methods that will facilitate conceptual change through problem-focused research" ("Theoretical Issues" 181).

SEWALL WRIGHT AND FITNESS SURFACES

Sewall Wright's metaphor of the adaptive landscape seems to have been designed specifically as an interdisciplinary boundary rhetoric, or a way of moving between disciplinary worlds. As one of the earliest writers of the Synthesis, Wright was immediately aware of the need to find new ways to connect the contextual knowledge and expectations of geneticists with those of the naturalists. His 1931 paper, "Evolution in Mendelian Populations," had provided a germinal demonstration of how a number of variables common to natural populations—such as mutation, selection, population size and structure, and random variation or genetic "drift"—could result in different rates, intensities, and directions of evolutionary change (Provine, *Wright*). But while this paper was immediately recognized as a major achievement, it was, like the papers of Fisher and Haldane, notoriously difficult to read. (It is, in fact, commonly agreed that almost none of the naturalists of the Synthesis could read or understand the work of the population geneticists in the "mathematical original.") Asked in 1932 to present a short, accessible, and nontechnical summary of his findings, Wright produced "The Roles of Mutation, Inbreeding, Crossbreeding and Selection in Evolution," the paper in which he first put forth his famous metaphor of the fitness surface, later expanded by other biologists into the notion of an adaptive landscape. Behind the mathematical complexities, Wright wanted to make the point that within a population a large number of genetic combinations are possible, some of which are inevitably more adaptive or more "harmonious" than others, and that different genetic combinations can produce relatively similar effects. To suggest the relative adaptive value of various genetic combinations, Wright offered the image of a topographical map, or fitness surface, where "harmonious" gene combinations are represented by "peaks" and less harmonious combinations that "fall off" from these peaks are represented by "slopes" or "valleys."

Wright's image of the adaptive landscape was immensely influential and quickly became a part of the generic vocabulary of evolutionary biology. It remains, according to evolutionary biologists, "the dominant metaphor for adaptation" (Kirkpatrick 142), "by all odds the most important metaphor in macroevolutionary theory in the past 50 years" (Eldredge, *Macroevolutionary Dynamics* 18). Kirkpatrick explains that "a lesson taught in university biology classes everywhere is that selection drives populations uphill, towards a fitness peak" (142). Similarly, William Provine, Wright's biographer and perhaps the foremost historian of the Evolutionary Synthesis, has claimed that the concept of the adaptive landscape or fitness surface "was one of [Wright's] single most influential contributions to modern biology":

> Few evolutionary biologists would question this assertion because most textbooks on evolution since the first edition (1937) of Dobzhansky's *Genetics and the Origin of Species* (with the notable exceptions of those of Mayr, Fisher, Ford, Cain, and Sheppard) have included representations of the famous fitness surfaces. I travel to many universities and centers where populations genetics is taught, and at most places graduate students talk as if natural populations lived on fitness surfaces rather than on the earth's surface in ecological settings. (*Wright* 307–8)

My argument is that this metaphor functioned as a powerful symbolic tool that allowed biologists to reconceptualize old problems in new ways. Entering into the generic discourse of evolutionary biology, the image of the adaptive landscape came to signify more than its original intent—that is, Wright's desire to "simplify" the quantitative concepts of population genetics into a spatial language understandable to naturalists. Instead, it served both an epistemic and a rhetorical function: the creation of a shared generic space where new typifications could be constructed and communicated to a variety of disciplinary readers. This interdisciplinary generic space is analogous to what Star and Griesemer have labeled a "boundary object," an analytic concept that—like genre—is social and cognitive, centrifugal and centripetal, product and process. Boundary objects are

> those scientific objects which both inhabit several intersecting social worlds . . . and satisfy the informational requirements of each of them. Boundary objects are objects which are both plastic enough to adapt to local needs and the constraints of the several parties employing them, yet robust enough to maintain a common identity across sites. They are weakly structured in common use, and become strongly structured in individual use. These objects may be abstract or concrete. They have different meanings in different social worlds but their structure is common enough to more than one world to make them recognizable. (393)

Boundary objects, in Star and Griesemer's view, facilitate "indeterminate" or "n-way translation" (412), a rhetorical process frequently characteristic of interdisciplinary projects, where the task involves much more than the "one-to-one translation" of an independent signified from one signifier to another. Instead, the challenge is to foster common understandings among multiple disciplinary worlds while at the same time allow possibilities for new knowledge and divergent points of view.

In the discussion that follows, I will examine how the metaphor of the adaptive landscape entered into the generic discourse of evolutionary biology through its appearance in two of the keystone texts of the Synthesis: Theodosius Dobzhansky's *Genetics and the Origin of Species* (1937) and George Gaylord Simpson's *Tempo and Mode in Evolution* (1944).[2] Dobzhansky and Simpson both used Wright's image of the fitness surface, and his original diagrams, to clarify the difficult mathematics of Wright's theories. But both also expanded the meaning of the image far beyond Wright's original intent. This dual use of the metaphor is characteristic of the both robust and plastic processes that boundary objects make possible.

THEODOSIUS DOBZHANSKY AND ADAPTIVE PEAKS

In 1937, Dobzhansky published *Genetics and the Origin of Species,* usually credited as the first major book of the Evolutionary Synthesis. As Leah Ceccarelli points out, part of Dobzhansky's ability to inspire scientists to traverse disciplinary boundaries lies in his ability to simplify Wright's theories in ways that were understandable and relevant to diverse disciplinary audiences. Dobzhansky specifically introduces an extended discussion of Wright's metaphor in response to one of the central problems of evolutionary theory in the 1930s (which it remains today): "the problem of the relative importance of the different agents [of evolution, such as selection, mutation, population size, environmental change, random drift]" (186). His answer is essentially a recapitulation of Wright's 1931 and 1932 papers: "A very interesting attempt in this direction has been made by Wright (1931a, 1932), whose lead we may partly follow" (186). Dobzhansky then reproduces Wright's diagram and argument in terms that, according to biologist Niles Eldredge, are "so purely Wrightian, that, beginning with the next paragraph, the language is lifted directly from Wright (especially 1932) without any particularly close citation to the direct passages that Dobzhansky is recapitulating" (*Unfinished Synthesis* 27). But in the next chapter, Dobzhansky also extends the metaphor far beyond Wright's original intent when he uses it to describe how species evolve:

> Related species occupy each a separate peak, and numerous peaks in the same field may remain unoccupied, since some gene constellations have never been formed and tried out. The adaptive valleys intervening between the peaks are mostly uninhabited, and some of them are so low as to be uninhabitable" (229).

In the third edition (1951), the metaphoric language becomes even more dramatic, as Dobzhansky places taxa above the species level—families and orders—on adaptive peaks:

> "Adjacent" adaptive peaks are arranged in groups, which may be likened to mountain ranges in which the separate pinnacles are divided by relatively shallow notches.... The feline adaptive peaks form a group different from the group of the canine "peaks." But the feline, canine, ursine, musteline, and certain other groups of peaks form together the adaptive "range" of carnivores, which is separated by deep adaptive valleys from the "ranges" of rodents, bats, ungulates, primates, and others.... (10)

Dobzhansky's use of adaptive peaks to represent the fitness of species and higher taxa sharply differs from Wright's, where points on the topographic map represent the genetic fitness of either individuals or populations. (Wright himself, according to Provine [*Wright* 311], is unclear which.) This metaphoric shift is important—both rhetorically and epistemologically—because it facilitates a significant conceptual move in evolutionary biology: the extension of theoretical arguments about micro-evolutionary processes of interest to geneticists (i.e., what happens at the level of genes, individuals, and populations) to macroevolutionary processes of interest to naturalists (i.e., what happens at the levels of species and higher taxa). The degree to which it is appropriate to explain between-species adaptation in terms of the mechanisms that operate for within-species adaptation was—and remains—one of the central debates in evolutionary biology (e.g., Eldredge, *Reinventing Darwin*).

Dobzhansky's use of the metaphor of the adaptive landscape is thus both very similar to and very different from Wright's. On the one hand, Dobzhansky offers an almost word-for-word paraphrase of existing knowledge. This recapitulation of Wright's argument and his language suggests the problems Dobzhansky and other biologists faced understanding the complex mathematical claims of the geneticists. But, on the other hand, Dobzhansky adapted Wright's metaphor for a very different argument, suggesting that its function went beyond simplifying the language of one disciplinary community for the interests of another. More powerfully, the adaptive landscape became a mediational means for reconceptualizing a new set of disciplinary problems of interest to biologists of the Synthesis. Ceccarelli has argued convincingly that Dobzhansky's extension of the metaphor of the adaptive landscape was successful in helping geneticists and naturalists better understand each other because it "takes[s] a mathematical abstraction of something that is happening in a real environment and returns[s] it to the spatial realm with an imaginary scenario" and because the "genetic alteration of populations inhabiting the 'field of gene combinations'" can be easily visualized as the movement of a "real population . . . to inhabit a new location" (97). The landscape metaphor is also effective, I believe, because it connects to larger canonical narratives of progress—going "up" to higher forms of life and "down" to valleys of death. But while the metaphor did seem to open up conversation between disciplinary groups, its equation of genetic "space" with ecological space is not a neutral move, just as the shift from mathematical language to spatial language is not unambiguous translation. (The implications of Dobzhansky's extension of the landscape metaphor from populations to species and higher taxa are discussed by Eldredge and Cracroft, by Gould ["Hardening"], and by Provine [*Wright*], all of whom argue that this move has serious conceptual consequences for the theoretical understanding of evolutionary adaptation.)

This dual use of Wright's arguments and language—borrowing and transforming—demonstrates the complexity of projects that have to connect the generic assumptions and language of more than one discipline. Julie Klein has differentiated two such kinds of projects: what she calls "interdisciplinarity" and "transdisciplinarity." Interdisciplinary work aims to show how the theory, methods, and findings of one discipline are consistent with those of another; such projects tend to borrow or modify the existing generic resources of the various disciplines involved, including creating intertextual links through citation, rephrasing specialist terminology, and suppressing differences in favor of emphasized points of contact. However, transdisciplinary work offers new conceptual frameworks and approaches that redefine existing disciplines and create new transdisciplinary knowledge; such projects, I have argued ("Jelliffe," "Synthesizing," "Re-Drawing"), often require the parallel transformation of existing discursive conventions to create new transdisciplinary genres.

The Evolutionary Synthesis was an example of both interdisciplinarity and transdisciplinarity, as Dobzhansky's use of the metaphor of the adaptive landscape makes clear. Dobzhansky's paraphrase of Wright's metaphoric language helped him integrate genetic theory with the extensive work already done on natural populations and species detailed throughout *Genetics and the Origin of Species*. But his transformation of genetic arguments—his extension of the adaptive landscape from micro to macro-evolutionary events—suggests the ways in which Wright's metaphor facilitated a new way to solve a new set of problems: how to explain the evolution above the population level, of species and higher taxa, a problem of distinct interest to naturalists. The metaphor of the adaptive landscape offered Dobzhansky and the biologists who followed him a new boundary object or sociocognitive resource —a new genre convention for thinking about and representing evolutionary processes.

GEORGE GAYLORD SIMPSON AND ADAPTIVE ZONES

If Dobzhansky is usually credited as author of the first general book of the Synthesis, Simpson is recognized as being the first to connect genetic theory specifically to the discipline of paleontology. Before the Synthesis, paleontologists were known for either advocating non-Darwinian explanations of evolution (such as orthogenesis or Lamarckism) or for shunning theory altogether in favor of empirical cataloguing (Gould, "Simpson"; Laporte, "Expansion"; Rainger). Thus they were perhaps the group of naturalists least receptive to the new theories of the geneticists. Simpson caricatures the rhetorical difficulty he faces at the beginning of *Tempo and Mode*:

> Not long ago, paleontologists felt that a geneticist was a person who shut himself in a room, pulled down the shades, watched small flies disporting themselves in milk bottles and thought he was studying nature. A pursuit so removed from the realities of life, they said, had no significance for the true biologist. On the other hand, the geneticists said that paleontology had no further contributions to make to biology, that its only point had been the completed demonstration of the truth of evolution, and that it was a subject too purely descriptive to merit the name "science." The paleontologist, they believed, is like a man who undertakes to study the principles of the internal combustion engine by standing on a street corner and watching the motor cars whiz by. (xv)

It is the general agreement of biologists that this situation changed with Simpson's *Tempo and Mode*, a work successful not only in demonstrating that the evidence gathered by paleontologists was consistent with the theoretical models of the geneticists but also in establishing that paleontology could be more than a descriptive enterprise at the service of genetics. *Tempo and Mode* is thus, like *Genetics and the Origin of Species*, both interdisciplinary and transdisciplinary. Simpson's latter, and perhaps more important, achievement was to demonstrate that paleontological knowledge about time (the "tempo" of evolution) completed the geneticists' atemporal models (what he called "determinants" of evolution), to produce a more coherent and original explanation of real evolutionary change (the various "modes" through which evolution occurs)—an explanation available *only* from the perspective of real organisms in historical time. Simpson's ability to combine paleontological description and genetic explanation is comparable, I have argued, to the combination of chronicle and plot that historiographers such as Hayden White describe as being the components of narrative history. *Tempo and Mode* thus represents a powerful and new kind of argument about evolution and a new genre for paleontology: an elaboration of what Simpson was later to call "The Historical Factor in Science."

To make this narrative argument, Simpson, like Dobzhansky, hinges most of his theoretical bridgebuilding on Wright, again using Wright's imagery of the adaptive landscape as the structuring principle of his presentation. And also like Dobzhansky, Simpson introduces Wright's metaphor both to simplify the complex mathematics of genetic theory and to make a new argument about evolutionary patterns. Specifically, Simpson addresses the role of time (the evolutionary dimension with which paleontologists are most directly concerned) by extending Wright's original metaphor into one of "adaptive grids," in which groups of organisms can shift, through time, from one "adaptive zone" to another. (Eldredge explains that while the two sets of imagery are "essentially equivalent," the "adaptive grid introduces time as one dimension, whereas the landscape depicts the adaptive scene at only one point in time" [*Unfinished Synthesis* 78].) Simpson then uses the zone-and-grid imagery, as well as detailed discussion of citations from the paleontological literature, to tell the "story" of equid evolution (his primary example of the mega or "quantum" mode of evolution). In this story, small populations of early horses move, through evolutionary time, from one zone to another: going down (through "random drift") one adaptive peak into a valley, then going up (through selection) a different peak to a new adaptive zone. Simpson thus transforms Wright's metaphor in three significant ways: (1) above the population level to species and families (comparable to Dobzhansky's extension); (2) from the genetic composition of organisms with which Wright was concerned (their genotypes) to observable physical characteristics (their phenotypes); and (3) to a much greater evolutionary time scale (Provine *Wright*). The result is to historicize the adaptive landscape, a move that has both epistemological and rhetorical consequences.

The narrative argument of *Tempo and Mode* for most contemporary readers represented a successful synthesis of genetics and paleontology. (See Laporte *Tempo* for a review of reviews.) But, as I have argued elsewhere ("Synthesizing"), the persuasiveness of Simpson's "boundary rhetoric" in *Tempo and Mode* may rest on his ability to synthesize not only the knowledge claims but also the genres of these two disciplines. In *Tempo and Mode*, Simpson transforms the values, principles, and assumptions of one discipline into the language and discourse forms of the other, making each seem accessible, relevant, and generically familiar. Specifically, he recasts paleontological genres of descriptive data into the quantitative language so important to the geneticists, and vice versa. Simpson's use of the adaptive landscape, like his use of mathematical equations in describing paleontological data, serves as one site for this renegotiation of disciplinary genres. Berkenkotter has pointed out the further sociocognitive resources of Wright's imagery: such "generic forms and conventions provide the symbolic tools that function as alternative thinking languages for readers knowledge-able of any one or more of these semiotic systems" ("Theoretical Issues" 183).

Wright's, Dobzhansky's, and Simpson's uses of the adaptive landscape demonstrate the multiple resources and effects of genre. The landscape metaphor is a *social* and *cognitive* object, providing a way to solve problems within the contextual assumptions of disciplinary groups. It includes both the *process* of that problem solving—creating, as Bazerman suggests "a resource" to help "see how evolution could be played out through genetic processes"—and the *product*, a thinking language that became a way to communicate that solution to others ("Influencing" 196). And it operates in ways that are both *communal* and *individual*, functioning within shared expectations—even helping to articulate those expectations—while it also opens up novel directions for future research.

The composing processes of Wright, Dobzhansky, and Simpson, as well as the evolutionary biologists who followed them, are obviously not understood solely in terms of genre, just as the intellectual achievements of the Evolutionary Synthesis are clearly not due only to landscape imagery. A complete picture, if possible, also would detail individual creativity and cognition, as well as provide a fuller picture of local social opportunities and constraints and other existing scientific tools and knowledge. This consideration of Synthesis writing from the perspective of one of its genre conventions is only meant as a partial view. Nevertheless, I believe that an examination of genre conventions can have important implications for our understanding of the intellectual work entailed in composing processes. First, in terms of theory, the adaptive-landscape metaphor suggests the ways in which genre knowledge is both epistemological and rhetorical, shaping thinking as well as writing. Second, in terms of method, examination of genre conventions such as the adaptive landscape shows the value of looking at texts—at products as well as processes—in order to understand the sociocognitive dimensions of writing. Finally, in terms of pedagogy, work on genre suggests that teaching students the conventions of professional writing is not just teaching them a set of guidelines to follow but helping them relate the specific situations in which they are engaged to the recurrent situations encountered by members of particular discourse communities and alerting them to that community's typical ways of responding to those situations.

Notes

1. That our categories of experience are constructed rather than mimetic or foundational is a hallmark not only of genre theory but also of much cognitive psychology and neurobiology (e.g., Edelman, Lakoff, Johnson, Searle) as well as other theoretical attempts to taxonomize experience such as evolutionary biology itself.

2. Of course, examining how a generic convention becomes established is only preliminary; the next task, beyond the scope of this chapter, is to illustrate its dispersal as a disciplinary norm. My primary evidence for the pervasiveness of this metaphor is the assertions of biologists and historians such as Eldredge, Provine, and Kirkpatrick. Eldredge discusses the history and development of the metaphor at some length in *Macroevolutionary Dynamics: Species, Niches, and Adaptive Peaks.* I can also add, more anecdotally, that every biologist I have ever asked has been familiar with the landscape metaphor, though not all are aware of its provenance. One of the latest incarnations is found in the title and structuring image of Richard Dawkins' recent book, *Climbing Mount Improbable.*

8

A Tangled Web of Discourses:
On Post-Process Pedagogy
and Communicative Interaction

Helen Rothschild Ewald

In 1988, Anthony Petrosky observed high school classrooms in the Mississippi Delta in a study funded by the MacArthur Foundation. Petrosky was drawn to two school districts in particular because of the students' consistently outstanding performance on mandated state literacy exams. In his observations, however, he did not, according to Evelyn Ashton-Jones, "find a pedagogy that might reasonably predict this success; rather, he discovered rote learning and unison drilled [choral] response" (Petrosky 65; Ashton-Jones 13). Ashton-Jones, who came to the Delta in 1992 to teach at the University of Southern Mississippi, assigned to her teacher education majors portions of Petrosky's published account. Her students' resistance *as Mississippians* to this account led her to conclude that she and Petrosky had "deployed a web of discourses" that essentially had entrapped her students. She concludes that both she and Petrosky were "spoken by larger-than-institutional discourses that we did not intend and perhaps believed were not operative in the classroom context" (20).

Although her account is not specifically directed to writing pedagogy, Ashton-Jones' observations introduce themes that, in themselves, form a web of discourses that has the potential to sustain or to ensnare those interested in post-process approaches:

- Ashton-Jones' students' resistance to Petrosky's right to speak on educational practices in their Delta embodies the theme of *agency/authority*.
- Her belated recognition of the importance of the social construct of Mississippians entails the theme of *perspective*.
- Petrosky's search for progressive pedagogies that would explain the outstanding performance of Delta students and Ashton-Jones' subsequent decision to use Petrosky's account in her class incorporate the

theme of *value* (here involving the choice of subjects and the uses to which knowledge about those subjects is put).

- Ashton-Jones' acknowledgment of the influence of cultural discourses entails the theme of *selection*.

I find these themes, also named in Joan E. Hartman and Ellen Messer-Davidow's *(En)Gendering Knowledge: Feminists in Academe*, particularly appropriate to discussions of post-process pedagogy because they entail epistemic issues, and I take for granted that knowledge making is the business of the classroom. Beyond this, I assume that any discussion of post-process pedagogy in the composition classroom needs to account for postmodern theories in the field. But, more particularly, I believe issues of selection hold the key to post-process pedagogical developments. Before turning to selection, I briefly review postmodern interrogations of agency, perspective, and value as a way of showing the tangle that awaits those committed to post-process approaches.

AGENCY

Postmodernism has been distinguished by its struggle with issues of agency, often discussed in terms of authority and authorship. Authority, which is thoroughly situated within a postmodern framework, is the source of considerable angst among theorists (Bizzell, "Antifoundationalism" 665). Postmodernists disagree regarding the place of individual authority within socially situated contexts. For example, whereas social constructionists situate the writer's authority in discourse communities, "externalists" see the writer having authority as an individual (although socially constructed) agent, who is *required to* assume a strategic attitude within the "circulation of discourse in society" (Kent, "Formalism" 84–91). Because externalism allows the *individual* authority to assume rhetorical stances and to construct texts, it allows seeing the subject as an individually accountable agent in a way that social constructionism does not.

Although some postmodern theorists regret or even refuse practical applications, the postmodern struggle with agency has had inescapable pedagogical implications. Lester Faigley posits that when the autonomous author of foundationalism becomes the situated subject of postmodernism, the result is an impasse of agency. That is, "the notion of 'participation' becomes problematic in its implication that the subject can control its location and moves within discourse" (*Fragments* 226–27). Composition teachers thus face the situation where, as Donald

C. Jones puts it, "[n]ot only does the apparent agency of some writers defy [theoretical] explanation, but also some postmodern pedagogies actually undermine the potential agency of student writers" (82). The postmodern subject, inscribed by language, is caught in a web of dominant discourses even as she or he tries to operate within and perhaps resist those discourses. As Douglas Hesse argues, the paradox of postmodernist pedagogy is that giving up the notion of foundational truths requires a teacher to take on a different kind of authority. Teachers must "invoke, seeming as foundational, the value of critical exchanges" even though such exchanges depend on having starting points (a text, for example) that are necessarily "provisional, transitory, exclusionary, or 'wrong' . . . " (230). In any case, the theme of authority represents a significant source of entanglement for those interested in post-process pedagogies.

This type of entanglement is shown by Paulo Freire in *Pedagogy of Hope* (1994). Freire recalls a 1973 trip to Santiago, Chile, where, amidst social and political upheaval, educators met to discuss educational reform. Outside the meeting hall, Freire noticed a poster designed to promote a new literacy campaign:

> A middle-aged workman, sitting at a table, was having showered over his passive head, by a strong, determined hand—as if it were crumbling something between its fingers—pieces of words. The vigorous hand of the educator was sowing letters and syllables in the purely recipient head of the worker. (188)

Needless to say, Freire was incredulous that such a poster expressing "a barefaced authoritarian ideology" and a "profound scientific ignorance of the nature of language" should be used to represent a progressive (and leftist) educational agenda. The disjunction between the physical representation of the Santiago program and its liberatory agenda captures the difficulties our discipline now faces when teachers try to translate postmodern perspectives on agency into pedagogical practice. So entrenched are traditional assumptions about authority and learning in the classroom that they resist escape, even when teachers make conscious efforts to do so (see Hull et al.).

PERSPECTIVE

Postmodernists have proven noticeably contentious regarding issues of perspective. These issues involve the positioning of writers or knowers in respect to subjects of inquiry by considering their social circumstances. Ashton-Jones invokes perspective when she reveals that both she and Petrosky had somehow overlooked the place of social constructs in their classroom observations and plans. Petrosky had not attended to the choral element of the classroom discourse he had observed. Ashton-Jones had failed to predict the negative responses of her students as Mississippians to Petrosky's account.

Hartman and Messer-Davidow identify four categories of circumstance that can inform perspective:

- affiliation with cultural categories (e.g., gender, race, class, sexuality)
- technical training, which differs not only across but also within disciplines
- personal histories
- critique of how these circumstances organize inquiry and shape knowledge (3)

In our discipline, infighting has erupted among various approaches regarding these categories.

A look at critical and feminist pedagogies provides a good sense of such infighting. Critical and feminist approaches share the same focus on cultural categories and the assumption that discourse relations reflect and constitute social relations.[1] Whether discussed in terms of transaction, dialogue, or reciprocity, communicative interaction is central to the type(s) of social relations recommended in these approaches. In the composition classroom, this concern for interaction has been instantiated in various instructional methodologies including conferencing, peer workshops, and computer-assisted interchanges. Despite this common ground, critical and feminist theorists often clash. For example, feminist Elizabeth Ellsworth criticizes the Marxist formula for dialogue for assuming "a classroom of participants unified on the side of the subordinated against the subordinators, sharing and trusting in an 'us-ness' against 'them-ness'"; she further faults Marxism for not confronting the "dynamics of subordination present among classroom participants, and within classroom participants, in the form of multiple and contradictory subject positions" (106). In other words, Marxism ignores the notion that a white, male student might bring to a group situation the personal privilege he enjoys in society. Such a student does not have to view himself as subordinate, especially with women and minorities as peers, and he enjoys discourse rights that allow him to reproduce the social relations of the culture at large within his small peer group. Conflicts among critical theorists and feminists are intensified by the fact that—as Jennifer Gore points out—these approaches are internally fragmented among those within each ideology who emphasize the "pedagogical project" (social vision) and those who focus on "pedagogical practice." This fragmentation creates a "struggle for pedagogies" among approaches that might more profitably be involved in forming alliances than in staking out distinct regimes of truth (Gore 43–49).

Accusations of cultural bias and uncritical cultural reproduction characterize exchanges between approaches emphasizing different categories of circumstance. For example, externalists draw fire from feminists for emphasizing technical training over cultural affiliation. Thomas Kent's *Paralogic Rhetoric: A Theory of Communicative Interaction* emphasizes the role genre, a component of disciplinary training, plays in communicative interaction. Because his work devotes little time to the influence of other public constructs, such as gender, race, class, and sexuality, it is open to criticism from affiliative approaches. Davison's work reveals a similar tendency to marginalize cultural affiliation. Initially, Davidson's articulation of prior and passing theory would appear to invite consideration of cultural affiliation in that prior theory sees both social constructs and a person's history with those constructs as important.[2] But the affiliation-neutral nature of "prior theory" leaves Davidson open to the charge that he is sanitizing or ignoring the powerful influence that cultural categories have on interpretation and communicative interaction. The externalist emphasis on genre rather than cultural categories may be attributed, in part, to externalism's repudiation of the Cartesian self. Because it denies the usual sense of the importance of self, externalism seems primed to marginalize those categories of circumstance readily associated with self, such as gender and race. Feminists have been particularly alert to such dismissal, taking to task theorists, externalist or otherwise, who seem to be reproducing an androcentric bias in their work. For example, Nancy Fraser critiques the social theories of Jurgen Habermas for an apparent indifference to gender, which she identifies as "masking a masculinist bias" (8). Equally sensitive to marginalization, leftists understand the affiliation-neutral pretenses of institutional discourses as evidence of cultural reproduction (see Freire, *Oppressed*; Shor; Giroux; Grossberg, Introduction).

The specter of cultural reproduction clearly haunts those pedagogies focusing on genre. As John Clifford argues ("The Subject"), those of us who teach students the dominant sets of discourse practices in an attempt to assure students further participation and success, in a very real sense perpetuate those practices. Those in first-year writing courses in particular must "think hard about the plausibility of the charge that in educational institutions writing is, in quite subtle ways, a servant to the dominant ideology " (39). Recently, a number of scholars in the field of rhetoric and composition have argued that literacy instruction in higher education must be seen as *acculturation* because of the nature of the literacy practices that are perpetuated (Lu, Herndl).[3]

VALUE

Hartman and Messer-Davidow see a causal relationship between the social positioning that informs perspective and the *values* that draw us to certain disciplines, "which in turn codify the values that influence our disciplinary *judgments* about subjects to investigate, methods to employ, knowledge to produce, and uses to which that knowledge should be put" (3). For our purposes, the values in our discipline that have fostered a "rush to theory" have contributed to the tangle that threatens to choke those interested in alternative pedagogical approaches. Gore's observations are particularly salient in this regard. Gore asserts that both critical and feminist pedagogies, in their failure "to see and acknowledge their location within the disciplinary power of institutionalized pedagogy," have promoted pedagogical practices that are "remarkably similar to, reminiscent of, mainstream or traditional pedagogies" (123–26). The same may be said of post-process composition pedagogies. That is, post-process pedagogies, occupied by the heroic jousting among theorists, risk not noticing the dragon shadowing the lists.

I think that it is encouraging in this regard that recent scholarship has begun to question the ascendancy of theory in the discipline. Kurt Spellmeyer remarks: "We are, perhaps, *trapped* in theory, and trapped so inextricably that even our most careful efforts to escape keep returning us to the isolation that drove us from theory in the first place" ("After Theory" 893). Marshall Gregory argues that teaching offers us a way of bypassing "the tangle of theoretical disagreements and gluing the fragmented pieces of our discipline back together again" (42). While I wholeheartedly concur that the respective value assigned to theory and pedagogy begs for renegotiation, I also submit that those pursuing pedagogy as a means of release need to see that pedagogies are often underwritten—and undermined—by educational paradigms and discourses that are all the more influential for being invisible or marginalized in our disciplinary discourses. We are, to paraphrase Ashton-Jones, spoken by *institutional* discourses that we neither intend nor respect.

SELECTION

Hartman and Messer-Davidow understand selection as a process that produces the paradigms and canons used to guide research, training, and teaching within a discipline (3). Both current paradigms of learning and received canons of classroom discourse represent a formidable challenge to post-process pedagogies.

A particular threat is the dominant paradigm of learning that assumes teaching necessarily involves knowledge transmission. Ironically, it is this paradigm that leads some to conclude that writing cannot be taught. For example, Kent explains the futility of Edward Corbett's frustration with teaching writing.

> Corbett's uneasiness derives, I believe, from his stalwart but misguided conviction that writing can be taught. He presupposes that writing—and probably reading, too—constitutes a body of knowledge, or a skill, or a process that may be codified in some way and then taught to others. Of course, I have been arguing throughout this book that discourse production and reception cannot be reduced to discrete processes, systems, or methodologies and, as a result, cannot be taught. (*Paralogic Rhetoric* 157)

Kent's claim here seems based on the assumption that the ability to teach a subject rests on its having a codified body of knowledge that can be transmitted.

Those dedicated to the principle that writing *can* be taught are equally vulnerable to the pervasiveness and reproductive quality of transmission models of learning. For example, these models have co-opted past movements in writing pedagogy. John Clifford notes that the process approach to writing has been easily appropriated by dominant approaches, which actually resist rather than represent change. He reports that one of his colleagues had "turned composing into such a labyrinthine sequence of prewriting heuristics, drafts, revisions, and peer-editing sessions that she has probably truncated years of bureaucratic socialization into three months." Clifford concludes that this practice created "a truly constructed subject, committed primarily to reinscribing the obvious and the known in hypercorrect and bloodless prose" ("The Subject" 48).[4]

But transmission models, and the cultural reproduction they represent, can cloud even the most progressive efforts. For example, using Dewey's educational goals and ideology, Fishman and McCarthy zero in on the process of making and redefining claims as a mark of transformative pedagogy. As they point out, claims, whether religious, political, scientific, or ethical, can be understood as social constructs and, as such, are subject to change (347). However, even though the ability to make claims is arguably a clear mark of agency, claim making itself can also be construed as a sign of cultural reproduction. That is, claims might be understood as a part of a phallocentric structure that characterizes traditional academic discourse and generally supports masculine styles of learning (Bleich, "Sexism").

I recently was caught in the tension between agency and reproduction when teaching claim making in my first-year writing course. Practice in claim making begins about midsemester, after students have submitted a number of written pieces, including some published in the first issue of the class's student-run magazine. In these pieces, students were to have worked on certain general rhetorical moves:

- coherence moves (having an understandable arrangement/paragraph structure unified by one subject)
- elaboration moves (including specific supporting details)
- "submission" moves (featuring formats designated by student editors, but including received methods of documenting sources and structuring sentences)

Perhaps it is not surprising that efforts for this first issue were largely narrative and many were quite good.

However, problems arose when I asked students to globally revise their first-issue contributions to reflect claim-and-support structures of academic discourse. In making this assignment, I thought that having students *use their own texts* would make the activity more meaningful. I was wrong. A look at the efforts of one student suggest how wrong. This student, who had effectively chronicled Tupac Shakur's unfortunate personal experiences and his important musical achievements, proposed the following revision plan:

> As for my article, I feel I could have added so much more, like how Tupac has helped the youth of today and about the projects he was recently doing. I could also have given more detail about how upset Tupac was growing up fatherless, but how in the last few years he met and got to know his father. There is much more I could have added, but the first time I didn't want to stray too far from the editor's call for articles on "current events." I also could have done much better proofreading. I now see a whole lot of grammatical and structural errors.

Predictably, I remarked that this plan represented local rather than global concerns and did not seem to address the assigned task of revising for academic claim-support structures.

The student then dutifully submitted a revised plan, using a handout I had hastily constructed as the assignment showed its first signs of missing its mark. Shown below is an excerpt of the student's revised plan and my comments, in italics. Students could list as many minor claims as they deemed necessary, and this student listed four, with the last looking more like a closure move than a separate claim.

> Major Claim: Although Tupac Shakur was criticized by many for his explicit lyrics and his lifestyle, to others his music was a story of his past and present life, which connected to and gave meaning to the lives of many others. *I see at least two claims in this underlined phrase. Will you be able to support all the claims that make up this thesis as it's currently worded? Could you reduce its scope?*

> Minor Claim: Many youth looked up to Tupac for surviving a rough childhood and becoming a very successful rap artist. *Right now I'm puzzled. How does this claim relate to your main claim?*

> Proofs: Tupac had a mother who was on crack. Tupac grew up not knowing who his father was. He was poor and lived in a poverty-stricken neighborhood, which made him not want to be who he was. *To me, this supports the rough childhood part, but not the rap artist part.*

> Minor Claim: Tupac was a great artist and entertainer. *More trouble: how does this directly support the major claim? Could you make the connection clearer? How is this different from the above claim?*

> Proofs: He had many fans who loved him. His music was effective and original. Some of his singles have made it to the top of the charts. His records sold millions. His concerts were always packed. He was inter-

viewed in a lot of magazines. Tupac starred in a few movies also. *These details might work well to support the part of your previous claim that asserts Tupac was a successful rap artist.*

The student revised her claims several times, seeing me individually to discuss her plans, ever trying to address problems with multiheaded claims, repetition, and unclear relationships. However, she never really abandoned the narrative structure of her first effort, nor did she produce a set of mutually exclusive claims.

I finally suggested that she just concentrate on constructing one paragraph using an academic claim-support structure. She used the claim "Tupac was looked up to by youth for surviving a rough childhood" for her paragraph:

> Tupac was called a gangsta rapper by critics, because of his explicit lyrics and his violent history. But to his fans, Tupac was a rap artist who could put reality into rhythm and song and make a person sympathize with his situation or connect the meaning of their own struggles to his. To Tupac's fans, he was like a guiding light, a man who had suffered many of the hardships and troubles of everyday youth. From selling drugs to living in poverty, being fatherless, and [having] a parent on drugs, he showed he could survive. For the youth of today, he was a sign that they could suffer and struggle and still be successful in life. His early lyrics were full of much hate, but as he grew in his career, and change could be noted in his music. [Quotes from Tupac's rap songs complete the paragraph.]

The fact that this student did not include in this paragraph the claim she had worked so diligently to construct clearly demonstrates how irrelevant the exercise was for her. Moreover, this paragraph, unlike her original narrative, is perilously close to plagiarism and as such reinforces the sense that she has lost control of her work. Regrettably, her experience was not uncommon. Instead of claim making being a sign of agency, it clearly was, in this assignment, a task so foreign to many of the students that it managed to alienate them from their own texts.

Canonical modes for classroom discourse represent another significant challenge to those who would pursue post-process pedagogy. In Bakhtinian terms, classrooms are "spheres of human activity and communication" in which specific sets of discourse practices or "speech genres" have developed that become generic styles shaping human activity and communication ("The Problem" 60). Classroom discourse research examines dominant patterns that define the speech genres of the classroom. Hugh Mehan reveals that the dominant pattern for classroom discourse is IRE—teachers *I*nitiate, students *R*eply, teachers *E*valuate (103). Other researchers identify lecture, IRE-style discussions, and individual seatwork as activities that dominate instruction in elementary and secondary classrooms (Nystrand, Gamoran, Goodlad). In her review of this research, Courtney Cazden concludes that the IRE pattern is so pervasive in American education that it can accurately be called the "default pattern—what happens unless deliberate action is taken to achieve some alternative" (53).

In light of these findings, I believe neither Petrosky nor Ashton-Jones need have been surprised when the pedagogy in the Delta schools featured "drill and kill" as choral response. The speech genres Petrosky observed there were perfectly suited for preparing students for the objective literacy tests. *Choral response,* a speech genre with which students were likely familiar from their community and churches can be seen as an inspired domestication of IRE, an institutional speech genre aimed at the reproduction of skills valued by the dominant culture. The expectation that stellar performance on objective tests should involve something other than IRE was an expectation appropriate to teachers who are characteristically not involved in "trying to correct our oral and written speech" (14).

As David Wallace and I argue in *Mutuality: Alternative Pedagogies in Rhetoric and Composition Classrooms,* the modes of discourse that currently serve as default speech genres in our classrooms reify the subject positions of teachers as providers of knowledge and students as recipients of that knowledge. Students, irrespective of cultural affiliation, are targets of exclusion as classroom speech genres exclude them as a group from being knowers.

I recently experienced the pervasiveness of these speech genres when teaching a graduate course in rhetorical theory. As the class was discussing disciplinary frameworks as a preliminary to interrogating them, I became involved in one of the very few teacher-student-teacher-student exchanges of the class session.

> *Helen:* So if we had made the distinction between internalists and externalists on the basis of whether they buy this Cartesian dichotomy, then you have . . . [noting on the board] internalists being cognitivists, . . . social constructivists, . . . how about expressivists? Class: . . . [long silence, fifteen seconds]

Karla: Why not?

Class: [laughter] . . . [silence, five seconds]

Penny: I think more just the inner, not so much the outer. You know what I mean. It's everything from within. It doesn't matter what the rest of the world thinks. It . . . I don't know how to say it. It doesn't matter so much what the rest of the world thinks . . .

Helen: Ah, say that again.

Penny: It doesn't matter what the rest of the world thinks . . . just to express yourself is the most important thing. . . .

Helen: Basing everything from within, it doesn't matter what the rest of the world thinks.

Class: . . . [silence]

Helen: You just made the dichotomy.

Penny: Oh! Okay. Yeah. Yeah!

Upon listening to this taped segment, Penny immediately identified for Wallace the difference in the pattern of interaction that the excerpt represented: "That's a little bit more teacher student, teacher student, than it had been, I think, during the rest of the class." Penny felt that I was "directing a little bit more [than normal] through this section."

> *Penny:* . . . I thought she did a good job of helping me see that . . . that I was creating a . . . dichotomy because I really . . . before she said that, I failed to see . . . there was the other part. . . . I was glad that she did that . . . because if she would have just let someone else go after my comment, I never would have realized or maybe not as clearly known [chuckle] that that's what she was driving at.
>
> *David:* Yeah. So it didn't bother you that she . . . you didn't see her response to you as . . . telling you had the wrong (*Penny:* No) idea or the wrong (*Penny:* No) response.
>
> *Penny:* Especially . . . Yesterday there was so much searching by everybody . . . and . . . any direction that she would offer, I was thrilled

My purpose in presenting this episode is that, at the time, I honestly did not intend to be directive, but I was trying to clarify for myself where *Penny* was in her thinking. However, the fact that both the student and the faculty observer interpreted my contributions as "leading Penny along" is a testament to the pervasive influence of IRE. Because the pattern of discourse here loosely resembles traditional teacher-student exchanges, it was interpreted as a teacher initiating questions in an attempt to direct the student's response. On the bright side, Penny clearly does not believe that I was searching for a "right answer."

Despite the postmodern angst over agency, it is fair to conclude that reports of the death of authority in the classroom have been greatly exaggerated. Dominant paradigms of learning and default patterns of classroom interaction virtually ensure teacher authority and control. Indeed, David Bartholomae argues that in college composition classrooms "there is no writing that is writing without teachers," and he identifies teachers as, at least, tacit tools of dominant culture: "To hide the teacher is to hide the traces of power, tradition and authority present at the scene of writing" (63).

In addition, past reports of the birth of student agency may have been equally exaggerated. Regardless of circumstance, dominant paradigms of learning and default classroom speech genres construct students as occupying object rather than subject positions. Dominant classroom speech genres work to minimize student authority. They instantiate the twin assumptions that knowledge is the result of a transfer (or, to use Freire's term, a "deposit") of information from teacher (in)to student and that language in the classroom transmits received knowledge or truth, which exists prior to classroom interaction.

Even so, communicative interaction in the classroom promises to be a salient feature of post-process pedagogies. To be sure, dialogic interaction is also crucial to Deweyan, Marxist, and feminist approaches, and an emphasis on interaction corresponds to Peshe Kuriloff's recent assertion that writing instructors should focus on teaching students the social skills required to interact well with their teachers and their readers (500). But a commitment to communicative interaction in post-process pedagogies requires research that articulates how classroom discourse might both reflect and construct transactional, as opposed to transmission, models of learning and alternative speech genres with teachers *and* students as subjects.

In advance of such research, however, we can envision how post-process pedagogies, celebrating communicative interaction, would look. Such pedagogy in the writing classroom would enjoy an intimate connection between instructional subjects and methods. Writing instruction could be organized around discourse moves—including moves to coherence, elaboration, and "submission" (where writers "submit" to the orthographic, graphic, and grammatical conventions of dominant/disciplinary discourses). Although this approach might be easily appropriated by transmission models of learning (for example, one can easily image a lecture on "five methods of coherence"), the focus on discourse moves even more naturally complements transactional models when these moves are defined by and subject to communicative interaction in the classroom. Differences in students' ages, training, personal histories, and cultural affiliations could ensure a multilayered understanding of discourse moves as rhetorical strategies.

Because of the inherent value of student contributions in an approach featuring subject-subject discourse relations, post-process pedagogies would conspicuously seek reliable links to students' prior knowledge. If it is true that, as educational psychologists tell us, you cannot learn something without knowing it (in Davidson's terms, there is no passing theory without prior theory ["A Nice"]), then focusing on discourse moves has the advantage that students have experienced communicative interaction since birth. Thus, when discussing closure moves in academic discourse, for example, students could draw upon past knowledge of punch lines of jokes, or two-minute drills in football, or endgames in chess or in video/computer games. Claim making could be similarly discussed. Despite the problems I had with my ill-fated assignment, students are certainly not strangers to claim making, especially given the ubiquitous presence of advertising in the culture. An emphasis on communicative interaction means that knowledge about discourse moves such as claim making would be constituted in the classroom discourse, with teachers and students alike involved in the knowledge making. Moreover, the selection of discourse moves to discuss would be situated in existing cultural, local, and personal forces.[5]

Because of the exchange value of teacher contributions, post-process pedagogies would readily offer the opportunity to explore jointly writing skills and pedagogical methodologies. Bizzell recommends teachers reveal their theoretical stances and ideologies to their students (*Academic Discourse* 271). I suggest they *uncover their methodologies as well.* For example, instead of assuming the value of global revision, a thoroughgoing post-process approach would invite classroom participants to discuss global revision not only as a strategic writing skill, but also as an artifact of previous composition methodology. Students might easily contribute by recalling other skills-based lessons (doing flexibility drills in sports, practicing scales in music) and other revisionist movements in education and in the culture (the "math in context" movement, revisionist histories on film).

At the same time, post-process pedagogies could address the contingent nature of instructional advice. For example, teacherly advice about writing often entails avoidance strategies, which are designed to save students from writing themselves into corners. Students can examine this function of pedagogical methodologies by interrogating the rules they learned in other writing classes. For example, the rule "You cannot start a sentence with *and*" makes sense if seen as advice given by elementary teachers to help students avoid fragments; the rule "You cannot use 'you' [and often 'I'] as a subject" makes sense if seen as advice given by secondary teachers to help students avoid switches in emphasis within paragraphs. Likewise, rules pertaining to claim making, which I blithely invoked in my admonitions, also make sense if seen as advice geared at avoiding certain writing pitfalls, such as unfocused organization, redundancy, and illogical development. Rules for writing could be compared to other rules designed to safeguard the inexperienced, such as "Don't talk to strangers" or "Hand baste your seams before you machine stitch." Through such exploration, students could construct a useful understanding of how writing conventions are situated in both disciplinary and instructional discourses.

Post-process pedagogies could, most obviously, use methodologies that required communicative interaction. In the class-magazine project mentioned earlier, communicative interaction was the main vehicle of decision-making and a crucial factor in composing the contributions. For example, students dialogically determined textual constraints for the magazine, which were then reflected in a call for papers and peer review guidelines. (It is significant that my student found the call "for current events" a meaningful guide for selecting details about Tupac.) Drafts of the call, the guidelines, and, later, the contributions were subject to on-line peer review. Furthermore, post-publication discussions elicited procedural changes, including a tighter due-date schedule and the stipulation that on-line peer review had to occur *on site* during designated class sessions.

In "Poststructuralism, Cultural Studies, and the Composition Classroom," James Berlin asserts that signifying practices in the classroom help define who we are, what is good, and what is possible (23). The pedagogy I have envisioned here defines teachers and students as knowers involved in communicative interaction that, in part, serves to demystify both writing and learning. Whether this demystification is possible depends in large part on our ability to research and re-envision the educational paradigms and speech genres that currently shadow our efforts.

Notes

1. This is an assumption shared by Deweyan approaches as well.

2. Passing theory constitutes on-the-spot interpretation or "hermeneutic guessing" regarding the meaning of an utterance. Prior theory is predictive, allowing the speaker and listener to express in advance how she or he is prepared to interpret the discourse.

3. I am indebted to David Wallace for these acculturation references. Patricia Bizzell, in *Academic Discourse and Critical Consciousness,* does an excellent job of examining the "reproductive difficulties" teachers face when focusing on academic discourse as a genre and invoking other forms of canonicity in the postmodern classroom.

4. Although not all implementations of the process approach have yielded such attempts to codify writing into a process fit for transmission and reproduction, the assumption that teaching involves transmission nevertheless often underpins how students are evaluated. Student work is often assessed in terms of their mastery of basic skills or of certain codifiable bodies of knowledge about language or types of discourses. Clifford notes that, despite empirical evidence that direct instruction in grammar does not have a significant effect on a student's writing, grammar instruction has continued because it privileges "upper- and middle-class language conventions against those of the working class and the poor" (47). Susan Miller also points to the ideological implications of continuing to measure writing achievement by how closely students can match their discourse to dominant codes of language use (*Textual Carnivals* 74). In this way, transmission models effect the reproduction of both language habits and social class, with the evaluation of students' performance in composition classes being a prime vehicle for exclusion.

5. Thomas Hatch and Howard Gardner use a similar tripartite explanation for the interaction among factors that affect learning. Hatch and Gardner are primarily concerned with describing how intelligence can be seen as distributed in social and cultural settings rather than as seated in individuals. David Wallace and I found their categories useful in discussing the implications of efforts to engage students as subject knowers in the social and cultural setting of the classroom.

9

Paralogic Hermeneutic Theories, Power, and the Possibility for Liberating Pedagogies

Sidney I. Dobrin

> No course can teach the acts of either reading or writing.
> —Thomas Kent, "Paralogic Hermeneutics
> and the Possibilities of Rhetoric"

In its most succinctly rudimentary definition, *post-process* in composition studies refers to the shift in scholarly attention from the process by which the individual writer produces text to the larger forces that affect that writer and of which that writer is a part. As Gail Hawisher and colleagues explain, "During the period of 1983–1985, composition studies absorbed the changes brought about by the new emphasis upon process and began to chart the course it would follow post-process, looking beyond the individual writer toward the larger systems of which the writer was a part" (65). That is to say, post-process composition studies began to focus on issues of social construction rather than on issues of the individual writer working within an individual process. The identification of larger influential structures afforded writing teachers the opportunities to teach definable, codifiable systems as conceptual schemes (Donald Davidson's phrase) that dominate discourse production. More recently, a few composition theorists have moved beyond this post-process inquiry and have begun to investigate ways in which the moment of communicative interaction supersedes and possibly refutes the constructions of "systems." Thomas Kent, for instance, has turned to the work of language philosophers Richard Rorty and Donald Davidson to propose that every moment of communicative interaction is singularly unique. In an overly simplified explanation, the systems by which we interpret are not codifiable in any logical manner since discourse does not operate in any logico-systemic manner and never remains static long enough to develop concrete understandings of the communicative interaction. In other words, there are no codifiable processes by which we can characterize, identify, solidify, grasp discourse, and, hence, there is no way to teach discourse, discourse interpretation, or discourse disruption. Individuals, then, communicate through paralogic hermeneutical strategies, and since there is no logico-system for codifying these strategies or even discourse, the act of teaching discourse becomes an impossibility, as I have quoted Kent in my epigraph.

At the outset, paralogic hermeneutic theories seem to be not readily translatable into manageable pedagogies; it is, as Kent claims, impossible to devise a pedagogy or even a simple classroom exercise from them. I have argued elsewhere that classroom application need not always be the measure for value of theory and that one of the greatest values of discourse theories, and paralogic hermeneutics in particular, is what they teach us about the interpretive act, not what they teach us to perform in the classroom.[1] However, my intention here is to examine the potential that paralogic hermeneutics holds for reinvisioning systems of power, and, in turn, how these theories might provide new access to liberating agendas of radical pedagogies. There have been relatively few attempts to derive pedagogies from work in paralogic hermeneutics, and those pedagogies that have used facets of these theories tend to fall short of the agendas of paralogic hermeneutics. While certain pedagogies are remiss in their use of these theories, discussions of paralogic hermeneutics have not theorized the role of power or ethics in their visions of discourse and communication and made themselves of use to the agendas of radical and liberatory pedagogies. By examining the role of power in paralogic hermeneutics in relation to particular pedagogical trends—both pedagogical theories and practices—these particular post-post-process theories of paralogic hermeneutics also should ask us to redefine dramatically both how we teach reading and writing and even how we conceive of the possibilities of teaching discourse without losing sight of liberatory agendas. I suppose, in some ways, my title is a bit misleading since what I offer here is not a pedagogy of paralogic hermeneutics but instead a two-fold examination of these theories and the possibilities it holds for reconceiving composition pedagogy. First, I examine a deeply rooted, self-perpetuating tradition of process that has pushed moments of inquiry into searching for codifiable processes via codifiable processes. Second, I examine a relatively unexplored facet of paralogic hermeneutic theories: the role of power in communicative interaction in relation to the agendas of liberatory learning theories and radical pedagogies, and the tradition of process thinking.

Perhaps because of its newness, perhaps because of the difficulties it offers in designing pedagogies (in fact, the impossibility), very little has been written regarding pedagogies that make use of paralogic hermeneutics. Those who have linked these theories to potential pedagogies—Thomas Kent, Raúl Sánchez, and Irene Ward, for instance—have not offered much as a point of departure for pedagogical application beyond the claim that these theories demand that we radically reconceptualize not only how and what we teach, but what we think teaching *is*. However, that is not to say that the discussions of paralogic hermeneutic pedagogy that these scholars/teachers promote are without value. In fact, there is great merit in the attempts made in these discussions. However, none are able to define the "true" paralogic hermeneutic pedagogy, nor, according to these theories, can they. Rather, each designs a pedagogy that contains elements of the larger understanding of post-process along with a few facets of paralogic hermeneutics, and upon closer examination, the pedagogies that have been forwarded are actually little more than redesigned radical pedagogies or dialogic pedagogies—pedagogies already accepted in the post-process era. For instance, the processes by which we define the substance of multiculturalism disinfects a radical substance and makes the multicultural classroom safe for institutional life. If we are to understand theories of paralogic hermeneutics for what they appear to be, then Kent, as I have quoted him in my epigraph, suggests that there is little room for them in the teaching of discourse or that we cannot teach discourse if we accept the theories. If we are to accept the premise of paralogic hermeneutic thinking, the current nature of how we envision *teaching* is obsolete, and that claim certainly leaves us at an interesting crossroads. As responsible teacher/scholars, we certainly do not want to devalue or dismiss these theories and what they teach us regarding language, writing, and reading simply because they do not offer direct links to pedagogies (as many frequently and ignorantly do). It is difficult for any of us to relinquish the idea that we, as members of the education mechanism, are not forwarding the process of education. The simple proclamation "I teach" is lifted from our repertoire, according to these theories, as the act of teaching is no longer possible. However, if we examine ways in which paralogic hermeneutics inform our understanding of communicative interaction, we can better access the agendas of liberatory pedagogies. Of course, the challenge becomes not creating the uncreatable paralogic pedagogies but redefining how we envision the very *nature* of pedagogy with these theories in mind.

The Tradition of Process

Certainly, one of the greatest resistances to theories that deny the possibility of teaching discourse is that as teachers, scholars, and human beings we have become deeply entrenched in the process paradigm.[2] While the phrase *process paradigm* in composition most familiarly refers to methods of teaching reading and writing, this paradigm of process is more deeply rooted in our understanding of the human animal. I would like to turn briefly to a predominant branch of philosophy studies to show what I mean. It is simple to identify through methods of science, history, cartography, archaeology, and so on that human inquiry has been guided by process, and, as recent postmodern critique has noted, these processes have been distinctively linear and frequently phallocentric. Process philosophy offers an opportunity to identify just how deeply rooted the larger process paradigm is in human thought.

In its most simple form, process philosophy dictates that process must come before substance. That is, things will always be subordinate to the processes that characterize, distinguish, and determine what those things are. According to Nicholas Rescher, "Process philosophy represents an attempt to come to intellectual terms with the world's empirical realities by deriving a framework of conceptions and ideas to integrate the products of modern inquiry into a coherent framework of thought linked to a metaphysical tradition" (3–4). In other words, process philosophy seeks to codify the "real" world, the things that make up the real world, and human understanding of that real world through an understanding of the process by which that real world is created. For most process philosophers, time, change, history, and other cartographies of process are, according to Rescher, the "fundamental categories for understanding the real" (25). John Dewey, for instance, forwards innovative processes of human development and individuality in order to better understand the reality of the human situation.[3] As it is currently studied, process philosophy is divided into two enmeshed (and often inseparable) categories: the first argues that the implications of studying process provide, as Rescher points out, the "most appropriate and effective conceptual instruments for understanding the world" (27). This thinking constitutes the *epistemic* branch of process philosophy. Rescher argues that the second part maintains that process is the "most pervasive, characteristic, and crucial feature of reality" (28). This branch is labeled "ontological." Though deeply entwined in one another, Rescher explains, "In its stronger version, process philosophy is an ontological reductionism that sees all physical things as reducible to physical process. In its weaker version, process philosophy is a conceptual reductionism that sees the explanation of the idea of a 'thing' as necessarily involving a resource to precessual ideas" (28). More directly, all physical things and all epistemological, ontological, conceptual things are products of process. Granted, this school of thought does conflict with other schools of Western philosophical thinking (Aristotle's primacy of substance, for instance); however, process philosophy *is* a dominant tradition in Western thinking.[4]

Making the leap between just about any field of inquiry and process philosophy seems fairly straightforward: historical events do not exist until we establish the process of historicizing those events; scientific laws are not determined until we have applied the process of scientific method; art does not exist until we have created it through process. Aristotle argued for "topoi" as a system for categorizing. Kenneth Pike promoted tagmemics as a heuristic for problem solving. Thomas Kuhn's scientific revolution and history of science argue for processes leading to new things, to new knowledges. Michel Foucault seeks process of history and power. Kenneth Burke identifies process as proceeding substance when he identifies the pentad—act, scene, agent, agency, and purpose—as answering the question "What is involved when we say what people are doing and why they are doing it?" (*Grammar* xv). The principles of process philosophy appear in almost all realms of inquiry. The notion of inquiry alone, in fact, calls for processes by which we come to better understandings of things and processes by which we identify things. Of course, this essentialized version of process philosophy is susceptible to postmodern critique from various angles, but I offer it in order to make a point regarding composition's process paradigm.

In making the simple connection between process philosophy and methods of inquiry, we see quite clearly how composition's process paradigm evolved. Moving from this tradition of process philosophy to the theories and inquiries that have shaped thinking in composition is a simple transition. The forces that have shaped composition's process paradigm—particularly the importance of cognitive psychology—are easily defined in terms of larger traditions of process thinking. Piaget's "genetic epistemology," for instance, codifies structures in knowledge in systematic ways. There is an assumed learning process that involves particular stages such as "abstraction" and "decentering." According to Piaget, these are the processes by which a child distinguishes its own perspectives from those of others; this is the process through which children move away from "cognitive egocentrism." In the discourse of process philosophy, perspective—the thing—does not exist for the child until that child has decentered—the process—and acknowledged its otherness from the rest of the world. In fact, the thing of the world does not exist to that child until it has gone through the process of identifying the world as thing. Likewise, in *Thought and Language,* L. S. Vygotsky—drawing on Piaget—examines the ways in which thinking processes involve the processes of inner speech and external speech that produce the thing of thought.

From these and other theories of cognitive psychology, compositionists developed the notion of cognitive processes that occur when human beings write. For James Britton, as well as other early proponents of cognitive process theories, all writers must deliberately initiate writing by deciding to engage in the act of writing in order to write. Once this step toward writing has occurred, the writer must engage in incubation, the process of deciding upon and understanding the topic about which one will write. Finally, the writer will produce the writing through several steps, pauses, and reflexive moves. While compositionists have argued over the exact nature of what the writing process is, traditional understanding of writing has argued that process precludes, subsumes, encompasses, characterizes, distinguishes, engenders, and determines what that thing of writing is to be. And that thing of writing, the product, is subordinate to the process by which that thing was produced. In fact, the very notion of "composing" suggests a process by which writing emerges.

Paralogic Hermeneutics, Power, and Pedagogy

Evidently, the deck is stacked in favor of process. While it has taken time for composition to shake free of some of the more romanticized notions of writing that expressive writing theories promote and to recognize the importance of process, particular notions of cognition and process also have begun to fade from dominance in composition research. Cognitive inquiry has certainly been crucial in the evolution of composition, but cognitive research has taken a back seat to other (postmodern) forms of inquiry that seek to identify forces that affect process. Important cognitive scholars such as Janet Emig and Linda Flower helped move composition in directions of process, but cognitive research does not receive as much attention as it once did.[5] Instead, current paradigms are dominated by scholarship and pedagogy of empowerment and liberation that examine larger systems and ways in which they affect discourse. The social constructedness of language; the power and oppressive nature of language; the role of gender, race, class, and culture in language are all prominent in composition scholarship. Yet even in this (supposed) post-process paradigm of questioning language in larger contexts, process still takes precedent in the teaching of discourse, in the teaching of reading and writing, not because process has necessarily provided accurate avenues of access to discourse, but because process thinking is so deeply entrenched in the human animal's way of thinking. Unfortunately, the processes that are taught are wrought with problems.[6] For instance, Sanchez notes, "The process-oriented classroom is often an unproblemitized environment, a 'content-course' in the worst sense of the words when the instructor acts as a dispenser of knowledge and the student is an empty vessel." Even in the most liberatory of classrooms where empowerment and critical consciousness are primary to the teacher's agenda, composition teachers still insist upon depositing—à la Freire—a particular process for writing, a particular process for becoming critically aware through understanding the oppressive nature of language. As Sanchez notes, the "writing process is often just the teacher's vision of process"—what prewriting is, what editing is, what revising is, what a final document should look like, what is oppressive, what is politically virtuous, how to become critically conscious, and so forth. Even in the most politically savvy classrooms, process is generally taught by simply reinscribing knowledge, by perpetuating process thinking, by perpetuating inscribed methods of inquiry—all under the guise of post-process inquiry. Students learn to repeat strategies rather than to manipulate discourse from communicative scenario to communicative scenario, just as they have with the five-paragraph theme in process pedagogies. As Joseph Harris contends,

> the advocates of process did not redirect attention to what students had to say so much as they simply argued for what seems to me a new sort of formalism—one centered no longer on textual structures but instead on various algorithms, heuristic, and guidelines for composing. This new formalism has proven little different from the old, as those versions of process teaching that don't work toward a very familiar set of technocratic ones. Both versions tend to move backwards, as it were, from an ideal version of the composition student: either the mature individual of one kind of humanist teaching or the expert practitioner of another more technical sort. The aim of teaching thus becomes to coach students toward either an emotional and intellectual maturity or an expert-level performance. What gets lost in this concern for development toward a known ideal are the actual concerns and perspectives students bring with them to their writing. (*A Teaching Subject* 56)

In his own words, Harris's critique is not "aimed against the proposition that writing is a process—which, again, strikes me as a claim that is true, banal, and of a real if limited use—but against a view of teaching that places some vision on the composing process (rather than an interest in the work of students) at the center of a course on writing" (*A Teaching Subject* 57). That is, while Harris notes that newer process pedagogies are not really that different from older current-traditional formalisms, current liberatory pedagogies also rely on similar process strategies for teaching writing.

Certainly, process pedagogy is convenient; process pedagogy makes it easy to define texts and to write texts. We can unproblematically, clearly present a body of knowledge and evaluate students' abilities to absorb and rehash that body of knowledge, that process. So even liberatory pedagogies that promote students' becoming critically conscious depend on process paradigms: multicultural readers, conflict in the classroom, and contact zones all prescribe processes by which students become "better" people and "better" writers. But these endeavors do not promote agency. Traditional process thinking does not allow the opportunity to name the world since prescribed processes take care of the naming. This activity means learning only the processes of a particular dominant discourse and simply reinscribing sets of processes. In many ways, this activity is exactly the sort of oppressive education against which liberatory pedagogies work. Since some idea of process has always been viewed as mediating between the writer and the world, the problem is recognizing these entrenched systems of process that are institutionalized and, hence, deny actual critical participation to both students and teachers. However, there is also little question that pedagogies of empowerment such as liberatory learning are more ethically sound; that is, as the argument goes, at least these (process) pedagogies are ethically "better" than other kinds of process pedagogies. What theories of paralogic hermeneutics afford are the opportunities to be critical participants in the very discourses that liberatory pedagogies promote or resist.

Perhaps one of the least discussed issues of paralogic hermeneutics is the ways in which communicative interaction accounts for power and ethics.[7] What makes current radical pedagogies so appealing is their focus on illuminating oppressive structures and affording human beings the opportunity to attain agency. In many ways, paralogic hermeneutics seems, at first, to deny this opportunity by denying that discourse can be codified into oppressive structures. However, it seems necessary, for various reasons, to discuss these theories in terms of power, including the current desire to examine power and ethics. Scholars who promote theories of paralogic hermeneutics have not adequately addressed these issues in the communicative moment.

To repeat and extend my overly simplified definition of paralogic hermeneutics, these theories argue that every moment of communicative interaction is singularly unique. Our acts of interpretation are not codifiable in any logical manner since discourse does not operate in any logico-systemic manner and never remains static long enough to develop concrete understandings of the communicative interaction. In other words, there are no codifiable processes by which we can characterize, identify, solidify, or grasp discourse, and, hence, there is no way to teach discourse, discourse interpretation, or discourse disruption. Effective communicative interaction relies on strategies of what Kent labels "hermeneutic guessing" wherein participants develop strategies based on previous experience to interpret discourse for that moment of communication. Kent draws his notion of hermeneutic guessing from Donald Davidson's theory of triangulation:

> Each of two people finds certain behavior of the other salient, and each finds the observed behavior of the other to be correlated with events and objects he finds salient in the world. This much can take place with-

out developed thought, but it is the necessary basis for thought and language learning. For until the triangle is completed connecting two creatures and each creature with common objects in the world there can be no answer to the question whether a creature, in discriminating between stimuli, is discriminating between stimuli at the sensory surfaces or somewhere further out, or further in. It takes two to triangulate. For each of us there are three sorts of knowledge corresponding to the three apices of the triangle: knowledge of our own minds, knowledge of other minds, and knowledge of the shared world. Contrary to traditional empiricism, the first of those is the least important, for if we have it we must have the others, so the idea that knowledge could take it as foundation is absurd. ("Production" 65–66)

More succinctly, as Anis Bawarshi explains it: "We come to know and understand objects in the world and each other only when our interpretations match others' interpretations" (73). Remarkably, Davidson's triangulation and Kent's hermeneutic guessing strategies—two major facets of these theories—are not that different from the process philosophy's claim that one comes to discover the objects of the world through processes of identifying objects. Theories of paralogic hermeneutic communication make the same claim: an individual comes to know an object through interpretive moves with other interpreters. The rudimentary difference—and ultimately what makes these the most post of post-process theories—is that paralogic hermeneutics contends that the processes by which we name objects are not codifiable into any recognizable or identifiable process since access to the world, to objects, to each other is afforded through the randomness of discourse, whereas traditional process philosophy seeks to identify, catalog, and predict processes and, as I have explained, many post-process pedagogies still depend on process teaching.

Kent explains, via Davidson, that triangulation is dependent upon two concepts: the passing theory and the prior theory. Prior theories are the interpretive strategies one brings to a particular communicative scenario—the hermeneutic guessing skills one has developed prior to a particular situation. Passing theories are the strategies one employs during the particular instance of communication. Each communicative act, then, becomes a unique moment in which a participant relies on particular prior theories to develop a passing theory in order to achieve successful communication with another. The skills we develop through prior theories, then, determine how effective our passing theories might be situation to situation. Kent, Davidson, and others acknowledge that a participant in a communicative situation might have obtained better hermeneutic skills than another member in the same communicative situation. In other words, one participant might be better adept at participating in triangulation than another. However, what is not discussed is the role of power in the moment of triangulation, in hermeneutic guessing. In fact, by not following up on what being "better skilled" at hermeneutic guessing might mean, it seems as though Kent and Davidson suggest that triangulation is egalitarian, that triangulation occurs on an equal interpretive playing field. Quite the opposite is true.

David R. Russell offers an example of how triangulation might work:

> [A] seven-month-old child who has not yet learned her first words reaches in the direction of a spherical object and babbles. Her parent, seeing this, puts the object in her hands and says, "Ball! You want to play with the ball?" Sooner or later—usually sooner—the child learns that adults may play with her using spherical objects and that certain sounds ("ball") and certain activities accompany human interactions with such objects. She learns through observing others' actions and her own that making the sound "ball" in certain situations often produces certain effects in others. Triangulation has been achieved. And learning.
>
> The child will eventually learn many words and effects for many kinds of spherical objects and many kinds of activities to go with them. But the crucial point here is that a linguistic system or conceptual scheme or community norm or discursive convention did not mediate between the child's mind and the object. Another human being, the parent, mediated between ("triangulated with" might be a better phrase) the child and the object. (181)

But what Russell, Kent, and Davidson do not identify in the instance of triangulation is the moment of power. In the scenario of the child and the ball, moments of power twist the triangle to result in particular effects: for example, the mother determines for the child what discourse is to be used to define "ball." In other words, a dominant discourse is established. The gender of the child perhaps determines how the mother addresses the child, as does the gender of the speaker. In fact, triangulation, as it has been defined, denies that culture, race, class, or gender affect at all one's prior theories which determine one's passing theories, which affect the moment of triangulation and communication. Certainly, the endeavor of becoming better skilled at hermeneutic guessing implies that participants in communicative interaction have learned to match their interpretations to others' interpretations in *particular ways* in order to be more effective communicators. Kent alludes to this when he writes: "When we communicate, we certainly share some conditions of a common interpretive method" ("Beyond" 501). And in Russell's scenario, the mother determines for the child what action is to be taken by asking, "You want to play with the *ball?*" If the child defines the object, in this case the ball, through triangulation and matches her interpretation with an (m)other's, then one participant in the triangulation has directed the interpretation of the other toward a particular site. In every communicative interaction, no matter how adept a participant is in his or her hermeneutic guessing skills, issues of power affect the manner in which triangulation occurs. In Russell's example, the child is at an interpretative disadvantage; in all communicative moments of triangulation, advantage and disadvantage perpetuate moments of power that when compounded with other instances of power take on the semblance of power structures. When the same prior theories consistently inform one's passing theories, the strategies that get used more frequently generally reflect structures of power. For instance, just as an oppressive regime may learn what discursive manipulations best control a populace, the mother in Russell's illustration will, during her communicative relationship with her child, develop prior theories that allow her to retain parental power over her child—until that child's own prior theories suggest ways of resisting the twist in the triangulation. This observation has significant ramifications for thinking about the important agendas of radical pedagogies and liberatory learning.

If we are to understand the moments of communicative interaction as being individually unique and as occurring in noncodifiable systems, then we must also identify how such notions of communication inherently set up particular moments of power and dominance in each communicative scenario and how those particular instances lead to recurring trends, recurring strategies that appear to create structures of power and oppression. As I read Kent, a communicative interaction is effective when the participants have hermeneutically guessed and interpreted until they are both satisfied with the action of the other. This resolution generally occurs in an unquestioned, unnoticed instance. For example, when I ask my students to turn in their writing assignments, I am satisfied that that particular moment of communicative interaction has been successful when they act and physically pass their papers to me. In this instance, I have a physical action on which to base my interpretation as to whether or not I have triangulated with my students. Inherent in this act is power. In my request, I have fashioned my interpretation during triangulation to lead my student to a particular action that I desired. My prior theories allowed me to develop a passing theory that engaged the other participants in this communicative moment and resulted in an action I desired, and my students' prior theories told them that they must respond in a particular way in order to avoid negative repercussions. At the most rudimentary level, each instance of triangulation is a battle for power and, finally, ethics. The mother who identifies the spherical object has leveled her position of power in that moment of triangulation in order to manipulate the outcome of this discursive act. Granted, the inability to codify the communicative interaction assures that we cannot always be sure our power push in triangulation will work, but we cannot overlook the factors that affect the relationship between participants in a particular communicative act. Nor can we overlook how the manipulation of triangulative moments allows for particular prior theories to dominate multiple moments of communicative interaction and, in turn, influence long-term discursive interactions that form structures of power and give substance to issues of culture, race, gender, class, and so on. It must also be noted that because these prior theories—with which communicators become comfortable and reliant—dominate moments of triangulation, the passing theories that actually get used begin to appear codifiable as discursive formations—à la Foucault. However, because each moment of communication is unique, the naming that we associate with discursive groupings—academic discourse, for example—is not as concrete as we would like to think.

Hence, if we are to accept this vision of paralogic hermeneutic theories, teaching students to become aware of oppressive discursive structures, such as academic discourse or other phallogocentric discourses, is less of a liberating pedagogical agenda than is giving students the opportunity to become more skilled in their own hermeneutic guessing skills and being able to resist the twist of triangulation. As Kent, Sanchez, Ward, and a few others have noted, this is the way in which paralogic hermeneutic pedagogy must be understood: students must become participants in communication; they must constantly engage in developing the skills needed to be adept triangulators. This vision of pedagogy takes seriously the notions of liberatory learning and student empowerment. Paralogic hermeneutic theory asks us to extend our focus beyond the notion of larger structures of power and to attack power at the instance where it begins. To employ a cliché, it asks us to think globally but act locally, and, as I will discuss, to observe power at its most local moment.

The Moment of Power and Self-Reflexive Critique

Once we re-evaluate post-process theories in ways that not only move beyond processes to larger structures but also beyond those larger formations to the individual acts of communication that create the perception of "power structure," we are able to see more clearly how triangulation creates prior theories that recur in oppressive moments. Certainly, we see moments wherein interpretive partners both unknowingly and willingly allow themselves to be lead in particular directions of interpretation. For instance, in both Russell's example and my scenario about asking my students for their papers, neither child nor students resist the moment of interpretation because they have not developed the prior theories that allow for critical questioning of where I or the child's mother lead the interpretive moment. That is, communicators in these situations met with particular experiences such as punishment or retribution for not responding in particular ways (my students would have received poor marks if they had not passed in their papers, for example.). Consequently, they developed prior theories that dictated passivity, for they did not have the prior theories that would lead to resistance or strong interpretive strategies. This process describes in part how manipulation actually occurs and helps explain, for instance, how centuries of communicative manipulation have led to oppression of women. We also may identify instances wherein the more adept hermeneutic guesser is all too skilled and the resistance of the other participant is futile. When we examine the moment of communicative interaction, we see that power determines how triangulation occurs, and each instance provides the experience on which we base our next move. So if we are expertly maneuvered, we may never even recognize that we have been led to a particular interpretation; the communicative moment becomes a moment of seduction, a moment of calculated manipulation.

But this point brings up an interesting question regarding how individual moments of communication, individual moments of triangulation, individual moments of oppression might lead to large-scale oppression and how pedagogies might benefit from paralogic hermeneutic theories that account for the moment of power during communicative interaction.

Pedagogical Possibilities

Ultimately, the greatest challenge composition faces with paralogic hermeneutic theories is finding ways in which these theories might create truly liberating possibilities for pedagogies without systematizing either the theories or the pedagogies. Unfortunately, that challenge seems beyond our grasp as our current conception of the nature of teaching keeps us pinned under a rubric of system and process. However, what we can reconceive via paralogic hermeneutic theories is the narrative character of education. What seems most frightening to me about the ingrained acceptance of process thinking is that we make process seem natural, organic, and by doing so we accept the narrative of education not as an artificial construct but as an inherent (and often naturally right) process. That is to say, if we are to understand oppressive structures not as codifiable systems but as conceptual schemes that occur at the moment of communicative interaction and that take on the appearance of an identifiable structure over a period of time, we afford students the opportunity to visualize, identify, and perhaps act more directly in moments of power. By giving students the opportunity to identify the moment in which power occurs and to possibly resist the triangulative power move, students attain agency in a more direct manner than many liberatory and radical pedagogies profess. In other words, by moving beyond examining structures that affect users of discourse to a critique of how individual moments of communicative interaction create the illusion of those structures, paralogic hermeneutics offers a critique of both process and system that gives individual communicators more opportunity for communicative action, not just communicative interaction.

By accepting the process-philosophy view of the world—that process presupposes object—we willingly accept process as natural. Natural processes inherently resist critique. This sort of thinking suggests that we are limited by linear process and that even recursive, self-reflexive critique must operate under the parameters established by process. By accepting the conventions of process, we have accepted particular ways of talking about teaching, discourse, and power that afford our students—afford us—little access to power. In fact, entrenched process thinking assumes innocent interaction. The machine of production pushes for teaching systemically in order to produce process thinkers.

Yet if we are willing to explore the paralogic nature of individual moments of communication, we furnish the opportunity for radical and liberatory pedagogies to be just that: radical and liberating. That is, just as composition scholarship appeared to move beyond the process paradigm (though still reliant upon process in inquiry and pedagogy) to inquire as to how larger structures affected those processes, we must now examine ways in which singular moments of communicative interaction account for moments of power and, in turn, establish prior theories that support triangulation/manipulation for the benefit of individual communicators. Paralogic hermeneutics removes process as a mediator and suggests the possibility for interpretive action that forces the unmediated, raw encounter between communicants and affords communicative room to critique the triangulative moment. That is, students who become more adept at participating in discursive moments are more likely to be able to resist the oppressive moments of triangulation and to wield more adequately their will when they triangulate.

As I mentioned earlier, I am not going to suggest ways in which pedagogies can or should be developed in order to accomplish the goals of these theories. I am not sure if such translations to practice are possible yet. I think Thomas Kent is absolutely correct in arguing that "if we are serious about finding better ways to help our students improve their writing and reading skills, we might rethink our traditional ways of doing business and attempt to account for the powerful paralogic/hermeneutic dimension intrinsic to the production and analysis of discourse ("Paralogic" 40). We cannot master discourse; we can only become better skilled in our hermeneutic skills, and by introducing students to paralogic hermeneutic theory, we are better able to help achieve their own agency at the moment of communicative interaction.

Notes

1. See Dobrin, "The Politics of Theory-Building and Anti-Intellectualism in Composition" and Dobrin *Constructing Knowledges: The Politics of Theory Building and Pedagogy in Composition,* particularly chapter 3.

2. In Elizabeth Hirsh and Gary A. Olson's interview, philosopher of science Sandra Harding argues that "we could pretty much go through every definition of what's distinctively human and notice that women have been excluded from it" (15). As I discuss the "human animal" here, I would like to recognize that much of intellectual tradition has been generated by patriarchal systems of process. Hence, inquiries of postmodern feminism such as Harding's questioning of scientific method and philosophies of science are critically important, but, for the most part, also must be identified as systems of process, albeit they are important reexaminations and challenges to traditional systems.

3. I recognize that my glossing of process philosophy does not do justice to this deeply rooted philosophical tradition. For more detailed discussions of process philosophy see Rescher or Muray.

4. Even with my limited knowledge of the subjects, I cannot help but notice the links that process philosophy seems to make to chaos theory.

5. Phillips, Greenberg, and Gibson's survey of *CCC* citations identifies just how prominent cognitivist research has been in composition. They identify more than twice as many citations of Flower than any other compositionist.

6. For an insightful critique of Flowers and Emig see Harris's chapter on process in *A Teaching Subject: Composition since 1966.*

7. I recognize the extreme difficulty in defining ethics. While I feel that issues of ethics must be more thoroughly discussed in terms of post-process theories, I will not do so here. Rather, my reference to the "moment of ethic" is intentionally left vague to suggest that ethics certainly plays an important role in the communicative moment and must be explored more thoroughly than here.

10

The Challenge of Contingency: Process and the Turn to the Social in Composition

David Foster

The rise of the process paradigm now seems one of the grand narratives of composition studies. In the seventies and eighties, writing teachers in American colleges and universities heard that real knowledge of how students wrote was coming on the wings of scientific research. Maxine Hairston wrote in 1982 that the new research would mean that "[f]or the first time in the history of teaching writing we have specialists who are doing controlled and directed research on writers' composing processes" in order to "find out something about how people's minds work as they write" (85). As articles and monographs about cognitive research accumulated, teachers were encouraged to help students become aware of the stages and sequences of their thinking and writing. Writing textbooks soon began reflecting this attention to process, as chapter sequences on prewriting, writing, and revision became common. In retrospect, says David Bartholomae, "there was a general shift away from questions of value and the figure of the writer in a social context of writing to questions of process and the figure of the writer as an individual psychology" (68). In Bartholomae's view, the attention process received in composition pedagogy made "schooling become secondary, not the primary scene of instruction, [but] a necessary evil in a world that is not well-regulated. . . . School [became] secondary, instrumental, something to be overcome" (69).

I see the impact of the process paradigm differently. In this chapter, I will begin by arguing that the process paradigm has enhanced—rather than diminished—the importance of schooling by naturalizing school writing within a framework of analytic conversation between student and teacher. This "process" conversation has helped teachers become more aware of the complexity of writing behavior, while encouraging them to identify apt points of intervention—thus foregrounding the importance of individualized relationships between teachers and students. In the nineties, however, there has been a marked turn toward the social in the scene of university writing, making collaborative and group relationships—rather than process-shaped individual relationships—the focus of writing-development efforts in the university. Along with this emphasis on the sociality of writing, there is increasing attention to "difference"—diversity in race, gender, socioeconomic status, sexual orientation—in the writing classroom. My thesis in this chapter is that the contingencies created by interactive groups of students diverse in ethnicity, culture, and socioeconomic status pose a fundamental pedagogical challenge. The turn toward the social and the emphasis on difference create unpredictable, often unstable interactions that can often lead to conflict. And by "conflict" I mean more than the clash of ideas or opinions; I mean the collision of divergent attitudes, values, judgments, and personal temperaments compounded in any classroom group dedicated to recognizing difference.

The pedagogical challenge of contingency may best be seen in contrast to the regularizing, interventionist tendencies of the process paradigm. This paradigm nurtured teachers' confidence that because each student writer followed the general stages of "the writing process," relationships between writing students and teachers could be individualized, yet also regularized by normative process-nomenclature and models. Teachers were trained to intervene at points where students' work stages seemed to offer the greatest opportunities for change. Process research provided a common vocabulary and analytic framework that could guide conversations between students and teachers. Such conversation could focus on the ongoing work of writing, and teachers began describing themselves as responding to—rather than "correcting" or "grading"—texts. These conversations naturalized student writing, encouraging students to see their drafts and revisions as legitimate stages of work in progress rather than failed attempts to produce a correct product. Teachers learned to make transactional in-progress comments to which students could respond, rather than evaluative "final" judgments. With a vocabulary for describing the production of drafts and revisions, teachers were encouraged to see a text as a set of strategies toward goals that they could help students reformulate as they worked. Observational research helped teachers understand the work of revising, allowing them to plan for and target appropriate moments for intervention.

Process research has also had institutional consequences; I will mention two specific effects of its individualizing influence. In the seventies and eighties when institutional enrollments nationally were climbing even as funding was squeezed, the process emphasis became a factor in English departments' efforts to resist pressure to put more students in writing classes. Deans and chairs in many institutions were able to argue that writing classes needed to be moderate in size in order to permit the instructor's attention to each student's writing process. This argument was especially pertinent to the issue of writing frequency. If revision was to be a major emphasis of writing instruction, then writing teachers had to be allowed the pedagogical time and space to work with students' specific developmental needs from revision to revision. In this way, English departments could point to labor-intensive teacher-student relationships in their bid for larger shares of institutional resources. In addition, describing composition pedagogy as increasingly grounded in research-warranted process knowledge helped legitimate writing programs in some institutions as separate academic entities with learning goals crucial to overall institutional missions. The growth of graduate programs in composition is itself partly attributable to the significance of process research, whose accessibility and repeatability offered rewarding research agendas for faculty and successive cohorts of graduate students.

The process paradigm thus has had some significant effects on institutional change and classroom practices. But in the eighties, the individualizing tendency of this paradigm began to be challenged by those arguing that describing writing and its teaching primarily within an individual psychological framework seriously limited the scene of writing. The writers' work is, after all, inevitably embedded in a large complex of variables that affect the production of any text at any given time. Since the process-research gaze can only see what moves before it—or to shift the metaphor, a process-research ear can only hear what is said to it—contextual and situational elements are often silent in such studies. The recent turn toward the social in composition studies is in part a critical reaction against the exclusionary force of the process paradigm.

There is a theoretical aspect to composition's turn toward sociality and contingency. In the view of some contemporary discourse theories, language acts are nonsystematic and paralogic in nature and are thus fundamentally contingent. Jean-François Lyotard's destabilization model of knowledge making describes paralogic moves toward new knowledge, which are "played in the pragmatics of knowledge" as sudden events. These moves are not "innovations," achieved "under the command of a system," but events that "destabilize the capacity for explanation" according to established rules (*Postmodern* 61). New knowledge cannot emerge unless under contingent and unpredictable conditions. A writer, continues Lyotard, works like a knowledge maker:

> the text he writes, the work he produces are not in principle governed by preestablished rules, and they cannot be judged . . . by applying familiar categories to the text or to the work. Those roles and categories are what the work of art itself is looking for. . . . Hence the fact that work and text have the characters of an event. (81)

The "roles" involved in the production of a text are created within the event that results in the text, not prior to it. Writing results from "the rules of *what will have been done,*" which always "come too late for their author" (*Postmodern* 81). A writer's moves emerge from a situation whose explanatory power can only be teased out after it is over, when its "rules" will have emerged. Language is the source of conventions, not the result of them, and they come to light only in the act of language making. Thomas Kent has pursued the implications of this paralogic view, emphasizing philosopher Donald Davidson's "externalist" view of the fundamental contingency of meaning making. Kent particularly cites Davidson's concepts of "triangulation"— that "each of two people finds certain behavior of the other salient, and each finds the observed behavior of the other to be correlated with events and objects . . . in the world" ("Externalism" 65)—and "passing theory"—"tenuous strategies for understanding . . . others that cannot be formulated in advance of a communicative situation" ("Externalism" 67). Meaningful language acts are thus created "by wit, luck and wisdom" ("Externalism" 68).

   In this view meaning making in language is situational and interactive, therefore also unpredictable and contingent. To follow this line of thought is to become deeply skeptical of a writing pedagogy that assumes regularity and transferability in writing behavior: since "writing is more than wiring," says Kent, "writing cannot be reduced to a systemic process and then taught"—a conclusion that, as Kent wryly points out, makes our customary and usual methods "exceedingly problematic" ("Externalism" 69). Writing becomes a meaningful event, in this view, not because the writer follows the right steps in producing the text, but because she reads the situation and the reader accurately and finds ways to adapt her language to the contingent requirements of the writing moment. Teachers can offer "only advice" for any student writer about to enter "specific hermeneutic interactions with others' interpretive strategies" ("Paralogic Hermeneutics" 37)—something like leaping into Conrad's "destructive element."

A thorough-going skepticism of this sort has the effect of undermining even the best-intentioned efforts to organize the scene of writing pedagogically. The process paradigm, after all, affirmed that writing can be taught systematically through individualized attention to composing and revising. The skeptical challenge to this confidence suggests that writing really can't be taught, and that teachers can only advise and collaborate in the scenes of writing. Such a conclusion certainly threatens to invalidate writing programs grounded in a consensus about individualized process instruction. But even as this skepticism challenges the totalizing pedagogy of structured writing programs, it makes its own argument on behalf of the complex implication of writing in all acts of learning. This affirmation of writing's crucial role in all knowledge making has helped energize the spread of university writing-across-the-curriculum programs, making writing a component of learning strategies in various disciplines taught by faculty who, though not generally trained in writing as process, believe in the central role of writing in the curriculum.

Other perspectives, though less radically critical of systematic writing pedagogy, are no less emphatic about the contextual complexity of writing. For example, the methods of process research—suspending the subjectivities arising from audience, form, and situation in favor of the writer's immediate consciousness—are contravened by the emphasis of ethnographic study on the complex situationality of the researcher and research situation. The objectivity posited as a necessary condition of process research is viewed by ethnographers as a slippery construct with the power to disguise the real complexity of the writing situation. Gesa Kirsch and Joy Ritchie say that research must "continually interrogate their relations with participants, working toward dialogic, mutually educative, caring relations while at the same time recognizing . . . the complex power dynamics between researcher and participants" (22). Kirsch and Ritchie adapt researcher Sandra

Harding's term *strong objectivity* to denote the recognition of contextual complexity in a writing situation: such objectivity "recognizes the historical, social, culturally situated nature of our motives and values . . . and searches for what is being eliminated, distorted, or masked" (24). Such a formulation suggests not only that writer, reader, and writing event are intertwined by both obvious and hidden variables, but also that meaningful research must try to account for, rather than simplify, those variables.

Recognizing and shaping the complex relationships in classrooms dedicated to preserving difference is a major challenge for writing teachers today. It is just here that the contingencies created by attention to difference come fully into play. The question posed by Carrie Shively Leverenz is apt in this regard: "[W]hat really happens when groups of students work together in writing classes that explicitly value difference" (168)? This fundamental question must be asked much more widely than it has been so far. Defining literacy as "social exchange," Maureen Hourigan declines to identify a particular pedagogy best suited to deal with the contingencies borne of difference and conflict in the classroom: there is "no specific pedagogy . . . for the increasingly diverse multicultural classroom, for good pedagogies must always be local ones, changing from one place to another" (xviii). Then what does the writing/reading classroom seeking to nurture complex differences among students really feel like? How does the scene of writing work when its primary charge is to articulate and confront differences among students? How does the contingency and uncertainty created by conflict impact the classroom, and how may it be managed?

A variety of collaborative models have been put forward in hopes of answering such questions. Advocates of collaborative pedagogy tend to offer one of two ways to respond to the effects of difference and its contingencies in the writing classroom. One is to emphasize the potential for cooperative pursuit of common goals. Kenneth Bruffee's version of collaboration, which gained influence in the eighties, aims at developing collaborative harmony within a discourse community centered on the teacher. In the classroom small "consensus groups" reach agreement on tasks set by the teacher and report back to the whole class. Thus the teacher's managerial skills are crucial. According to Bruffee, "skillfully managed classroom collaboration" will help students "enjoy the freedom to reinvent in the class the collaborative peership . . . [of] their everyday lives" ("Collaborative Learning" 27) and students will be rewarded with a sense of belonging to "a new community," one that will provide "a powerful force changing" those who participate ("Collaborative Learning" 20). For Bruffee, then, collaboration minimizes conflicts by unifying students around common goals and a common discourse controlled and enacted by the teacher.

The harmonizing tendencies of Bruffee's model open it to critique, however, by those who hold that classrooms should seek not to harmonize differences, but to articulate and preserve them. Conflict within student groups should be foregrounded because "substantive conflict during collaboration is not only normal, but also can be productive, in large part because it gives collaborators more time to generate and critically examine alternatives," maintain Rebecca Burnett and Helen Rothschild Ewald (22). In order to foreground the play of difference in the classroom, John Trimbur proposes a "rhetoric of dissensus" which redefines consensus as "a matter of conflict" (608). The dynamics of classrooms should shape not "collective agreements" but "collective explanations of how people differ, where their differences come from, and whether they can live and work together with these differences," says Trimbur (610). In the place of consensus, we should "recognize the inexhaustibility of difference," which requires that we find "a way to orchestrate dissensus and turn the conversation . . . into a herotopia of voices" (Trimbur 615). Such a "herotopia" would be a scene of fundamental contingency as the claims of cultural, gender, and racial differences collide unpredictably in discussions and group interactions. Indeed, Trimbur's use of the word *orchestrate* seems problematic in this context, given that the group's goal is to formalize dissonance. In fairness, it should be said that Trimbur does not write toward a practical pedagogical model. Yet in the absence of any consensus awareness, each classroom situation would require some form of maneuver among disagreements and oppositions. What happens when unpredictable conflicts meet with the purposefulness of a writing/reading classroom?

The meeting point between contingent conflict and pedagogical design is well illustrated in the description David Bleich provides of his "pedagogy of disclosure" ("Collaboration"). Bleich foregrounds contingency as a basic principle of writing/reading classrooms. Collaboration is a purely "contingent" and "local" activity whose success depends upon the outcomes of "disclosure." He argues that group members must discover how to make knowledge out of self-revelation because "what each person brings to the classroom must become part of the curriculum for that course," because "each member of a classroom *actually has* an individual history" (47–48). Since self-disclosure introduces thoughts and attitudes unwritten by the teacher/course planner, "curriculum is contingent" upon self-disclosure and cannot be structured or planned by the teacher. In literature courses grounded in self-disclosure the topics for class discussion are constructed by the students, who in responding to texts disclose those personal stories and experiences which shape their responses. In a basic writing course cited by Bleich, "ethnic and gender antagonisms" themselves become the basis of classroom study, from which emerge *"a contingent strategy of letting the class's language determine the curriculum"* ("Collaboration" 50). No one form of knowledge is privileged over another by virtue of its being vested in the teacher or in those students more agile in a given knowledge area.

The eruptive potential of self-disclosure brings a fundamental unpredictability to the scene of writing here. Bleich cites an incident in his course on Jewish identity in literature illustrating "a risk of dysfunction" affecting "the academic and pedagogical identity of the course" ("Collaboration" 59). Recriminations were "stirred up" as students positioned themselves within Jewish and gay identities, while new issues generated "new alignments" within the classroom group ("Collaboration" 60). Disclosure of difference proved so destabilizing to classroom dynamics that Bleich's skillful personal negotiations were required to reconstruct student relationships. Ironically, a course intended to be student-centered required the teacher's personal intervention to restore its dynamics. Bleich's forthright account of the unpredictable collision of attitudes suggests the potential for conflict in a class grounded in the unpredictable interplay of personal differences.

Other recent studies demonstrate that unequal and unstable power relations are the primary source of conflict in writing/reading classrooms. For example, in an effort to test Trimbur's "dissensus pedagogy," Leverenz describes her observation of how a class "designed to be multicultural and to value difference" is divided by power alignments that shifted between whole-class and small-group interactions. The class consisted of sixteen African American students, two white students, and one Asian student. In classroom discussions the instructor—also African American—encouraged students to give equal privilege to various interpretive perspectives, including both textual analysis and personal-experience responses. Studying the interactions of one small, multiracial peer response group within the class, Leverenz notes that while in whole-class discussions the African American students generally supported experience-based personal responses to texts, in one multiracial, small group a white student—an experienced academic reader and writer—dominated the discussions with other group members (an African American and a Korean American) by advocating a traditional text-based perspective. "In the larger classroom setting" where discussions were guided by the instructor, says Leverenz, the white student's claims were "a minority view loudly opposed by many of the other students," but in the separate response group, the white student "was able to assert her views without opposition" because "neither [of the other two students] had the experience or success with reading and writing about texts that might have given them the confidence to oppose [her]" (181). These other students, both women of color, remained silent but resentful of the white student's power: the African American student wrote privately against her peer's dominance, but "in the public arena of her group and her class, the dissensus represented by [the African American student's] writing went unarticulated and unheard" (184).

I detail Leverenz's findings because they illustrate vividly the silencing force of conflict arising from unequal power relations. The conflict was neither articulated nor addressed collaboratively by the students; it was expressed only in private writings and one-on-one interviews with Leverenz herself. Tellingly, as in Bleich's situation, it was the teacher's authoritative negotiations that maintained an equitable cohesion within the whole-class group. In the small group, absent the direct authority of the teacher, hierarchical power relations created conflicts that were neither addressed nor resolved.

Though Trimbur does not speak directly to the issue of whether classroom conflicts should be resolved, the instances described by Bleich and Leverenz suggest that unresolved conflict destabilizes the classroom scene. And as Trimbur forthrightly acknowledges, students are both uncomfortable with unresolved conflict and eager to avoid dissensus as a group climate: students often seek "noncontroversial consensus without considering alternatives" (603). They perceive the unpredictable potential of conflict as a threat to learning: disagreement interferes with the sense of purposefulness students identify with in a functional classroom. Perceiving this difficulty, instructors are drawn in to negotiate differences that among themselves students cannot resolve. Indeed, say Julia M. Gergits and James J. Schramer, students in their collaborative-writing classrooms uniformly seek "prescriptive or authoritative intervention"; they quote one student as saying that "'the strain of the project itself accompanied with uninvolved and uncooperative members resulted in more of a headache than a constructive learning experience'" (198). They suggest that their task is to resist petitions for intervention and to allow the unpredictable interactions of student differences to play out.

Students' avoidance of conflict in classrooms dedicated to preserving difference is also recorded by Amy Goodburn and Beth Ina. A peer response group of three African American and two white students dealt with "issues of difference" primarily by not addressing them in direct fashion. In response to a collaborative assignment these students constructed "separate stories connected only by nominal transitions, enabling them to "keep their negotiations about difference in a more nebulous or unscrutinized [oral] context and to avoid having to give definitive answers" (139). Having avoided conflicts that might have arisen from trying to write a single unified text, these students left themselves free to negotiate among themselves in informal discussions. These students "value[d] collaboration because it enabled them to form friendships and a sense of community by overcoming difference" but engaged in "a free-ranging discussion of politics and social issues" (139). However, they were able to do this only by creating personal relationships outside regular classroom proceedings. Faced with the institutional pressure to assign a grade, the instructor responded to the moves of this group by repositioning their work within the "official" norms of academic evaluation and giving the group project a C, which did not please the students in the group.

This episode illuminates the impact of conflict arising from intimacy and disclosure in any classroom relying on collaboration. On the one hand, Bruffee is optimistic that willing collaboration among students will overcome interpersonal conflict. He represents conflict as a temporary dysfunction that the instructor's authoritative presence should resolve; if students cannot "get along with others," then the teacher must remind students of group rules, must insist upon politeness, or perhaps revise group memberships to defuse problems, Bruffee advises ("Collaborative Learning" 27). On the other hand, Susan Jarratt asserts that "differences of gender, race, and class among students and teachers provide situations in which conflict does arise, and we need more than the ideal of the harmonious, nurturing composition class in our repertory of teaching practices to deal with these problems" (113). In classrooms, small-group reports intended to help construct knowledge claims for whole-class discussion can indeed be destabilized by conflict within a group, as Bleich and Leverenz report. In any writing/reading classroom in which collaboration is coupled with the intent to acknowledge and preserve difference, interpersonal conflict is a possibility whose effect on the work and goals of the group cannot be predicted.

An important challenge for composition studies today is to think carefully about the effects of dissonance and conflict upon classroom scenes of writing and reading. Edward Pauly's study of classroom success in public schools has strong implications for contingency and conflict in university writing/reading classrooms. He views classrooms at all educational levels as radically differentiated: "[E]very classroom is different from other classrooms," including others taught by the same teacher, others taught within the same curriculum, or others with the same students taught by different teachers (173). Thus, argues Pauly, "the important differences" in comparing learning experiences "are between successful and unsuccessful classrooms, differences which cannot be traced to . . . teachers, curricula, [or] teaching methods" but to complex situational variables within each classroom (33). As a consequence, Pauly warns, the outcomes of large-scale curricular planning are entirely dependent upon the complex interactions of teachers and students in specific classroom scenes: "[T]he consequences of an education policy are determined by the choices of teachers and students" (142). This conclusion parallels Hourigan's admonition that all pedagogy is "local." That is, planned elements of most writing programs—common objectives, strategies, and assignments—make far less difference than any of the variables that can neither be predicted nor planned for: the particular mix of students, teachers, motives, and backgrounds generated by the faculty assignment and student registration processes. But Pauly does not conclude from this that successful classroom experiences occur arbitrarily; he believes teachers must be prepared for them. Because "the classroom crucible" is the core of learning, teachers must be given maximum freedom to evaluate and respond to situational factors in their classrooms.

The fact that students and teachers together must cope with unpredictable conflict in their classroom work does not require a stoic submission to chance and good luck. Indeed, as the studies I have
cited suggest—and as common sense dictates—dealing with contingency requires careful, proactive planning. I will conclude with some
thoughts about the kind of planning that should inform writing/read-
ing courses committed to valuing difference.

First, if the play of difference and its contingent outcomes are to be
nurtured in the writing/reading classroom, they must be framed in
an interactive structure that is clearly laid out for all participants.
As the studies cited above show, and experienced teachers are well
aware, classroom interactions may be shaped in a variety of ways that
bring attitudes and values into view and perhaps into conflict. Bruffee's
well-known model of collaboration positions student collaboration
within an agenda set by the teacher, whose expertise within the
discourse field represented in a particular course is the ultimate
authority of the class. Bruffee's model has been given wide attention
and has exerted considerable influence in composition studies, in part
because it makes clear the kinds of interactive dynamics needed
for successful learning as defined by Bruffee. It is hierarchical, however, privileging the teacher as the ruling authority within the discourse field the class is exploring. The teacher's role in Bruffee's model
is to maintain a positive authority in the class and enact the expertise
of the discipline.

But reliance on hierarchical authority to control the classroom situation is anathema to some advocates of collaboration, who insist that
students must be guided toward undermining—and ultimately working free of—top-down authority. Students must rehearse collaborative
work, says Thia Wolf, by learning their power within the classroom:
"I must be honest with them" by representing "the context in which
we are situated" so that "I can set the stage for a different kind of conversation" (102). Wolf emphasizes the need to prepare students for
their roles: "[I]n the rehearsal stage . . . students develop tools for challenging structures and injustices immediately at hand," challenging the
teacher's agenda-setting authority by redesigning the syllabus and taking over the classroom activities" (103). However, the problem with
this model is that it does not clarify how students should deal with
conflicts among themselves as they pursue liberatory goals. If the
teacher's authority is to be set aside, in what ways will students themselves be prepared for the contingencies of interpersonal conflict? Clari-

fication of this question is essential in planning any writing/reading course in which student collaboration and interaction are the primary modes of learning.

Second, teachers must prepare themselves and their students for the personal tensions created by dissonance and conflict. Teachers need to preconceive the contingencies their classes will face and think through their possible outcomes. They must be prepared to decide what to do with conflict: ameliorate it through negotiation, help students find ways to resolve it, or prepare the students to face it as an ongoing condition. The crucial variable is whether an interactive or collaborative structure proposes a privileged role for the teacher in dealing with conflict, or whether teacherly authority is to be restrained in favor of student efforts to manage conflict. Rebecca Bell-Metereau describes a hierarchical model similar to that advocated by Bruffee, foregrounding student responsibility but relying on the teacher's oversight and conflict-resolution skills: students organize their own group interactions and leadership, while "the [student] leaders in turn report to me any concerns they cannot handle on their own" (255). For Bell-Metereau, "The existence of such a hierarchy gives structure to what might otherwise be a chaotic free-for-all," each group operating independently until conflict becomes irresolvable within the group; then the problem is referred to the teacher "if [the students] feel the system has gone awry in some way" (255). Such a policy is also implied in Bleich's model, wherein the teacher's persuasive intervention is essential to help student groups through their most divisive conflicts. The virtue of such a structure is that students are made aware that they can avail themselves of teacherly authority if they feel conflict undermines group interactions.

However, many writing/reading teachers accept Trimbur's eloquent call for a dissensus model of collaboration, which foregrounds conflict and seeks "explanations of why people differ" rather than efforts to harmonize or resolve those differences. Patricia Bizzell has argued that well-meaning efforts to develop community in classrooms made up (as most university classrooms are) of middle-class majorities who do not recognize their own privilege, inevitably silence disempowered others ("Marxist"). Similarly, Susan Miller is uncompromising in her insistence that "no amount of mutuality, sympathy or collaborative, 'dialogic' and dialectic interaction [can reduce] this difference" that makes me "always an 'object' to you, even in 'public' spaces where we write collaboratively" ("New Discourse" 298). Consequently, she maintains, a normative idea of community must not cause us to "channel our energy into overcoming our disunity, especially in efforts to respect 'pluralism'" because "valorizing a rational 'healthy pluralism,' ultimately makes it necessary to exclude those who do not 'identify' with a community" ("New Discourse" 298). Teachers who want to follow Miller's injunction to avoid normative communalizing in writing/reading classes would have to ask themselves what a classroom feels like in which difference and its conflicts play themselves out, where tensions and oppositions remain to generate discord. Miller does not offer a practical pedagogy for such a scenario, and it is not my purpose to propose one here. Clearly, a classroom structured *around* conflict as its mode of being, rather than one developed to *use* conflict as a dialectical strategy, makes very different demands of all participants. If such a scene is to be developed pedagogically, teachers must anticipate and plan for contingencies that may develop.

Finally, it has to be said clearly in classrooms valuing difference that articulating (in Trimbur's words) "how people differ" is personally risky, stressful, and sometimes painful. Of course, students are accustomed to classroom disputes over opinions and values, but interrogating difference at the personal level can elicit the personal fear and resentment usually kept out of classroom environments. When an African American male tells his predominantly white classmates angrily and with contempt for their ignorance that he has often been stopped by white police while driving to visit friends in white suburbs, his white peers may remain silent in dismay, deny their own involvement in such bigotry, or dispute that honest police officers would do such a thing. In this scenario and countless others like it, students experience distress as the price of articulating difference; it is no wonder that most students avoid such efforts. Indeed, the unwillingness to risk direct confrontation over issues of differences is, as Goodburn and Ina demonstrate, a perfectly logical stance for students to take, for they have well internalized the view that all students have the right to their own narratives proceeding from lived experience. In classrooms dedicated to articulating differences, students must be challenged not to take refuge in the I'm-OK-you're-OK relativism in which differences of culture, class, and gender are given the status of opinions not to be interrogated. Yet, if such interrogation is to occur, students must be persuaded that it is worth the risk. This is perhaps the greatest challenge of a new pedagogy of contingency.

11
I Was a Process-Model Baby

Nancy C. DeJoy

My experience as a process-model baby began in 1978 when I entered a two-year state college in the Northeast. There, my male composition teacher used what he called "personal-based" writing to elicit essays from his students. (I vaguely remember using Peter Elbow's *Writing Without Teachers* in this class.) From his reactions to our first papers and clues we were getting in class, a group of us figured out that the way for females to get an "A" from this man was to tell stories of sexual experience—particularly stories of sexual experiences that were frightening and/or painful. The code cracked, we proceeded to meet in the hall lounge to make up stories for the teacher (each of us was responsible for creating her own "invention packet" to hand in with her final version). If I remember correctly, English 101 was the only class I passed that semester. I was put on probation until the end of the next semester when I flunked all of my courses and was invited not to return the following year.

This experience marks my introduction to what I later came to know as "the process-model approach to writing." It was not the only time I knew that the real game behind process approaches could be to produce a teacher-identified discourse from prewriting strategies such as brainstorming, freewriting, clustering, and journals. And it is not the only kind of experience I have had using process approaches to writing, although I did have more of these kinds of unpleasant experiences throughout my career as a student. These unpleasantries did not occur only when I was instructed to use an expressive approach, as in the case just described. Similar issues arose when using Edward P. J. Corbett's *Classical Rhetoric for the Modern Student*, a text required in a two-course sequence in my undergraduate writing major (here it was more the assignments than the textbook that caused such similarities). Similar issues also arose when I was instructed to use a cognitive problem-solving approach in my technical writing class.

These, then, are the complexes that defined my introduction to and various undergraduate experiences with traditional, dominant, process-model approaches to writing: (1) confusion about the question "A process of what?" in response to various calls to be "in process" (e.g., saying what the teacher wants to hear; inscribing ethos, logos, and pathos "effectively"; defining problems and solutions in capitalist terms, and so forth); (2) a clear sense that invention could, and often did, mean the creation of something false (e.g., a false past; a false ethos, pathos, or logos; a false consciousness); (3) a vague and disconcerting feeling that teachers had their own unspoken reasons for requiring certain kinds of invention work. (It never occurred to me until graduate school to think about this requirement as something that was imposed only because it was going to make me a "better" writer. In fact, I was quite shocked when I went to graduate school and found out that this was the controlling argument about process in our field.)

Being a process-model baby, then, was not always easy; it came with its own complexes, especially if one wanted to gender the issue. And in what I now see as repercussions easily paralleled with sexist Freudian notions of female complexes, I was accused more than once of being confused and/or hysterical, of not understanding, for example, the "universal" quality of any or all of dominant process models' conceptualizations of audience, invention, and so forth.

For a while, I looked at the research—the protocols, the observations of professional writers, the classic essays, the cognitive proofs—to discover grounds for the claims to universality behind the traditional heuristics for invention, arrangement, and revision that define the prewrite, write, rewrite activities of those dominant models. Over time, it became clearer that the claims were more about certain types of discourses, certain aims and modes, if you will, than they were about other kinds of discourses. This realization led me through a process of another kind, a counterprocess informed primarily by three moves: the move from mastery to analysis, the move from identification to alternative routes to subjectivity, and the move from persuasion to participation. I am convinced now that the absence of invitations to make these moves within writing classrooms explains the more generalized absence of a critical aim or mode in the constitution of dominant process-model approaches to composition that currently drive our field. We can see these absences in the best-selling textbooks in our country—*St. Martin's Guide, Writing with a Purpose, Simon and Schuster's*

Handbook for Writers, The St. Martin's Handbook, and *The Prentice Hall Guide for College Writers.*[1] Even a cursory glance exposes the absence of a critical aim or mode outside of some textbooks' inclusions of discussions about explicating literature, an unfortunate pairing (since literature was the "Other" of the process movement) but one that may help explain the repression of critical aims and modes in the model.[2] We see this absence in other texts marking the process model's domination of the field—Edward Corbett's *Classical Rhetoric for the Modern Student,* Erika Lindemann's *A Rhetoric for Writing Teachers,* Lindemann and Gary Tate's *An Introduction to Composition Studies,* James Kinneavy's *A Theory of Discourse,* and Peter Elbow's *Writing with Power.*[3]

As a grown up process-model baby, my goal is to establish as firm a position in composition studies for critical aims, modes, and purposes as dominant modern process-model frames have established for expressive aims and modes, persuasive aims and modes, classical paradigms, literary explication, narration, and so on. Let me also say that it is no coincidence that both critical discourse and the rhetorical strategies of feminist discourse were constructed largely as absent possibilities as the field of composition constituted the system of aims and modes currently driving composition pedagogies for the majority of writing teachers in this country.

In fact, I believe that this coinciding absence of feminism and of a ground for critical discursive practices in dominant process-model frames is no coincidence; this absence stems from the uneasy discovery that the assumptions of those frames—theoretical, pedagogical, practical—are not necessarily in conflict with the constitution of a critical aim or mode. Rather, dominant process-model approaches have gone about the business of reading and writing *as if* this absence were indeed a necessity, and feminist discourse is the mother of invention that had to be ignored in the process. The necessity of this absence has been constituted within the profession as a response to product-centered approaches to the over-valuing of explication and the products being explicated, in response to the devaluing of student writers' processes and products in that model. Yet it is equally informed by the field's attempts to validate itself by grounding itself in the dominant and dominating male classical and modern frames from which it hoped to gain authority.[4]

More recent analyses also expose the absence of feminist and other alternative rhetorical strategies in the texts upon which the process-model movement institutionalized itself as the ground of composition studies. Miriam Brody's *Manly Writing* exposes these absences by discussing the masculinization of style in many of the texts from which our profession has drawn authority. Other recent texts such as Andrea Lunsford's edited collection *Reclaiming Rhetorica* and Krista Ratcliffe's *Anglo-American Feminist Challenges to the Rhetorical Traditions* illustrate the history, reality, validity, worth, and absence of feminist rhetorical strategies in modern process-model approaches to composition. What these works show is that critical discourse can exist in relation to the dominant process-model paradigm—theoretically, pedagogically, and in practice—if we do more than merely include discussions about feminist discourse and feminist rhetorical strategies as we construct that relationship. Particularly, some feminist discourses that were ignored as modern process-model paradigms came to dominate composition pedagogies can now do for process-model approaches what classical rhetoric did for product-centered paradigms if revision rather than inclusion informs our purposes. Here I will concentrate on ways that feminist discourses allow us to accommodate critical practices within that dominant frame—a strategically important consideration if we are to establish a firm ground for critical discourse in contemporary composition studies. I will look first at the move from mastery to analysis and the moves toward participation which it invites. I then consider other-than-identificatory routes to subjectivity and issues of participation.

From Mastery to Analysis

One of the things that has silenced me the most as I struggle to create a place for critical discursive practices and pedagogies is the process-model ideology best expressed by Donald Murray in his opening essay in *Eight Approaches to Teaching Composition*—a quote used as a blurb to sell the book: ". . . making meaning with written language cannot be understood by looking backward from a finished product" (1996 NCTE College Catalogue 21). Even if we bracket the concerns such a statement makes about our abilities to analyze our own and others' texts (and histories) in any but the simplest of ways, there are still major issues to deal with here. One such issue raises questions about the validity of justifying our field by referring to its roots in the products of classical rhetoric. For have we not looked at *those* products precisely to construct ideologies for the making of meaning as we constituted process pedagogy as the dominant approach to composition over the last thirty years? Another set of issues arises if we consider this configuration of product in relation to the equally widespread process-model ideology, which asserts that the model represents a recursive process, one in which any stage can, in theory, send us to any other stage of the writing process in infinitely unrestrained ways—although the demands of deadlines, due-dates and other "external" concerns may limit us in practice. At this point, we can only imagine the implications of such assertions for a primarily progressive (rather than recursive) discursive aim.

Both of these silences have been modified by my understanding of how the process-model assertion—the assertion that products cannot teach us anything about meaning making—refers to specific kinds of products and approaches to products, those most usually canonized and held up as models in "Western" traditions within literary studies. The tangle becomes understandable if we consider that in process-model critiques of product-centered approaches "product" refers not only to a certain kind of text but also to a certain way of reading that brackets all but what Louise Rosenblatt named the "efferent stand," one that "makes reading [and writing about what we read] a process of deriving correct answers . . . an approach whose aim is not audience participation but audience persuasion" (Hallin 291; Rosenblatt).[5] But the move from mastery to analysis positions textuality in a more response-able way in relation to writing.

Within this move, we look not only at processes and products but also at means of production (including process-model means). Of course, this move is more possible when we look at some texts rather than others, surely more true for texts traditionally silenced as the process model built up claims about the deficiencies of products and product-oriented pedagogies—more true for feminist texts, for example than for the products referred to, although never explicitly named, in the claims against product-oriented approaches themselves. In fact, it is possible that neglecting feminist discourses' tendency to be overt about process was not merely an oversight, that this silence operated more generally as a necessary absence shoring up these claims about "products" and their deficiencies. The move from mastery to analysis is not just about dramatic changes in how we read; it is also about re-valuing texts that put into question the claims of process-model theory and the activities for writing that they assert as universally applicable. It is about putting two texts such as Aristotle's *Rhetoric* and Virginia Woolf's *A Room of One's Own* next to each other and asking questions such as "In which text is a writer more overtly in process?" and "In which text does process most overtly stand as a vital mode of production for the work of the author?" And it is about admitting that there are obvious ways in which we must respond that, at the levels of analysis and practice, Woolf wins out. For it is true that one can take Aristotle's *Rhetoric* as instruction, but from the text one learns little to nothing about Aristotle's or anyone else's process. In fact, by putting these two texts side by side, one learns that Aristotle's *Rhetoric* positions mastery of the system itself and of one's audiences as the end of writing, while Woolf discusses mastery as a physical place that is systematically made unavailable to specific parts of the population. Perhaps one could argue that it is not fair to put two texts from such different times and contexts in relation to one another. One might use what Steinem calls the "he was a man of his time" argument, homogenizing history and historical subjects and playing the double standard game (*Outrageous Acts* 32–35; "Phyllis," 12). Fine. Put Audre Lourde's 1977 essay "The Transformation of Silence into Language and Action" next to Linda Flower and John Hayes's 1977 "Problem-Solving Strategies and the Writing Process." Or put Lourde's 1977 "Poetry Is Not a Luxury " next to James Kinneavy's discussions of the aims and modes—for example, *A Theory of Discourse* (1971) and "An Introduction to the Modes of Discourse" (in *Writing—Basic Modes of Organization* 1976). Compare Chernin's 1988 discussion of writing for discovery in *Reinventing Eve* with discussions about writing to discover in writing textbooks of that time period. Put the invention strategies discussed and used by Gloria Steinem in her 1963 essay "I Was a Playboy Bunny" next to the discussions of invention in our field's publications of that time period.

What you will find is that there are not only very different notions about the activities in which one engages when creating texts but also that invention, arrangement, and revision are conceptualized and practiced differently in the feminist texts than they are in those upon which our profession founded its process-model movement. Most significantly, attempts at other-than-only-textual revision tend to drive feminist processes and to inform the creation of invention strategies. This move marks a significant difference from more dominant—and dominating—systems where enthymemic logic, identification, and mastery of the advantages of preconstructed cultural assumptions rule over invention.[6] This new positioning of literate subjectivity inserts alternative analysis activities into writing processes in new other-than-classical ways. These processes do not assume *identification with* cultural assumptions and the production of discourses for the purposes of persuasion based on those assumptions as the unquestioned and/or inescapable basis for, and end of, all writing. Krista Ratcliffe gives us one example of this difference when she discusses the rhetoric of Mary Daly's work in *Anglo-American Feminist Challenges to the Rhetorical Traditions. Be-Spelling* is Daly's word for the process of revising language in ways that expose previously repressed meanings that challenge our usual assumptions; it is what allows Daly to position writers as people who make up new words, who give old words new meanings, who invent new forms and styles (cultural and social as well as textual). She shows that "breaking through foreground meanings is a context-bound possibility, not simply a utopian desire" (74). As Ratcliffe notes, "whether conscious or unconscious, Be-Spelling choices do not culminate in static stylistic rules that all feminists should follow. Rather, these choices embody visual ruptures in texts that force readers to become aware of, and reflect on, the foreground function of language" (93).

But "context" here is not a place where *identification of* dominant cultural assumptions and/or processes and products which valorize *identification with* those assumptions is the only, or over-valorized, route to literate subjectivity. In fact, the activity of *identification with*—while it may require reproduction of some master narrative—cannot on its own create contexts for critical literacy at all, not in relation to products or to processes; not in relation to reading or to writing; not in relation to issues of invention or to issues of revision. This Be-Spelling is why the move from mastery to analysis leads to and is informed by acknowledgment of the possibilities of and for other-than identificatory routes to subjectivity.

To be clear, I am not interested in the mere inclusion of feminist texts and/or processes. My belief that dominant process-model frames could have accommodated feminist rhetorical traditions it chose to ignore does not mean that it can now include them without revisioning what it means to teach writing as a process. There is a difference between inclusion and revision, a difference that is either all too often ignored or used to reproduce the status quo. bell hooks makes the difference between inclusion and revision clear in *Killing Rage:*

> [I]t has been easier for white people to practice inclusion rather than change the larger framework; . . . it is easier to change the focus from Christopher Columbus, the important white man who discovered America, to Sitting Bull or Harriet Tubman, than it is to cease telling a distorted version of U.S. history which upholds white supremacy. Really teaching history in a new way would require abandoning old myths informed by white supremacy like the notion that Columbus discovered America. It would mean talking about imperialism, colonization, about the African who came here before Columbus (see Ivan Sertima's *They Came before Columbus*). (187–88)

I invoke the difference between inclusion and revision as one of a growing number of people who were both composed by dominant process-model approaches to composition at the undergraduate level and who studied rhetoric and composition at the graduate level. I believe that this articulation of the realities of being previously subjected to and contemporarily implicated and/or involved in composing (rather than merely being composed) marks an important moment in our history in general and in our profession in particular—a moment in which those who hope to participate in the profession also have firsthand experience as undergraduate students who were subjected to the dominant pedagogies driving our professional existences. As a result of these different positions, process-model babies' relationships to the process-model paradigm are not always informed only by identification-driven responses to that model. This kind of complexity marks the unexplored revisionary territory of our profession, providing a basis for explorations of the history driving dominant configurations of pedagogical practices in contemporary composition studies. Analyzing rather than merely mastering the theoretical, pedagogical, and practical terms of dominant approaches to process is a significant heuristic informing these explorations, especially for those of us who write. For it is this analysis that enables the possibility for critical understandings, making revision—rather than either reproduction or rejection—an option in relation to the models themselves.

In fact, it became necessary for me to create a frame to move from mastery to analysis and from persuasion to participation if I wanted to think about critical discourse as an institutionally rhetorical possibility at all. Committed to an idea of writing that was not founded on the process/product binary, I began to work through the terms of the binary itself. At the heart of the matter from both sides—product and process—was the repression of certain questions and the underlying assumptions about the structure of literate rhetorical realities driving those repressions. I began by triangulating the process/product binary by reinserting matters of production.[7] Then I doubled the questions I asked about products and production to make room for this addition. Instead of asking "What is invention?" and limiting myself and others to preconstructed responses (e.g. ethos, logos, and pathos; brainstorming, defining rhetorical situations, a heuristic process through which a writer explores a subject), I allowed myself and others to respond with a difference. To double the question, I asked not only "What is invention?" but also "What is being invented?" After much thought and a number of attempts at analysis and production, I created a set of six paired questions: What is invention? What is being invented?; What is arrangement? What is being arranged?; What is revision? What is being revised?[8] These questions allowed me to explore, identify, and see as challengeable the terms for making meaning inscribed by dominant process-model approaches, those employed in a number of feminist texts, and the differences between the two. My ability to acknowledge approaches to literacy that configure analysis as a vital part of the process of literacy created alternatives to holding out as the end of writing mere identification and accurate reproduction of someone else's invention, arrangement, and revision schemes. The need for alternative routes to subjectivity, then, is the issue at hand.

Other-Than-Identificatory Routes to Subjectivity

As the driving force behind the constitution of self/other relations (i.e., self as writer/other as audience), identification has claimed an overarching hold on translations of rhetorical activity that position mastery (over) as the end of writing. The power of this hold always strikes me most when I think about experiences with and discussions of audience in process-model theories, pedagogies, and practices. As a student, I was expected to draw conclusions about audiences in relation to issues of age, gender, occupation, habits, hobbies, educational background, and economic and social class. (I was never asked to consider issues of race in relation to audience, an absence that I now understand as a necessary part of the model's attempt to suppress the dangers of this process of drawing conclusions and its repercussions.) In attempts to get my audiences to identify with my writing, I was supposed to create effective appeals from assumptions based, for example, on people's age, gender, or class standings. I remember asking what conclusions I was supposed to draw about a person from these bits of information; I received two kinds of responses. The first were either very vague or insinuated that, once again, I just did not get it. The second constituted myself and the majority of the professors in my academic environment as exceptions to the general assertions we could make about other people our age, gender, or class. (The fact that we were exceptions was always put forth as a positive thing, and, for a while, I was flattered to be included out.)

However, I see now that at the heart of this dilemma was an idea I could not articulate in those days—the idea that *identification of* those stereotypes was supposed to lead to prose *identified with* those stereotypes. It took me a long time to name this monologic dialectic—*identification of/identification with*—as the thing I was resisting. It was not so much the identification of the stereotypes that bothered me but the idea that my job was to reproduce them rather than to engage in activities that explored their sources, ramifications, and the falseness of their inventions (falseness in relation both to how they created and to what they created). hooks notes,

> Stereotypes, however inaccurate, are one form of representation. Like fictions, they are created to stand in as substitutions, standing in for what is real. They are not there to tell it like it is but to invite and encourage pretense. They are a fantasy, a projection onto the Other that makes us less threatening. Stereotypes abound when there is distance. They are an *invention,* a pretense that one knows when the steps that would make real knowing possible cannot be taken or are not allowed. (38, emphasis added)

What I have learned from refusing to identify with the call to stereotype is that the process models' failures to distinguish between identification of and identification with not only positioned mastery as the end of writing and the teaching of writing but also effaced the realities and textualities made possible by that split. This disruptive split between identification of and identification with is what could have led to alternative explorations of the process of stereotyping in which I was expected to engage—and sometimes still must resist—as

I became literate through dominant process-model frames. Had I not struggled, by studying feminist discourses, to find ways to understand that this split could exist, the split would not be part of my repertoire now. I would not be able to talk about critical discourse as a way of writing different from those dominant calls to literacy that positioned me as a consumer and reproducer rather than as an analyzer and creator of rhetorical practices. hooks is correct about this: "the pretense" of other as audience made "the steps that would make real knowing possible" an absent possibility in most of my writing education.

I turn now to a discussion of some of the feminist strategies for interrupting the monologic dialectic of identification of/identification with that I have discovered in my struggles to make critical discursive practices understandable within contemporary composition studies. Each strategy creates breaks between identification of and identification with, breaks that open up the possibility for critical discursive practices. Some of these strategies are the following: reversal, considerations of other-than-identificatory routes to subjectivity, considerations of absence in the creation of meaning, transposition, contextualization, and entering the context with a difference.

Reversal is a strategy that, as Gloria Steinem notes, exchanges subject for object. In "Womb Envy, Testyria, and Breast Castration Anxiety," Steinem reverses Freudian gender positions by creating a character, Dr. Phyllis Freud, who shows us what Freudian theories about maleness and femaleness would look like if the terms for making meaning remained the same but the binarized gender terms were reversed. Returning to a strategy she used much earlier in her 1978 essay "If Men Could Menstruate," Steinem gives us a way to identify the terms for making meaning without assuming that our response should be reproduction of those terms. Because reproduction of that logic is not the purpose of the essay, the reversal invites something other than *identification with* that logic. In her introduction, Steinem is quite overt about her own reversal process. Analysis of her discussion identifies a number of activities informing the writing of this version of the essay. While they are too numerous to mention here, it is important to note that actually doing the reversal occurs late in the process and is preceded by many kinds of activities (social, written, research oriented, emotional, as well as others).

What is most important, the process not only clarifies and articulates the terms for making meaning in the system being reversed and in the process of revising, but it also opens up a system in which the terms for making meaning are other than identificatory. The process of reversal raises our consciousness about how meaning is made while inviting us to understand the possibility for changing those terms. As my students and I have discovered, this awareness means that we may have to revise the order of Steinem's process, adding stages she did not need or skipping stages of the process unavailable to us or unnecessary in our own endeavors. Steinem makes it clear that if writers want to do reversal, they must "add water," contributing something new to the process of doing reversal itself (*Moving Beyond Words* 11). That is, this heuristic, like the others I will discuss, calls up critical rhetoricians rather than reproductive rhetors.

Gerda Lerner has given us many examples of the historical sources informing the need for other-than-identificatory routes to subjectivity in the creation of critical forms of literate consciousness. In *The Creation of Feminist Consciousness* she states: "The creation of the authentic self which defines its own creativity is a historical phenomenon which for women was possible only much later in history than it was for men" (47). Throughout her text, Lerner shows how counter-identification and dis-identification with this generalized exclusion are two process activities informing the creation of feminist consciousness.[9] Historically positioned as excluded from dominant constructions of self-hood and the social institutions through which self-hood is constructed, female consciousness is never a monologic process but one for which identity is a dialogic in which identification and other routes to subjectivity converge and conflict.

The importance of consideration of other-than-identificatory routes to subjectivity becomes apparent in relation to issues of selves, audiences, and subjects (in its traditional sense as referring to topics) in feminist texts . Naomi Wolf makes this point clear in her introduction to *Fire with Fire: The New Female Power and How to Use It* when she states: "I will look at how women must recount the all too real ways in which they are often victimized, without creating an *identity* from that victimization (xxvii, emphasis added). In *Playing in the Dark*, Toni Morrison dares to propose topics for critical investigation that challenge the assumption that the end of writing is identification with either the texts we investigate or with the result of our investigations. She states: "Let me propose some topics that need *critical* investigation" (51, emphasis added). The list of topics following this statement shows that identification of can raise critical issues previously ignored if identification with does not drive processes and their purposes. This understanding is strongly grounded in a critical strategy I call "considerations of absence in the creation of meaning," a heuristic that also lies behind a number of other feminist texts. In fact, consideration of the absences in my own process-model education, and a refusal to identify with those absences, is the main heuristic strategy that has allowed me to create a discussion of critical discourse at all.

The split between identification of and identification with, then, invites us to revise the terms for creating self/other relations and the ways in which we find subjects for writing. Specifically, it gives us the opportunity for doing identification of the terms for making meaning without pre-scribing reproduction of those terms as the end of writing and/or as the measure of mastery. Such explorations create the possibility of con-texts and/or ways to enter into conversations with a difference. Kim Chernin gives us an example of the creation of a context when she uses the Gnostic gospels to "reinvent" the scene at the garden of Eden. She writes:

> I imagine the scene. I reinvent it. The anguish of the woman who has eaten. Who knows that her husband is still blind. There she is, with a single bite of the apple, light years ahead of him. She knows that the male Authority in the garden has puffed himself up with a false grandiosity, had been lording it over them out of ignorance. (171)

Although the next strategy, transposition, has been used in literary theory to discuss the move from one genre to another, here it names the process of moving a subject (in both senses of that term) across disciplinary, cultural, historical, and other sorts of boundaries, especially boundaries that block con- and counter-texts. One of my favorite examples of this strategy occurs in Naomi Wolf's *The Beauty Myth*. Here, beauty moves from the realm of the aesthetic into the realms of work, sex, religion, and culture. Thus transposed, considerations of beauty cross over issues of appearance and into considerations of women's family and work lives, female medical issues and health trends, spending trends, and speculations about the future in a kind of "contact" zone activity. These heuristics are discussed or overtly applied by the feminist writers I have discussed as well as by many other feminist writers before and after them. They are not places or topoi but possibilities that are currently constructed as absences by the terministic screams of dominant process-model theories, pedagogies, and practices.

Let me conclude by pointing out that all of these heuristics reposition writers as participatory subjects, rather than as the persuaded or persuading audiences of composition studies. As a process-model baby, this awareness has been a necessary crossing for me as a writer, thinker, and teacher. Pedagogically, it has resulted in the constitution of a new approach to writing, one I have been using with the students in my sections of Critical Reading, Writing, and Researching (the name of our first-year composition sequence), and in critical writing seminars and feminist writing seminars at Millikin University, as well as in women's studies courses. The major revision informing the con-text for writing that now informs all my teaching is this: instead of stepping in with pre-scribed and pre-scribeable notions of process, my students and I begin exploring our own, one another's, and various other meaning-making processes by posing the six questions I discussed earlier: What is invention? What is being invented? What is arrangement? What is being arranged? What is revision? What is being revised? We think about these questions in relation not only to our literacy pasts, in relation to the history of literacy more generally, and in relation to texts but also in relation to our classroom. Such considerations do not force us to efface our classroom context, but instead invite us to rearrange that context, to see and challenge its limitations.

These questions have changed the texts (experiential, popular, and literary) at which we choose to look, how we look at them, what we do in response, and how we interact. It has made us feel more able and welcome as rhetoricians in a field that has tended to position us as the physical, conceptual, and linguistic subjects through which other people's notions of process are reproduced. It has invited us to look in new ways at the texts that attempt to define this reproduction as excellence and, as a result, to feel freer and more prepared to choose to adopt, adapt, or reject what we find there in relation to our new understandings of ourselves and our possibilities for participation. It has, in effect, unearthed the absent possibility for critical practices—discursive and otherwise—informing most of our literacy educations. It has rearranged our relationships to literacy. We are no longer process-model babies, mastering and being mastered. We are revising subjects with possibilities for participation, possibilities that may not be included in the dominant models of literacy we encountered in our past or across the realities of our presents. These considerations invite us to respond to the gaps created by the absent possibilities informing our relationships to literacy, allowing us to acknowledge and revision our realities and their absent possibilities as they present themselves to us.

Notes

Special thanks go to Tim Lord and Susan Jarratt for their support of this project, even through times of unclarity and confusion. As always, my work remembers Jim Berlin and his contributions.

1. My source for this information is a person in the textbook industry who has asked to remain anonymous.

2. My observation about the absence of invitations to discover, create, and engage in critical discursive practices in these textbooks should not be misinterpreted as a critique that faults the texts for not doing what they set out to accomplish. I understand that the texts I list here make no claim about their intention or ability to engage in critical practices themselves or to invite others to engage in such practices. In fact, the possibilities for critical discourse in these texts are either subsumed by matters of explication or, more usually, by discussions about dealing with one's own text as one revises for the purpose of illustrating one's mastery of the skills valorized by the book itself. Some of these books are beginning to ask students to think about what their texts imply about their beliefs after the texts are written. Some even ask students to write about these implications informally and as a separate writing assignment, detached from the paper itself (see, for example, *The St. Martin's Guide to Writing*).

3. My observations of the lack of discussions about critical discursive practices and the construction of a critical aim or mode in these texts should not be misinterpreted as a dismissal of the texts. They are important texts and books I have used and found helpful both as a student and as a teacher. Moreover, the authors of these texts have made important contributions to our field, and I have a great deal of respect for them and for their works. However, the habit of constituting critical discursive practices as absent possibilities in the history of modern process-model composition studies is an important trend, one we must acknowledge and address to continue the process-model movement's commitment to improving writing instruction in this country.

4. As Kathleen Welch has shown in *The Contemporary Reception of Classical Rhetoric: Appropriations of Ancient Discourse*, the attempt to ground contemporary composition in the authority of classic rhetorical texts often led to practices of "accessibility-through-formalizing" which presented rhetorical activity as the application and mastery of preconstructed processes, forms, and grammatical structures (22). Welch names the "Heritage School" as the site upon which formulaic renditions of rhetorical activity build their contemporary homes (1–67). I would add that the best-selling composition textbooks of our time—as well as many of the most

widely read introductions to composition studies that take teachers and graduate students as their audiences—are similarly constructed architectures in the field of composition studies.

5. I am only just beginning to understand the extent to which our field has tended to ignore analysis and the ways in which the rift between communication studies and composition studies has fed our ignorance in relation to this issue. Edwin Black's *Rhetorical Criticism: A Study in Method* is a good place to start thinking through the ways this split has created some of the major terministic screens of modern process-model approaches to composition studies.

6. Whether these assumptions are translated into composition studies in relation to standards for grammatical correctness, adherence to some value or set of values, or the positioning of students as rhetors rather than rhetoricians, they take reproduction as their primary aim.

7. For a discussion of the implications of inserting issues of production into the process-model frame, see my "Critical Discursive Practices and Literate Subjectivities: Redefining the Terms of Composition Studies Through the Work of James A. Berlin."

8. These questions raise issues about historical contexts, social arrangements, and institutional practices and not merely questions about texts. Although I agree with Sharon Crowley, Kathleen Welch, and others when they discuss the problems connected to dropping memory, style, and delivery out of the rhetorical canon, I have found that within a revisionary context these issues exist in relation to issues of invention, arrangement, and revision, and not separately from them.

9. For an extended discussion of counter- and dis-identification see my "Critical Discursive Practices and Literate Subjectivities: Redefining the Terms of Composition Studies Through the Work of James A. Berlin."

12
The Ethics of Process

John Clifford and Elizabeth Ervin

We are both compositionists committed to praxis, to a composing process that promotes in rhetors both critical reflection and an informed and ethical impulse toward intervention into the public sphere. We both think of ourselves as post-process, conceptualizing a composing sequence from invention and drafting to revision and copy editing as secondary to our emphasis on a range of literate activities that challenge sociohistorical subjects caught in a flawed social order to enact a democratic rhetoric. But we have arrived at this professional ground from circuitous paths, across generations, genders, geography.

John has been teaching literature and writing since the sixties, moving from a high school in Brooklyn, to Queens College, to a state university in North Carolina. With a degree from New York University in literary theory and English education and a dissertation in composition, he has focused on finding ways to make these disciplines coalesce under a progressive rubric. Betsy has been teaching full time for four years. She received her Ph.D. from a well-established doctoral program in rhetoric and composition at the University of Arizona. This point is itself worth emphasizing: in only thirty-some years, composition has not only emerged as an academic discipline in its own right but has even begun to define itself *against* disciplines such as rhetoric and literary theory with which it was originally, sometimes uncomfortably, aligned.

Naturally we have diverse perspectives on the process movement; on the evolution of composing studies; on the influence of ethics and postmodernism; and on the status of public intellectuals. We want to trace some salient moments in our respective journeys through the discipline, to offer reflections from two representative members of two generations of compositionists, two meditations on process, two visions of where we have been and where we might go to be faithful to the intellectual and democratic possibilities of our profession.

1975–1984: JC

It felt as if I were at the center of the blast. In the late seventies at the City University of New York, the universe of composition theory was radically expanding, and the catalyst was process. Working in the writing program at Queens College with Don McQuade, Marie Ponsot, Rosemary Deen, Judy Fishman, and Sandy Schor, committed, energizing talk about composing was ubiquitous. Bob DiYanni and I planned our first book walking to a distant parking lot after class; Ken Bruffee was a frequent visitor, as was Mina Shaughnessy; Janet Emig was just across the Hudson at Rutgers. At the same time, I was finishing my dissertation on collaborative writing at New York University where Sondra Perl, also teaching at CUNY, was conducting her case studies of composing. The *zeitgeist* was invigorating. After teaching high school English for ten years in Brooklyn and getting an MA in literature, I was thrilled that composition was finally becoming a serious topic of intellectual inquiry. Spurred on by the necessity of addressing the literacy needs of thousands of underprepared open-admissions students, process seemed a pedagogical breakthrough: not only as a fresh way of thinking about writing for professionals but also as a cogent explanation of composing for the deans and provosts who would fund the burgeoning remedial writing programs. Like New Criticism a generation earlier, process gave writing professional credibility. It could generate theory while allowing for an accessible pedagogy.

A discipline was forming, and theorists and practitioners began gathering to help shape the emerging paradigm, armed with varied intellectual tools from educational research, cognitive psychology, literary theory, and linguistics. A motley community of scholars was deciding what ideas were worth exploring, what work needed to be done. After studying reader-response theory with Louise Rosenblatt, I was already predisposed to translate her ideas on the process of reading literature to the process of writing. I also was influenced by Bruffee's theories of collaborative learning. Indeed, for my first five years as a compositionist, process and collaboration seemed to be two sides of the same coin: a full composing sequence the goal and collaboration the means. In retrospect, Bruffee's idea was quite simple, even commonsensical: students learn better if they can help each other through a composing sequence from brainstorming to drafting and revision. Bruffee's strategy was to "arrange optimum conditions" for students to learn ("The Way Out" 470). This suggestion dovetailed with another influential voice, that of Carl Rogers, who theorized that teachers interested in enacting process produced "more creative and independent learners" (119).

For me these ideas, extensions really of techniques floating around since the late sixties, gave not only philosophical and professional substance to process but also an ethical dimension that was nowhere to be found in the current-traditional obsession with error, form, and syntax. Of course there was the professionally responsible move to actually teach basic writers how to compose rather than merely expecting them to, but there was another impulse animating my sense of process's possibilities. The writing process seemed as potentially empowering as Rosenblatt's insistence that readers create meaning over time. Meaning was not some reified entity found in the hidden interstices of poems but something for which readers and writers negotiated themselves. It seemed to privilege the voice of the individual over mere skill.

Just as the formalists focused on the ordered critical essay as the unseen, mysterious distillation of a complex interpretive process, so too traditional compositionists focused on highly edited products, ignoring the unique composing routes of diverse writers. This seemed pedagogically bankrupt and worth fighting against. Decidedly anti-authoritarian and fluid, process and collaboration seemed strong threads in the democratic fabric progressives had been struggling to weave since John Dewey. Process seemed to push against certainty and rigidity, against language as a mirror of reality, against the idea that writing was simply a record of what was already thought out in the mind. Process seemed an exciting antithesis to the vapid essentialist rhetoric of the day.

However, as I look back on the articles I published then, there is a surprising emphasis on technique, especially in an essay in *Research in the Teaching of English* where I elaborated on an elongated collaborative sequence concerned with evolving meaning as writers shape, refocus, and revise. I was inspired by Mina Shaughnessy's idea that "meaning is crafted stage by stage" (81). Like others at the time, I wanted to establish in rigorous empirical terms the credibility of process against the old skills-and-drills formulation.

And although I felt process was more democratic, more in tune with participatory impulses latent in the profession, I see now that I privileged the desire to establish a disciplinary ethos acceptable within the university community, one that promised more competent writers, more disciplined thinkers. Although I claimed that process "allowed writers the freedom to say something worth the effort" (39), and later that combining the process of reading and writing would help students "examine personal and cultural assumptions" (40), the explicit progressive philosophy underlying process was marginalized. And as process became more institutionally acceptable and entrenched during the Reaganite eighties, the progressive engine that powered process in the first place slowed down. Process no longer seemed a more democratic way to know, but simply a technique, a way to proceed, ten steps toward more effective writing, as easily adaptable to teaching executives at IBM as basic writers in South Brooklyn. The expanding universe of composition seemed to me to have lost its democratic purpose. But not for long.

1990: EE

There was no "big bang" for me as a new professional in composition: no subversive thrill, no illicit paradigm shifting, no ground zero. By the time I attended my first 4Cs in 1990, composition's epistemological break from a product orientation for the most part was complete and taken for granted, and "the writing process" had become as fuzzily synonymous with composition as "rhetoric" had been a century before. So what was invigorating about my entry into composition was not the sense that I was part of something "radical" and new but that I felt immediately in sync with the questions our discipline was contemplating at the time—questions related to diversity, marginality, and identity; questions of how to rethink traditions and rewrite racist, patriarchal, and elitist narratives. These were the concerns around which composition theories and practices were then developing, and since I shared those concerns, it never occurred to me to ask how our profession had arrived at them. More specifically, it never occurred to me to ask what process had to do with those issues—how, some might argue, process made possible the very *consideration* of those issues within the field of composition studies.

My primary reason for attending our discipline's flagship conference was to present a paper entitled "The Language and Rhetoric of Courtship: An Examination of Personal Ads" as part of a panel called "Critical Thinking about Mass Media." The session was packed, and the discussion was lively, leading me to conclude that my work was part of the professional mainstream. In addition to my speaking position, I served as associate chair of a roundtable discussion on "Gender and Multicultural Concerns: Transforming Ourselves, Our Students, the Curriculum, and the Profession." Although a comparatively minor role in terms of program status and responsibility, my participation at this session nonetheless served as a more vivid introduction to the field in 1990 than "Critical Thinking about Mass Media." My only duties were to distribute handouts and count the number of attendees—mundane tasks, to be sure, but tasks that vividly conveyed to me the significance of the event: the smallish room to which the session had been assigned was filled to overflowing, much to the surprise of the panelists, who had not brought nearly enough handouts. Despite the cramped quarters, people were enthusiastically engaged in the session from start to finish. I, too, was excited, if slightly clueless: don't "we" always talk about this stuff?

Before attending the 4Cs, I had been advised that the real action took place at the parties—the "hidden conference," so to speak—and I zealously plunged in. I was admittedly starstruck at glimpsing, hearing, or actually having a conversation with people in the field whose work I admired. One evening, for example, Sharon Crowley and Jasper Neel stood behind me in a buffet line. Having just read Crowley's *Teacher's Introduction to Deconstruction* and Neel's *Plato, Derrida, and Writing*—and buoyed by the appreciative response to my presentation earlier that day—I longed to be a part of their conversation, but the shrewdest insight I could muster was, "I've enjoyed your books so much." These and other awkward overtures represented my first steps into this profession: I had read some "important" books, books that other people were talking about; I was thinking about connections between composition and critical theory, gender issues, media, just like (I told myself) veteran members of the field. Being even marginally part of these disciplinary conversations supported and shaped my own emerging professional identity, and, furthermore, assured me that these issues represented what the profession was "about."

Where was process while all this was going on? Everywhere and nowhere at once. Everywhere in that references to "the writing process" were ubiquitous, and in that there were, according to the program, seventeen sessions at the conference devoted to "Theories of Composing," making it among the most well-represented "areas of emphasis" on the program proposal form and subsequently at the conference itself. (It is significant that this number dwindled to eight in 1991, and by 1992 theories of the composing process was eliminated altogether as an area of emphasis on the program proposal form; it has been resurrected as a subheading in recent years.) Yet process was also nowhere in the sense that I neither circled in my program nor attended at the conference a single session expressly devoted to that topic. Process, in short, was invisible—part of the ideological landscape of composition studies, but naturalized, unremarkable, understood. I had a vague sense of what "the writing process" *was*—prewriting, drafting, revising; a recursive system; and so on—but no sense whatsoever of the ethical or political ideals out of which it had emerged. And, frankly, I was content to be ahistorical.

Which makes me part of composition's Generation X, I suppose—those professionals who were not present for the process revolution but who nevertheless passively accept it as a fact, even a "right," just as many of my own students passively accept their access to higher education or their right to vote or the "fact" of equal pay for equal work. "We fought that war. Things are better now. Move on," these students tell me in their complacent, blasé way, believing that these issues are resolved and that there are different, more important ones to worry about. The Generation X of composition—believing, likewise, that "the writing process" is the least of our discipline's problems—has moved on to other preoccupations, including such "selfish" concerns as whether we actually will have jobs after grad school or whether we will be among the part-time "freeway fliers" who, as Pauline Uchmanowicz describes it, teach ten to twelve composition courses a year but whose lack of full-time presence at any one institution "force[s their] exclusion from departmental 'reindeer games' that sometimes go hand-in-hand with job security" (426). This generation might be more aware than ever of the problematic authority of the composition teacher, of the ways in which knowledge and expertise are constrained by discursive conventions and in which we transfer these constraints to our students, of our precarious professional esteem. These are the ethical dilemmas that define my professional generation. So maybe composition studies always has been post-process for me.

1985–1991: JC

Process clearly helped create the discipline of composition and rhetoric, but it did not prove rich enough to sustain the diet of those theorists interested in moving beyond pedagogy, exploring the complex interpenetration of the writer and society. In retrospect, the process movement seemed necessary but finally insufficient in the progressive attempt to make reading and writing comparable ways of knowing, of discovering meaning, of being in the world. And, naturally, when process became the major theme of commercial rhetorics during the eighties, theorists lost control of its classroom direction. Unmoored, process was quickly co-opted by the larger socializing function of the university.

The surprisingly effective conservative renaissance of the eighties caught most progressives off guard. Many soon began paying more attention to the social dimension of their scholarship. Around this time it was obvious that composition too was taking a social turn. Although John Schilb notes that the initial focus of the social typically involved the ritualistic invocation of "RortyKuhnFish" (*Between the Lines* 63), my growing interest in theory was galvanized by Frank Lentricchia's reading of Kenneth Burke. Previously I was struck by Burke's similarity to Rosenblatt, especially his notion in *Counter-Statement* that readers surround each word with "a unique set of imponderable emotional experiences" (78). However, Burke can be read many ways, and through Lentricchia's perspective as an engaged intellectual, Burke's radical social agenda was dramatically foregrounded. I wrote an essay, "Burke and the Tradition of Democratic Schooling," that reflected my sense of urgency in extending the process movement outward to the social world beyond the classroom. At first that simply meant I used Burke's pentad to problematize typical mechanistic invention devices. Burke's dialectic encourages writers to identify themselves with a sociopolitical context so they can acknowledge who they are aligned with, who they serve, who they defend. This seemed an important step for me, yoking rhetoric, power, and form, reconnecting writing to the larger social world. Even as pedagogically astute a text as Knoblauch and Brannon's *Rhetorical Traditions and the Teaching of Writing*, which is critical of the debasement of process into a performance recipe, does not highlight rhetoric's embeddedness in the social. At the time compositionists still clung to the illusion of the inside and the outside, of the teeming world of politics and the reflective world of the university.

But Burke inevitably lead me beyond these polarities to see that students are indeed socio-historical subjects, always ideologically situated, always imbued with the assumptions, biases, and values of specific communities. Behind all writing, Burke notes, the mind is a social product. For me the social seems to have led quite naturally to an investigation of ideology. Indeed, my movement from process to social construction to ideological critique seemed to happen quite rapidly and was rooted in the disciplinary epiphany that the composing process enacted in institutions was never going to be disinterested. Chillingly, it could be an even greater instrument for discursive socialization, for a pedagogical interpellation to occupy an uncritical subject position. As I noted in "The Subject of Discourse," process could become such "a labyrinthine sequence of prewriting heuristics, drafts, revisions, and peer-editing sessions" (48) that the darkest predictions of Althusser and Foucault would be validated. Ethically, I wanted to resist the academic socialization of passive, apolitical rhetors. And after reading Gramsci, I did not want to be pessimistic about the possibility of being a transformative intellectual. I did not want to be the shepherd, in Burke's analogy, that "acts for the good of the sheep" by raising them for the market (*Rhetoric* 27). I wanted my students to write well, a goal James Berlin clearly champions in his posthumous text, but also for them to see that the arbitrary strictures of form could be self-reflectively problematized. In other words, I wanted to allow simultaneous subject positions: one competently articulate about normal discourse, the other so weary of being interpellated that they would vow never to lose sight of the democratic narrative that is our responsibility as ethical rhetors to evoke. Next to this renewed sense of social purpose, the writing process seemed anemic, its goals pedestrian, its methods politically suspect. For me writing had become not only a way of being in the world but also way to be an ethical agent of change.

1992: EE

About midway through my doctoral program, I got tired. I had been in school my whole life—had sat in classrooms, dutifully reading the assigned texts and writing the assigned papers, for twenty-one years without stopping to ask what I was doing or why or how it was done.

I had never even changed my major. After so many years in school, I was not prepared to leave my graduate program, but something had to give. It was around this time that one of my professors invited me to drop his required rhetoric course and take it as an independent study; he thought I had a bad attitude and would distract other students who were genuinely interested in the material. Though I was inclined to react defensively to his "invitation"—and in fact, some of my peers suggested that I document the conversation as evidence of harassment—I knew that it was just the incentive I needed. So I declined my professor's offer, opting instead to perform what felt at the time (remember, I had spent my life in school) like the ultimate act of in-your-face resistance: I cast aside the course syllabus and began reading almost exclusively in the areas of feminist political, epistemological, and historiographical theory.

I became completely absorbed in the work of Joan Wallach Scott, Sandra Harding, and others. Their ideas about the inevitable situatedness of knowledge validated and explained my growing frustrations with school. When I read Dorothy E. Smith's assertion that "[a] man's body gives credibility to his utterance, whereas a woman's body takes it away from hers" (30), I began to think differently about the sexist comments in my course evaluations and what I perceived as condescension from peers. When I read Lorraine Code's argument that "[t]here is no more effective way to create epistemic dependence than systematically to withhold acknowledgment; no more effective way of maintaining structures of epistemic privilege and vulnerability than [to evince] a persistent distrust in someone's claims to cognitive authority. . ." (*What Can She Know?* 218), I began to contextualize my anxiety over producing work that was by turns irrelevant or ignored. While these theories were natural outgrowths of the interests I pursued when I first entered the profession, it was only now that they began to influence my composition teaching in tangible ways. I began explicitly to discuss issues of positionality and subjectivity with my students—why it is not only rhetorically appropriate but also politically significant to use "I" in one's academic writing, for example, or why Verónica's response to Ellen Gilchrist's story "Traveler" might be different from Stephanie's—and incorporated a variety of ethnographic projects into my composition syllabi. The ethical implications of such practices seemed obvious: when we begin to challenge traditional assumptions about who has the authority to know and what counts as knowledge, we create new possibilities for epistemological and discursive agency. This was liberating and, to use a word that was getting stale even in 1992, empowering.

But this position was in fact more complicated than it might appear, for it existed simultaneously with an incongruous position, one that regarded students as ethically suspect. I arrived at this position by way of two developments at the University of Arizona, the institution where I taught at the time, that were not adequately anticipated by the composition program there. The first was the enthusiasm and sophistication with which our students embraced computer composing. The university had several well-stocked computer labs, and many of my students composed their entire papers onscreen, printing out hard copies of their drafts only when they needed them for class, specifically, peer review days, conferences, and due dates—or, if they procrastinated, only due dates. This situation introduced two problems in my teaching. The first, which Paul Heilker describes in "Revision Worship and the Computer as Audience," was "imposing a linear notion of writing process and placing revision as a separate stage at certain points along that production line, most typically at the end of the line" (62). Not surprisingly, this linearized version of process was based on my own writing process, conceived and refined before computers became so accessible: I handwrite some notes and an informal outline, do some drafting on the computer, revise on hard copy, transfer these revisions to disk, and so on. As a teaching assistant, I was advised by supervisors and more experienced peers to require students regularly to print out hard copies of their drafts, even if they did not need one for peer conferring, even if they did not normally revise on hard copies or preferred to revise onscreen, even if they had ethical convictions against wasting paper, even if they normally did not revise at all. The penalty for no drafts? A one-letter grade reduction. In implementing this policy, Heilker suggests, I became an enforcer "of mandatory, institutionalized revision," perpetuating the notion not only "that there is one best kind of writing process" (63) but also that students who are "unable or refuse to revise [according to this process] . . . [should be] punished with lower grades in the hope that they will mend their ways" (62). Though I did not recognize it at the time, my pedagogy suggested that revision should be practiced for its own sake—"it's only a matter of hitting a few keys, after all; it's not like you have to rewrite the whole thing . . ."—rather than as a means of "re-seeing" an idea and hence deepening and strengthening one's writing.

This set the stage for a related problem. Students who did not produce hard copies of early drafts aroused my suspicions: their final drafts seemed to materialize out of thin air, process-less, illegitimate, and yet somehow perfect. My wariness about accepting such drafts stemmed less from my own experience than from that of a fellow TA, Tim, a technophile who encouraged his students to submit their work on computer disks, with their drafts identified by separate file names. Near the end of the semester, one of Tim's students handed in his disk with only a final draft file, but the onscreen "trash can" was bulging; Tim opened it, expecting to find the earlier drafts, but what he found instead was the same final draft with another student's name on it. When this story spread, TAs once again were advised to require writing students to hand in all "process work"—not as a means of understanding their drafting strategies or mapping their revision decisions but in order to preclude messy confrontations about plagiarism. I still adhere to this policy, despite its ethically objectionable assumption that all students are potential cheaters (see Murphy) and its perversion of "writing process" into an injunction to "show your work"—that is, account for your authorship.

Learning-disabled students were similarly suspect. Like many schools, the University of Arizona sponsored a comprehensive academic support program for LD students, and I regularly had several such students in my composition classes. When I looked over their drafts, I occasionally found revisions made in someone else's handwriting. Although privately I was troubled by this, I never questioned it until I worked with a student, Joe, whose revisions—obviously written by someone else—amounted to substantial "corrections" of everything from spelling to sentence structure to content. I met with Joe's tutor, who insisted that Joe was an intelligent and trustworthy young man, that he had made those revisions orally and she had simply written them on his draft; she assured me, furthermore, that this was standard tutoring practice for learning-disabled writers. I have since learned that such practices are in fact highly controversial among experts in the field of learning disabilities, many of whom believe that they impede the development of muscle memory and foster dependence and passivity on the part of LD students (Dunn 77, 108–9). But my point here has less to do with this specific practice than with the unsettling realization that I held my writing students in contradictory ethical positions and that my distorted conception of writing process seemed to trap me within that contradiction: even as I valued students' ethical authority (in this case, I agreed utterly that Joe was an intelligent and trustworthy young man), I was mistrustful of their ethical intentions. "Process" had become an end in itself or at best a means of "catching" students not doing . . . the process.

Perhaps I should point out here that I did not "disagree" with theories of composing processes or consider their pedagogical manifestations obsolete. When Sondra Perl says that "writers must have the experience of being readers" ("Understanding" 369), I still believe her. When Peter Elbow advises writers not to "read over your freewriting unless you can do so in a spirit of benign self-welcoming" (*Writing with Power* 17), I still nod in agreement, certain of the wisdom of that advice. But, though I assiduously guided my students through freewriting exercises and peer review sessions, I was becoming further and further detached from the genuinely sound rationales for these practices. Like my colleagues untrained in composition, I had been going through the motions with the writing process—"doing process" for no better reason than because that is what you do when you teach composition.

I should also point out that although I continued to go to 4Cs, teach writing, and pursue my doctoral studies (albeit in a rather loosely interdisciplinary way), I was largely ignorant of developments in the field of rhetoric and composition during this time—not because nothing there supported my concerns but because, as Michael Polanyi observes, "as human beings, we must inevitably see the universe from a centre lying within ourselves and speak about it in terms of a human language shaped by the exigencies of human intercourse. Any attempt rigorously to eliminate our human experience from our picture of the world must lead to absurdity" (3). In other words, my professional identity developed according to the idiosyncratic confluences of my personal life (including my life in school, the catalyst for my interdisciplinary reading), various professional conversations, and the larger political scene that I was observing, overhearing, and in which I was slowly working up the courage to participate. And I would suggest that the identity of disciplines, too, develops in these ways.

1991–1997: JC

Some six years later, the present moment seems more a natural extension of my thinking about the possibility of agency than the radical readjustment that occurred in the early eighties when the profession began to sense the limitations of process. That felt like a paradigmatic shift from technique to philosophy, from modernism to post-modernism, from community to difference, from the language of the isolated classroom to an interconnected web of overlapping and contradictory social and political discourses. Along with many others, I am trying to come to grips with the implications of a social-epistemic rhetoric. Drawn to its appealing dialectic among writer, language, and the sociopolitical, as well as its imaginative mix of postmodern theory and political activism, I am still wrestling with the awesome ethical and logistical demands of enacting such a rhetoric with today's passive, apolitical students. The interrogation of signifying practices that James Berlin adapts from the Birmingham Center (especially in *Rhetorics, Poetics, and Cultures*), for example, requires a daunting melange of Fredric Jameson, Stuart Hall, Louis Althusser, Antonio Gramsci, Goran Thorborn, Jacques Derrida, and many others.

I certainly want to act on postmodernism's insights about the decentered self, the power of discursive interpellation, its distrust of metanarratives and epistemological absolutes, and especially its rejection of the modernist belief that knowledge claims can be free of situated persuasion and power. But I am hesitant to employ a cultural studies pedagogy that leads to *a priori* conclusions. It seems to me antithetical to the spirit of postmodernism, to its self-conscious affirmation of indeterminacy, heterogeneity, and contradiction to employ invariant heuristics in the classroom that lead students to see, for example, how symbolic capital is imbricated in sustaining ideology. I certainly agree that we should raise our students' consciousness, allowing them to understand that they are not as free as they assume. That seems an ethically responsible destination. However, the paths students are asked to travel need to be more flexible, more focused on their awareness rather than on political conclusions. Encouraging students to take responsibility for their ethical decisions as readers and writers seems closer to the antifoundational impulse that initially helped us all resist the formulaic process of the early eighties.

That ethical values are contingent few theorists would dispute. But that, of course, as Rorty and Barbara Herrnstein Smith remind us, does not mean there are not values for which it is worth fighting. Ethical absolutes are suspect for obvious historical reasons, but a commitment to ethical decisions should never be under a cloud. More than ever, we need to encourage writers to enact a critical literacy that employs all sorts of processes: reading, thinking, interpreting, composing, and critiquing. We need to encourage a dialectically literate environment that foregrounds an interaction with a variety of texts. Recently, in an essay-writing course, I used Patricia Bizzell and Bruce Herzberg's new historicist anthology *Negotiating Difference,* but I also used *M. Butterfly,* a memoir by bell hooks, and even a conventional short story by Barry Hannah called "Water Liars," a piece that poignantly illustrates our culture's enduring tolerance for the double standard. In "Water Liars," a married couple plays a dangerous game: the husband tells his wife about the lovers he had before they were married and then asks her to do the same. She does so honestly and with devastating emotional consequences for the "crucified" husband. I asked my students first to read the story and write a response, but then I asked them to compose a parallel narrative from their own lives. Later I asked them to critique their stories, to interrogate the cultural values motivating the characters in their own text.

We spent considerable time creating explicit mappings of the ways our ideas, attitudes, and values are written by various discourses from neighborhoods, religions, class affiliations, racial beliefs, and political and sexual orientations, as well as ethnic, gender, and familial associations. This self-reflective process provides a metacommentary on their original responses, allowing them to see that their earlier "autonomous" belief that men should or should not have more sexual freedom than women is ineluctably a dimension of the multiple discourse that both constrains and enables our ethical agency. It does not take long for these typical middle-class students to see that the wife in particular and women in general are made to function as the other. It takes more time to understand how and why the double standard is maintained, who it benefits, and who it diminishes. Some students reproduce the truths of their received discourse, but others contest these norms. I encourage them to use this dialectic to move beyond disciplinary objectivity, to engender commitment, to risk an emotional stake in the subsequent analysis of their response to Hannah's story as cultural artifact. In this way, I hope to subvert the academy's suppression of subjectivity without resuscitating the expressionist illusion that simply baring one's soul is a democratic gesture. A rhetor who sees the ways we are constructed occupies a subject position capable of reinscription, of composing a counternarrative where the writer can sense the ethical necessity to intervene in our vexed democratic polis. I am encouraged by the numbers of students who refuse to write what is always written, who seem willing to challenge received norms by taking responsibility for the construction of an alternative symbolic narrative.

1995–1997: EE

For the first several years of my professional life, the ethical questions posed by writing process had mostly to do with students' behavior, not with mine as a teacher. Process still represented a way of decentralizing the authority of the teacher—a remnant of the original process *zeitgeist* that fit nicely with the goals of what might be called the "diversity paradigm"—but it was also a way of pre-empting plagiarism problems and of shifting to students all responsibility for creating meaningful contexts for their writing. These are inconsistent goals at best, but I persevered in my efforts to bring them into alignment. I still required students to hand in their drafts; however, I also frequently encouraged them not just to write about topics in which they were genuinely interested but to adapt our assignments in ways that would allow them to accomplish multiple purposes and reach multiple audiences. When Christy proposed an alcohol awareness component to new student orientation, for example, I urged her to send it to the chancellor's office. And when Lauren worked through her own end-of-semester stress by exploring the range of opportunities for spiritual development on campus, I suggested that she shape it as a feature for the student newspaper. "Lots of students are feeling the same way," I said. "They'd probably welcome this information." Neither student followed through, and though I was disappointed, I was not exactly surprised: having already imagined my students as ethically suspect—prone to cheating or at least taking unsanctioned shortcuts in their writing—it was not such a stretch to conclude that they also were apathetic, lazy, and passive.

What *was* a stretch was to confront the ways in which I was implicated in my students' inertia. I checked out Paul Rogat Loeb's *Generation at the Crossroads*, which is based on interviews with college students all over the country, hoping to get some insight into why my students seemed so reluctant to engage in even the most benign po-litical acts—or more specifically, *literate* acts that served civic functions outside the context of our classroom. What I learned was that few stu-dents trace their political commitments back to their professors—a fact that, according to Loeb, "speaks to the failure of . . . decent and con-cerned professors, of whatever political stripe, to teach their students to act as involved citizens" (94). Upon reading this, I began to exam-ine my own tangled ethical impulses.

By 1995 I was out of graduate school and so grateful to have a ten-ure-track position that I hesitated to engage in any activity that might be perceived as boat rocking. But even as I constructed a fairly con-ventional academic identity, I yearned for a role in what I rather ro-mantically imagined as the "real world." Dana Polan suggests that "one of the great self-comforting affectations of academics is to refer to everything outside the university as the 'real world,' as in the phrase, 'I'm going back to the real world now' (said when one's day of teach-ing and committees is over)." Furthermore, he argues that this belief represents "the intellectual's simultaneous hope and fear that nothing he or she does matters to the world 'at large'" (353–54), and such was indeed the case for me. Though I experienced intermittent urges to participate in what Walter Fisher calls "public moral arguments" and even contemplated running for political office, I was terrified to so much as write a letter to the editor: what if someone who knows me reads it? will I look ignorant? bring shame upon my department, my university, the academic world? will I lose my fragile credibility, or my job? And as with many would-be activists, my hopes and fears had coalesced into an uncomfortable lethargy. It occurred to me that basic tasks of literate citizenship ought to be part of college composition curricula, but I wondered how I could reasonably require my students to do a kind of writing that I did not value enough to undertake in my own life outside school.

Clearly, my ambivalence about civic participation had influenced my writing pedagogy, including the conflicting assumptions about and expectations for my students. By surreptitiously focusing on plagia-rism I had represented writing as a decontextualized process, circum-scribed by school conventions, school purposes, and school schedules. By suggesting alternative audiences and purposes for my students' writing, I had co-opted their political intentions, thus undermining the very actions I was hoping to encourage. In short, by displacing my own ethical contradictions onto my students, my curriculum, and my pedagogy, I had become one of those "decent and concerned" but ultimately ineffectual professors who bemoans her students' indifference from the comfort of her academic office. Allowing my uneasiness with the ivory tower image of the university classroom to guide my academic inquiries once again, I vowed to overcome my reluctance to engage in public writing. So during the summer of 1995 I wrote my first letter to the editor and coauthored, with a colleague, a response to George Will's critique of college writing instruction. The following fall, I undertook two community writing projects with my students—an annotated timeline of the history of a nearby beach community and a sourcebook for the study of African American history.

My transformation into a "civic writer" was swift and thorough, and, moreover, led me back to scholarship in composition studies, where a burgeoning service-learning movement was beginning to gain momentum. I was particularly influenced by James J. Sosnoski and David B. Downing's "A Multivalent Pedagogy for a Multicultural Time," which addresses the difficulties of building a composition course around "writing directed at actual audiences in 'live' situations" instead of "artificial exercises" (309). The authors acknowledge the complex ways in which conflicting allegiances and implicit, unrecognized agendas interact in a classroom organized around such principles; given the erratic and exhausting nature of my own service-learning efforts, their ambivalence about creating alternative "intellectual spaces" for college writing was oddly reassuring. Furthermore, they validated my determination that notes and drafts and revisions had become less central to my composition classes than what my students and I were doing with our writing—the purposes that informed the writing, the actions that it promoted, and the interactions that were necessitated by our endeavors. Although writing process was not exactly irrelevant to such a classroom—it still happened—it was in a sense beside the point, and certainly seemed at odds with my growing conviction that the purpose for writing and the responsibilities of writers ought to precede and inform any further decisions about process and that this is what we should teach in college writing classes. "Process" no longer seemed like the most useful set of propositions to inform my professional ideals or direct my practices as a writing teacher.

While process seemed to trap me in a series of ethical inconsistencies, the notion of praxis has enabled me to reconceptualize both the purpose of writing instruction and the dynamic ways in which my roles as teacher, writer, and citizen overlap. Praxis is certainly not a new concept in rhetoric and composition; it was theorized as early as Aristotle, was popularized in recent decades by Paulo Freire, and is a featured term in two new disciplinary sourcebooks, *Keywords in Composition Studies* and *The Encyclopedia of Rhetoric* and *Composition* (see Fitts, Swartz). Broadly speaking, it seeks to blur distinctions between theory and practice, integrate ethical and political purposes, and promote critical reflection that leads to informed action and civic virtue within the context of a polis. The problem with this definition, of course, is that the diverse and fragmented ethical systems that manifest themselves in American culture no longer resemble a coherent polis, and the communities that sponsor our academic institutions no longer welcome our pedagogical values without some degree of suspicion. And yet, according to Susan Wells, academics persist in envisioning a unitary public as "a location in space, always available, with secure and discernible borders." Wells argues that such a conception dooms our efforts at public discourse to failure and that we would do better to think of publics—plural—"as questions, rather than answers," "as a richly determined practice," as "discontinuous and associated with crises," as "provisional" (326–27, 335). A pedagogy that supports this approach "might begin by valuing what is difficult, and direct itself to the connection between discourse and action" (337).

This, I believe, is where the process approach to writing instruction falls short in today's hyperpoliticized, postmodern culture. It is also where praxis—with its emphasis on obligations and agency, actions and their consequences—might assist us in contemplating a post-process future for our discipline. A praxis orientation to composition studies need not be limited to public discourse, but neither should it be limited to student writing, academic writing, or even teaching writing. For those of us who see the composition classroom as a vehicle for promoting democratic values and behaviors, any discussion of our professional future must be predicated on honest appraisals of our own civic behaviors, including the ways we embody and act upon our ethical assumptions outside of the classroom, where no one—and everyone—is watching.

The process movement of the late seventies is exhausted: simultaneously overburdened by the manifold aspirations of a discipline and depleted by the normalizing propensities of academe. Its democratic impulses, once brimming with liberatory potential, have been domesticated by inertia and routine; its subversive intentions have been co-opted by the institutional power of the university; even its tireless commitment to critical consciousness is, well, tired. As composition teachers, we are tired, too. The social turn of the eighties heightened our profession's awareness that the autonomous writer of modernism is in fact deeply embedded in a variety of discourse communities, thus complicating our understanding of process as well as our notions of a democratic ethic for composition studies. We are frustrated with the failure of process to sustain a democratic rhetoric, and we are anxious over the limitations of social construction to see the resiliency of the ideological web that circumscribes even our efforts to struggle against it. But we also remain optimistic that we can continue to do what engaged, oppositional compositionists do best: encourage students to be literate agents not objects. By rethinking the guiding idioms of our discipline, sociopolitically alert rhetors might be better poised to resist domination and exploitation. Their heightened awareness of the imbrication of writing, ideology, and power might someday translate into the restoration of democratic energy to composition studies, a process worth the effort.

13
Reprocessing the Essay

John Schilb

A post-"process" approach to composition studies would not necessarily ban the term. But certainly it would critique how process has been represented in the analysis and teaching of writing. Here I want to question how the term has figured in recent calls for making the essay central to composition courses and the English curriculum at large. To be sure, such calls rarely honor every conceivable type of essay. Rather, they privilege the type traditionally labeled "personal," "familiar," and/or "exploratory." Thus, they can be charged with insufficiently considering the attractions of other essay forms. To simplify the following discussion, though, I myself will use the term *essay* to mean the particular subspecies they prize.

Furthermore, let me say at once that I am not out to thwart the reading and writing of essays. I myself like to use them in my writing classes, I regularly teach a course on Modern Women Essayists, and I even read essays outside of school. Although it is hardly the case that some of my best friends are essays, some of my favorite texts are. Also, I believe fans of the genre are right when they argue that it has yet to achieve the foothold in English studies it deserves. But their embattled enthusiasm for it has led them to engage in some dubious moves. Especially problematic are their invocations of "process."

Mind and Text

Repeatedly, fans of the essay have praised it for modeling the very dynamics of the author's mind. To them, it reflects the messy, circuitous processes of writing and thinking that the essayist allegedly experienced. According to O. B. Hardison, "The essay is the enactment of a process by which the soul realizes itself even as it is passing from day to day and moment to moment" (20). For Kurt Spellmeyer, "the essay dramatizes a process of negotiation and revaluation concealed by other genres, a process never wholly methodical or disinterested" (*Common Ground* 101). Pamela Klass Mittlefehldt contends that the essay "allows us to see the process of contemplation that results in understanding that in turn leads to action" (198). William Howarth links the essay directly with the writing-process movement, observing that practitioners of the genre "think less *about* writing than *through* it: they watch it unfold and grasp its meaning as it emerges" (642). Even when they do not mention "process," many of the essay's champions express sentiments like these. "[I]n an essay," Phillip Lopate asserts, "the track of a person's thoughts struggling to achieve some understanding of a problem *is* the plot" (76). According to William Gass, "The hero of the essay is the author in the act of thinking things out, feeling and finding a way" (20). In keeping with this theoretical tradition, Paul Heilker climaxes his recent NCTE book *The Essay* by proclaiming that the genre is "kineticism incarnate" (169). More precisely, Heilker claims, "In the act of essaying, we write in a perpetual movement toward knowledge and wisdom; in reading essays, we witness writers perpetually moving toward wisdom and understanding" (183). *Process* may indeed be an appropriate term for essays. In content and form, many of them do seem to validate uncertain exploration rather than mere delivery of established truths. Also, I myself have often been captivated by an essay's account of its writer's musings. But a student of essays ought to bear in mind that the processes they represent may differ from those their authors actually experienced.

Some champions of the essay do admit that its portrayal of the author's mental flux may be fabricated. For example, G. Douglas Atkins acknowledges that the essay "produces the artistic or literary *effect* or *illusion* of witnessing thinking in progress, in process" (emphasis mine). Yet Atkins immediately withdraws these intimations of fictiveness, adding that the essay "*is* the act of thinking through writing" (6). In fact, rarely do the essay's advocates linger on possible differences between art and life. If pressed, no doubt they would concede that there are some. Sooner or later, though, they prefer to suggest that the essay imitates its author's real state of mind.

Take Heilker's remarks in his chapter entitled "The Practice of Some Contemporary Essayists, or Living in the Real World." (In the following quotations, I have italicized various words for emphasis.) Discussing the first paragraph of Aldous Huxley's "Music at Night," Heilker comments that "Huxley *apparently* piles up his sense-sparked thoughts one after the other as they come to him." Here, Heilker holds back slightly from declaring that the paragraph mimics Huxley's actual cogitations. At the same time, he does not explain why the qualifier *apparently* is in order. Moreover, just a few sentences back, Heilker has praised Huxley's essay for "effortlessly connecting his thoughts" (66), as if a critic could tell from the text itself how much sweat Huxley really put into it.

Later, in discussing Joan Didion's "On Keeping a Notebook," Heilker again resorts to qualification, noting that Didion "*seems* to present her thought as she experienced it" (68). But once more the qualifier is not explained, and elsewhere in this section Heilker's tone is more confident. For him, "Didion's work accentuates how the essay *enacts* the evolution of an author's understanding over time, how the essay *embodies* an author's skeptical groping toward an uncertain truth" (67). Moreover, he claims that Didion is "*showing* us where and when she achieves an understanding" (68). Moving to a discussion of Charles Simic's "Reading Philosophy at Night," Heilker again hesitates a bit: "He evidently presents his thoughts as they were experienced on the spot rather than being later systematized and rearranged" (71). But qualification fades as Heilker proceeds to note "Simic's groping efforts toward understanding" (72) and climactically asserts that Simic's text demonstrates how the essay as a genre attempts to "offer the reader the unsorted wholeness of the writer's experience" (73).

Later, discussing Gretel Ehrlich's "Looking for a Lost Dog," Heilker comments that certain of her words "seem to allow her to present her thoughts as they occurred to her on the spot" (81): at the time she was searching for her dog. Earlier, however, he echoes his conclusion about Simic's essay, claiming that Ehrlich's is "presenting the reader with unsorted wholeness of the writer's experience." Furthermore, he remarks that her "present-tense verbs . . . enact the linear order in which Ehrlich's thoughts are developing over time" (80). Heilker's own use of the present tense ("are developing") is confusing, since presumably Ehrlich wrote her essay after the time period it recalls. Her use of the present tense is clearly an artistic device. The thoughts she had while actually writing about her search may have differed significantly from those she had during it. Indeed, perhaps her essay incorporates sheer invention at least as much as reportage. Moreover, Heilker's word *unsorted* suggests a more chaotic text than Ehrlich has produced. Shuttling back and forth between narrative detail and philosophical comment, she puts her alleged experience into a definite framework.

In fact, I always like to begin my Modern Women Essayists course with Ehrlich's piece because it exemplifies some of the ways essays are typically crafted. I inform students that many essayists get autobiographical and that often they recall journeys entailing intellectual as well as physical shifts. In addition, I point out that many essayists resemble Ehrlich in mixing personal anecdotes with philosophical statements, so that their texts, like hers, seem at first glance to wander. Actually, Heilker's book is useful as a guide to these and other conventions that essayists follow. Yet, like many commentators on the genre, he does not pause at length to consider how the existence of such conventions undercuts the belief—or the hope—that essays can offer barely mediated glimpses of their authors' real psyches. Of course, conventionality is not tantamount to deceit. If essayists have codes and formulas for rendering experience, they are not necessarily engaged in falsifying experience. But neither are they presenting it directly. Rather, they are simulating it, and the signifying practices to which they resort in doing so merit sustained analysis.

Contexts

By identifying the essay with processes of the individual writer, its advocates also have tended to neglect the *social* processes through which essays are generated, circulated, and read. *These* processes, I would argue, deserve much more attention than they currently receive in most classes and textbooks devoted to the genre, even at a time when social constructionism is supposedly all the rage. Noting that recent homages to the personal essay more or less assume that it furthers the cause of democracy, Joel Haefner wisely calls for greater caution. Among other things, he recommends that students be asked "to reconstruct the cultural context in which personal essays are written" (133). In the same spirit, I suggest that they also be encouraged to analyze contexts of circulation and reception, tracing the "journeys" that essays take once they are produced.

Louise Smith offers a good model for this work in discussing how she teaches Alice Walker's much-anthologized essay "In Search of Our

Mothers' Gardens." Originally, the essay was Walker's keynote address at the 1973 Radcliffe symposium The Black Woman: Images and Realities. Subsequently, she published it in the May 1974 issue of *Ms.* magazine. Smith has her classes examine the changing rhetorical circumstances that Walker faced. The first time round, Walker was giving a speech to a group of elite black women; next, she was putting it into print for a broader audience. Interestingly, the *Ms.* version ends with three new paragraphs. In considering Walker's essay, Smith's students ponder its change of forum, its shift from orality to print, the different audiences that thereby encountered it, and Walker's revision of her text.

Unfortunately, I find few indications that Smith's way of teaching essays is being widely adopted. Hence, I want to affirm and build on it here. Specifically, I will point out what students can learn from examining the shifting contexts of another much-anthologized essay by Walker, "Beauty: When the Other Dancer Is the Self."

The key event in the essay occurred when Walker was eight. Her right eye was blinded and disfigured when one of her brothers fired his BB gun at her. Prior to then, Walker recalls, she was perceived as "the *cutest* thing" (386), whereas afterward her appearance made her ashamed and withdrawn. To a large extent, the essay's structure is chronological. It begins by depicting her as a two-and-a-half-year- old complacent about her beauty, details the shooting incident, describes her subsequent years of misery, refers to an operation that considerably improved her appearance, and chronicles her increasing ability to accept herself once more. At certain points, however, Walker departs from strict chronology. Four times, for example, she reports her mother and sister's belief that the shooting did not change her. Also, when noting her eventual success in high school, she mentions what eventually happened to one of her classmates: "Ironically the girl who was voted most beautiful in our class (and was) was later shot twice in the chest by a male companion, using a 'real' gun, while she was pregnant. But that's another story in itself. Or is it?" (390). Furthermore, in discussing her recent unease over being photographed for a magazine cover, she looks back at three events. The first is a conversation with one of her brothers about the day she was shot. Next is her first visit to a desert, when she became aware of the beauty possible in this kind of landscape. Finally, Walker recalls the moment when her daughter indicated that she was not troubled by Walker's blind eye. Specifically, her daughter exclaimed "Mommy, there's a *world* in your eye" (393). This comment, Walker reports, moved Walker to look at herself in a mirror and acknowledge that she, too, had learned to accept herself. The essay ends with an echo of this mirror scene: in a dream, Walker joyfully realizes that the person she is dancing with is herself.

Given Walker's tampering with chronology, a reader may experience her essay as rather discontinuous. Reinforcing this impression is her division of her text into several discrete units. Acknowledging this feature, Carl Klaus sees "Beauty" as a typical "disjunctive" essay, which he defines as a kind that

> often seems to be occasioned, at least in part, by an impulse to evoke a sense of the rich array (one might even say, the disarray) of images, observations, recollections, and reflections that may have come to mind during the process of exploring or thinking about a particular subject, experience, or aspect of existence. (46)

Of course, Klaus himself is a typical commentator on the essay in his invocation of "process." But he is right to suggest that Walker gives the appearance of ever-so-gradually working things out right on the page. If anything, this image is strengthened by her almost constant use of the present tense, even when she is recalling the past.

My students always love Walker's essay. They are gripped by her story of mutilation, and they enjoy thinking about the issues it raises, especially the issue of how beauty ultimately should be defined. Whenever my classes discuss this text, various students go so far as to proclaim their identification with Walker. The most spectacular of these testimonies occurred on the day that a woman student said she recently had been shot, and a man sitting near her confessed that he had once shot his brother. More commonly, women students identify with Walker as a victim of male violence and of society's notion of how women should look. Even most of my male students empathize with her, although some get uncomfortable when she appears to criticize men who like guns. In general, my classes find that Walker's essay has mimetic power.

Hence, Walker's mirror scene is quite appropriate. My students perceive her essay itself as a mirror and recognize themselves in it. Her daughter's observation that "there's a world in your eye" has a related resonance. I think many essayists hope that even if they are writing about their own lives, their readers will feel moved to say what her daughter said. At any rate, my students feel that Walker manages to

capture their world; they sense themselves to be part of her "eye"/
"I".

Furthermore, Walker's text inspires them as they proceed to write
their own essays. Many of them describe their own physical ordeals,
their own encounters with male violence, their own conflicts with
society's aesthetic standards. Quite a few of them try for the first time
to recount past events using present tense. And the result, I am de-
lighted to report, is some of the most powerful student writing I have
ever read. In short, I am glad to teach Walker's piece.

Yet, I worry that my students too readily accept this essay as a mirror of their own lives. After all, the other dancer is never completely
the self, as one can tell even from the essay's content. This is hardly a
text that suggests everyone is in the same situation. Besides mention-
ing gender differences, it alludes to racial differences. Walker recalls
that her father's employer, a "rich old white lady" (384), expected her
mother's services, too, and for a mere pittance. Near the end of the
essay, she quotes her brother Jimmy's account of how race mattered
on the day of her shooting: "A white man stopped, but when Daddy
said he needed somebody to take his little girl to the doctor, he drove
off" (391). The text's explicit references aside, Walker surely wants
readers to bear in mind that concepts of beauty have been racially
biased. Until recently, Miss America was also Miss Caucasian.

It is partly because I would like to have students think about
differences as well as mirrorings that nowadays I introduce them to
the various incarnations through which Walker's essay has gone, the
different turns it has taken. As I said before, another motive for such
inquiry is the importance of pondering social processes rather than
focusing solely on textual images of the writer's processes. In the case
of Walker's essay, I would add that its history is worth studying because we can thereby track key ideas and debates in the history of feminism.

"Beauty" first appeared in the May 1983 issue of *Ms.* magazine.
Many of today's students have read or scanned copies of *Ms.*, and others at least know about it. But for various reasons, plenty of students
remain unacquainted with it. Moreover, everyone can stand to be reminded of just how important *Ms.* was in the seventies and eighties,
both as a conduit for feminism and as an image of the movement. There
are various ways of alerting students to this history. Among other
things, I show my classes the illustration that accompanied an article

I published in the April 1982 issue of *Change: The Magazine for Higher Education.* The special topic for that issue of *Change* was women's studies, and my own article concerned my experiences teaching as a man in such a woman-oriented field. The illustration showed a man sitting at his desk reading a copy of *Ms.* Obviously, the artist's goal was to depict economically my interest in feminism, and at the time, *Ms.* could serve as a metonym for that.

In the May 1983 *Ms.*, Walker's piece was one of several devoted to the topic "The Beauty of Health." Evidently, the wording of the topic was an attempt to revise conventional notions of beauty and get women thinking about sheer well-being. It implied that up until then, women had been discouraged from linking "beauty" with "health" and from valuing the second word at least as much as the first.

Many people would argue, and rightly so, that "beauty" continues to be privileged over "health," despite protests by Walker and later social critics such as Naomi Wolf. Indeed, if various commercial enterprises now invoke health, often they do so because they see it is a device for marketing beauty. To be sure, some ads still promote beauty products and services with icons of anorexia like Kate Moss. But many others out to commodify beauty now resort to a different strategy. As my women students will attest, these ads lure them by celebrating the image of the "healthy," "fit," or even "buffed" woman. If Kate Moss has not made an exercise video Cindy Crawford has. Articles in women's magazines often project the same ethos. Analyzing one such magazine, *Shape,* Ruth Conniff points out that its "articles on diets, relationships, and thin thighs" amount to a "fitness hype" that "blends right into the rest of the fashion and beauty market" by "exalting physically 'perfect' anatomical features over every other human attribute, quirk, and endeavor." "Page after page," she observes, "features anonymous bottoms, bellies, and breasts—nary a whole woman to be seen" (549). In other words, connecting "beauty" with "health" can result in a publication akin to *Playboy.*

Needless to say, the two concepts can be linked in more feminist ways. Clearly *Ms.*'s editors hoped so in 1983, when they published their issue "The Beauty of Health." But students should be encouraged to identify ways in which the issue's contents may be at odds with its goal. Consider the issue's ads. Nowadays, thanks primarily to increased foundation support, *Ms.* is able to do without ads entirely. In its first several years, though, it depended on them, and often they contradicted the political messages of the magazine's articles.

In the May 1983 issue, grim irony looms as Walker's essay is interrupted by a full-page ad for soap. Lying directly opposite the page on which she recalls her shooting and her subsequent "hideous cataract" (387, *Ms.* 72), the soap ad proclaims that "Neutrogena is going to clean your face. And clean it perfectly. . . . There's nothing in Neutrogena that could cloud the bar and your complexion. There's nothing in Neutrogena that can linger on your skin after you rinse and cause your face to feel dry and uncomfortable" (*Ms.* 73). Indeed, as if it were deliberately defying the spirit of Walker's essay, the entire issue is packed with ads affirming the pursuit of conventional beauty. The products include Clairol's Ultra Blonde hair coloring, Revlon's European Collagen Complex, Maybelline Cover Stick, Maybelline "Expert Eyes" Eye Shadow, Maybelline Moisture Whip Make-Up (modeled by Lynda "Wonder Woman" Carter), Herbitol Weight Loss System, Clinique Skin Texture Lotion, Dexatrim weight loss pills, Max Factor Le Jardin (with a picture of the ever-lovely Jane Seymour), Pond's Essential Cleaning Lotion and Makeup Remover, and the Schick Personal Touch razor ("Get silky smooth, show-off legs"). Furthermore, conventional images of white female beauty are prominently featured in the issue's abundant ads for cigarettes, panty hose, deodorants, and liquor.

Seeing these signs of orthodoxy, present-day readers may feel morally superior to the *Ms.* staff of the early eighties. In particular, feminists may feel that they have come a long way since. Even back then, however, *Ms.* played a key role in making the women's movement popular. Besides, many of us would hesitate to acknowledge what our own degree of feminist consciousness was or would have been back then. Furthermore, many of us have yet to abandon all cosmetic aids, no matter how much their manufacturers and advertisers promote gender stereotypes. Also worth noting is that probably most of *Ms.*'s staff back then barely tolerated the magazine's ads, seeing them as at best a necessary evil. Therefore, when my classes study the ads that surrounded Walker's essay on its first appearance, I discourage whiggishness. Rather than have them simply condemn the eighties *Ms.* or, for that matter, simply revere it, I have them focus on identifying the complex forces shaping this forum for Walker's work.

Relevant to the ads is a remark that Walker quotes near the end of her essay. It is a statement from the "gorgeous woman and famous journalist" who came to interview her for a magazine story. Walker reports her as saying, "Decide how you want to look on the cover. . . . Glamorous, or whatever" (390, *Ms.* 142). At this point in the *Ms.* version of Walker's essay, an asterisk directs readers to the following footnote: "See 'Do You Know This Woman? She Knows You—A Profile of Alice Walker,' by Gloria Steinem, June, 1982" (*Ms.* 142). I will return to the footnote in a moment. Right now, I simply want to point out that both in the June 1982 and May 1983 issues of *Ms.* ads repeatedly promote a conventional notion of female "glamour." However, through her use of the word "whatever," *Ms.* editor Steinem raised the possibility of finding other notions of "beauty" more in keeping with feminist ideals.

Of course, by not being more specific, Steinem intimated that such notions remained as yet a vague hope. Thus, her "whatever" is an example of catachresis, the rhetorical figure used to name the unnameable. As a subject of theoretical discussion, catachresis had a comeback in the seventies and eighties. Deconstructionists such as Paul de Man often employed the term as they traced what they took to be the fundamental indeterminacy of language. Yet this kind of work threatened to make catachresis merely a term for linguistic conundrums. In analyzing the various contexts of Walker's essay, students might find it more useful as a term for social and political difficulties, including Steinem's effort to imagine more feminist concepts of "beauty."

Back to the footnote, which is hardly as conspicuous as the ads but just as provocative. As far as I can tell, this footnote appears only in the *Ms.* version of Walker's piece. When Walker subsequently made the essay the concluding one of her 1983 book *In Search of Our Mothers' Gardens,* the footnote vanished. Nor have I found it in any of the many composition anthologies that went on to include "Beauty." Remember that students are most likely to encounter Walker's essay in just such a volume, with very few students now getting the chance to see it as it appeared in *Ms.* Thus, usually students leave the essay wondering exactly what woman, magazine, and cover story Walker had in mind.

The initial inclusion and later deletion of the footnote raise interesting issues. My students enjoy debating, for example, whether it should really be considered part of Walker's *Ms.* text. Given that she went on to drop the footnote, probably the editors of *Ms.* inserted it in the first place, with Walker never thinking of it as her own. Often my students agree that this was likely the case. Nevertheless, they must then decide whether and how authorial intent is important. Should Walker's own thinking matter a lot as they try to distinguish her "real" text from mere supplements to it? Many students argue that even if the footnote is deemed integral to the original essay, the noteless version of "Beauty" in Walker's book should be seen as her definitive text since it is the most recent. Yet not every student wants to establish the identity of a text purely on the basis of its latest form. Some like to invoke aesthetic criteria, asking whether dropping the footnote makes Walker's essay more effective. Is the footnote genuinely informative, or does it just provide fodder for gossip? Is its specificity engaging, or do its details make Walker's reference to the "gorgeous woman and famous journalist" less thought-provoking? Naturally, a student could take all kinds of positions on these issues. Here I simply want to emphasize that the issues are worth considering and that at present the English curriculum rarely encourages students to grapple with them. This is true even when the text being taught is not an essay but a work of fiction, poetry, or drama.

On the one hand, in the *Ms.* version of her essay, Walker could have precluded any need for the footnote by providing right up front the information it contains. Moreover, including its details in the body of her text would hardly have seemed odd. To specify *Ms.* when Walker's essay is appearing in the magazine at that very moment; to name Gloria Steinem when she is the magazine's editor; to give bibliographical data for a cover story that exalted Walker—these moves would probably have come across as logical even if rhetorically debatable. By omitting such information from her main text, Walker in effect distances herself from *Ms.* and Steinem. In doing so, she is actually being consistent. After all, as she tells of the journalist's visit, Walker indicates that she was intimidated by the journalist's glamour and leery of being photographed for the magazine's cover. Therefore, with her account of the visit as well as with her omission of names, Walker emphasizes difference.

On the other hand, the footnote can be said to emphasize commonalities, by keeping Walker within the *Ms.* family. Besides functioning as an advertisement for the magazine, it reminds us of Walker's previous associations with *Ms.* and Steinem. Similarly, in her June 1982 article on Walker, Steinem is cozily familiar: over and over, she refers to Walker as "Alice." If, as seems likely, the footnote was *Ms.*'s device rather than Walker's, the attempt to sustain an air of bonding is especially interesting. At any rate, whereas earlier I proposed having students examine how they differ from Walker, here I encourage having them consider how the footnote may obscure differences between Walker and the *Ms.* staff.

Steinem's article on Walker in June 1982 is worth sustained attention, even if a class is ultimately more concerned with *Ms.*'s publication of "Beauty" in May 1983. Take, for example, Steinem's brief account of Walker's childhood injury and its aftermath. Whereas "Beauty" is primarily about Walker's injury and gives Steinem only a small role, Steinem's article is primarily about Walker's entire career and gives the injury only a small role. In fact, Steinem's reference to Walker's suffering is moderately informative. Though only three paragraphs long, it packs in a lot, with the aid of direct quotations from Walker herself. Still, the "Beauty" essay is a much more substantial history.

The differences are most apparent in the two pieces' allusions to Walker's eventual success in high school. Steinem reports Walker saying, "I was Valedictorian, voted 'Most Popular,' and crowned Queen!" Commenting on the tone of this testimony, Steinem adds that Walker "is laughing at herself, but much of the pain of those earlier years is still there" ("Do You" 92). In "Beauty," however, Walker gives no sign that she is laughing as she recounts her high school career. Also, she proceeds to tell about the more attractive classmate who was shot later on by a man. *This* story casts a shadow of irony over Walker's own triumphs. In part, it reminds us that other women, even conventionally beautiful ones, still suffer from male violence.

Steinem should not necessarily be criticized for her different version of Walker's high school years. For one thing, Walker may have told her only so much. Besides, throughout her article Steinem's attitude toward Walker is downright worshipful. Reverence is evident in its very title, "Do You Know This Woman? She Knows You." Indeed, when I see Walker staring out at me from the cover—almost as if she were looking into a mirror—and I am then told that she knows me, I sense that once again what is being suggested is that Walker reproduces our own selves as she confronts hers. "Mommy, there's a *world* in your eye."

I think it is important for students to realize that the early eighties was a time when the feminist movement was beginning to reel from charges that it was overwhelmingly white and middle class. Exactly one year before *Ms.*'s cover story on Walker, the National Women's Studies Association tried to address such charges by devoting its annual conference entirely to the subject of racism. (Audre Lorde's now-classic essay "The Uses of Anger: Women Responding to Racism" was one of the keynote speeches.) By celebrating Walker and regularly publishing her writing, *Ms.* was working in tandem with a larger effort to expand feminism's concerns and broaden its base.

Today, plenty of people argue that feminism is still far from this goal. Meanwhile, others hold that it has made ample progress, becoming notably more sensitive to issues of race. In any case, even diehard fans of Walker might be troubled by *Ms.*'s 1982 claim that she "knows you." For that matter, they also might be troubled when readers of "Beauty" feel moved to say the same thing. Clearly, *Ms.* was trying to acknowledge differences, especially racial ones, by publicizing Walker. But the magazine actually curtailed exploration of differences when it stressed Walker's ability to leap over them and know everyone.

As I noted, Walker's essay subsequently appeared as the conclusion to her 1983 collection of essays entitled *In Search of Our Mothers' Gardens: Womanist Prose*. The opening dedication of the book directly connects to "Beauty":

> *To My Daughter Rebecca*
>
> Who saw in me
> what I considered
> a scar
> And redefined it
> as
> A world.

Next, Walker defines the term *womanist*, giving it four meanings. A class would benefit from examining all four, but here I will concentrate on the first two. In the first definition, Walker points out that a womanist is a "black feminist or feminist of color" and that the term is derived from *womanish*. The latter, she explains, is a "black folk expression of mothers to female children. . . . Usually referring to outrageous, audacious, courageous, or willful behavior" (xi). Although Walker indicates that *womanish* has often functioned as an insult, she herself puts a positive spin on the word, and she does so as well with *womanist*. This reversal of value is echoed in "Beauty," where she ultimately seems to find aesthetic merit in her damaged eye and soul. Furthermore, Walker's first definition of *womanist* implies that "Beauty" and the other essays are to be seen as grounded specifically in Black feminism as distinguished from feminism in general.

However, this emphasis on difference is in tension with the second definition. There, soon after explaining that a womanist is "[a] woman who loves other women, sexually and/or nonsexually," Walker also points out that such a person "[s]ometimes loves individual men, sexually and/or nonsexually"; stands "[c]ommitted to survival and wholeness of entire people, male and female"; is "[n]ot a separatist, except periodically, for health"; and is "[t]raditionally universalist" as well as "[t]raditionally capable" (xi). Much of the second definition, that is, implies that "Beauty" and the other essays should be seen as calls for uniting feminists of all colors. The emphasis seems to be on wide commonality among women, rather than racial distinctions among them.

Yet before she is through with this second definition of *womanist*, Walker engages in a more complicated interplay of difference and commonality. It emerges as she elaborates the phrases *traditionally universalist* and *traditionally capable*. Her example of a traditionally universalist sentiment takes the form of a question and answer. The question is "Mama, why are we brown, pink, and yellow, and our cousins are white, beige, and black?" The answer is "Well, you know the colored race is just like a flower garden, with every color flower represented." Similarly, Walker uses two different speakers' remarks to exemplify traditionally universalist. The first speaker says, "Mama, I'm walking to Canada and I'm taking you and a bunch of other slaves with me." The second speaker replies, "It wouldn't be the first time" (xi). With both phrases, the traditions to which Walker refers seem specifically black. At the same time, she returns to the idea of commonality insofar as she emphasizes that "the colored race" includes several colors and generations rather than being a narrow, isolated tribe. Again, a similar complexity can be said to inform "Beauty," making it a most appropriate finale for the book. Besides considering how much it matters that the author and protagonist of "Beauty" is a black woman, students might think about the similarities and differences that the category "black" harbors, a kind of inquiry that the book's opening definitions invite.

The word *our* in the title of the book suggests that even if the essays draw heavily on Walker's personal experience, in doing so they will have implications for the larger collective body of *womanists*, no matter how this group is defined. Nevertheless, Walker is engaging in a provocative move when she makes the very last word of "Beauty," and thus the very last word of the book, the personal pronoun *me*. Specifically, Walker is describing her relation to the other dancer she is dreaming of: "She is beautiful, whole and free. And she is also me" (393). The scene is one of self-acceptance, self-coincidence, and self-integration. Understandably, many a reader has left it feeling that Walker has earned such bliss. More debatable, though, is her implication that by focusing on "me," she has managed to capture the core experiences and concerns of the larger group designated by "our." In fact, what is her relation to other womanists? To other women in general? This is basically the same issue that arose with *Ms.*'s claim that Walker "knows you."

And it is an issue that I hope will remain for students as I have them consider Walker's most recent use of the shooting episode. Up to this point, they will have examined the different packagings of Walker's entire essay. It seems just as important, though, for a class to analyze how essayists recycle parts or elements of their writing. Walker recalls the shooting incident at the beginning of her 1993 documentary film *Warrior Marks*, which she did in collaboration with Pratibha Parmar (who is listed as director). She recalls it, too, at the start of her book based on that film, *Warrior Marks: Female Genital Mutilation and The Sexual Blinding of Women*, also done in collaboration with Parmar. Both the film and the book report on clitoredectomies in Africa and Europe, making extensive use of interviews that Walker did with victims of this procedure. Walker introduces both the book and the film by using the story of her own shooting to identify herself with her subjects. In the book she declares, "It is true that I have been marked forever, like the woman who is robbed of her clitoris," and she adds, "I was eight when I was injured. This is the age at which many 'circumcisions' are done. When I see how the little girls—how small they are!—drag their feet after being wounded, I am reminded of myself. . . . Instead of being helped to make this transition, I was banished, set aside from the family, as is true of genitally mutilated little girls" (18–19). In the film, this testimony is intercut with images of African women, another way of equating Walker's situation with theirs. Later in both the book and the film, Walker tells Parmar that the shooting left her with a sense of "great isolation" and oppression that she finds "mirrored in the rather callous way that little girls are taken to be mutilated" (26).

Once again, the concept of "mirroring" disquiets me. Personally, I think it admirable of Walker to investigate female mutilation and report her research in print as well as on film. I do not mind that she puts herself fairly often in front of the camera; by making herself the star of the film, she undoubtedly increased its chances of being seen. Moreover, her moral condemnation of female mutilation seems entirely justified. Yet her insistence on absolutely identifying herself with the victims of it is troubling. To me, such "mirroring" seems a presumptuous and unnecessary denial of difference. As I have found in class, not everyone agrees with me; still, the issue makes for lively discussion.

With this issue in mind, I am especially struck by a moment late in the film, since it brings up differences otherwise obscured by Walker's autobiographical musings. Recall that "Beauty" ends with a dream in which Walker is dancing with someone and realizes the other person is herself. As I have said, the scene suggests that Walker is in tune with many people besides herself. By contrast, the film of *Warrior Marks* briefly features a scene in which Walker observes a group of African women dancing. Although they are performing a ceremony designed to welcome Walker and her assistant as "sisters," Walker is not shown becoming one with them. Rather, she is merely a laughing, applauding spectator on the margins of their circle. At least in this moment of her life, the other dancer is not herself. She is not even dancing. In short, the scene highlights the cultural distance between Walker and the other women. Whether this emphasis is intentional, and whether it is appropriate, are issues that a class might ponder.

Conclusion

All along, I have been referring to processes. Yet the pedagogy I am recommending is not, I think, the process pedagogy familiar to composition studies, especially to that subdivision of the field centered around the essay. Contrary to many aficionados of the genre, I would ask students to think of such texts as at most representing, rather than re-enacting, their authors' composing processes. Furthermore, I am suggesting that a class on essays attend to social processes involved in their editorial histories. This pedagogy can begin with, and frequently return to, students' own responses to whatever essays they are studying. After all, the class would be yet another context for these texts, part of their ongoing circulation.

Most readers of this book are interested in helping students produce their own essays, as well as other kinds of texts. I have the same goal. Whenever I teach a course on essays, my ultimate aim is to have students add to the corpus they are studying. Some people may fear that students will feel disinclined to do this if their teacher emphasizes what I have been emphasizing here: namely, that essays never mirror the writer's experience and always appear within particular social frameworks. But the news can be energizing rather than discouraging. Once they have recognized the sheer craft of essay writing, my own students have grown more eager to practice it. Moreover, seeing essays travel through different contexts has driven them to identify situations that their own writing might affect. I would add that whether as readers or as writers, all of us would do well to think about the social positions we ourselves occupy. In what ways do we resemble and differ from other dancers, other selves?

Works Cited
Contributors
Index

Works Cited

Altieri, Charles. *Subjective Agency: A Theory of First- Person Expressivity and Its Social Implications*. Oxford: Blackwell, 1994.

Anderson, Gary L., and Patricia Irvine. "Informing Critical Literacy with Ethnography." *Critical Literacy: Politics, Power, and the Postmodern*. Ed. Colin Lankshear and Peter L. McLaren. Albany: State U of New York P, 1993. 81–104.

Anson, Chris M., and L. Lee Forsberg. "Moving Beyond the Academic Community: Transitional Stages in Professional Writing." *Written Communication* 7 (1990): 200–231.

Applebee, Arthur N. *Curriculum as Conversation: Transforming Traditions of Teaching and Learning*. Chicago: U of Chicago P, 1996.

———. "Problems in Process Approaches: Toward a Reconceptualization of Process." *The Teaching of Writing. Eighty-Fifth Yearbook of the National Society for the Study of Education*. Ed. Anthony R. Petrosky and David Bartholomae. Part II. Chicago: National Society for the Study of Education, 1986.

Applebee, Arthur N., et al. *The NAEP 1992 Writing Report Card*. Washington, DC: GPO, 1994.

Aristotle. *The Rhetoric and Poetics of Aristotle*. Trans. Ingram Bywater. New York: Random, 1954.

Ashton-Jones, Evelyn. "Putting Resistance in (Its) Place: A Localized Reading of Classroom Discourse." *Composition Forum* 6 (Winter 1995): 13–21.

Atkins, G. Douglas. *Estranging the Familiar: Toward a Revitalized Critical Writing*. Athens: U of Georgia P, 1992.

Axelrod, Rise B., Charles R. Cooper, and Alison M. Warriner. *The St. Martin's Guide to Writing*. 4th ed. New York: St. Martin's P, 1994.

Baars, Bernard. *The Cognitive Revolution in Psychology*. New York: Guilford, 1986.

Bahri, Deepika. "Coming to Terms with the 'Postcolonial.'" *Between the Lines: South Asians and Postcoloniality*. Ed. D. Bahri and M. Vasudeva. Philadelphia: Temple UP, 1996.

Bakhtin, M. M. "Discourse in the Novel." *The Dialogic Imagination: Four Essays by M. M. Bakhtin*. Ed. Michael Holquist. Trans. Caryl Emerson and Michael Holquist. Austin: U of Texas P, 1981. 259–422.

———. "The Problem of Speech Genres." *Speech Genres and Other Late Essays*. Ed. Caryl Emerson and Michael Holquist. Trans. Vern W. McGee. Austin: U of Texas P, 1986. 60–102.

Bartholomae, David. "Writing with Teachers: A Conversation with Peter Elbow." *College Composition and Communication* 46 (1995): 62–71.

Bawarshi, Anis S. "Beyond Dichotomy: Toward a Theory of Divergence in Composition Studies." *JAC* 17 (1997): 69–82.

Bazerman, Charles. *Constructing Experience*. Carbondale: Southern Illinois UP, 1994.

———. "Influencing and Being Influenced: Local Acts Across Large Distances." *Social Epistemology* 9 (1995): 189–99.

———. "Intertextual Self-Fashioning: Gould and Lewontin's Representation of the

Literature." *Understanding Scientific Prose*. Ed. Jack Selzer. Madison: U of Wisconsin P, 1993. 20–41.

——. *Shaping Written Knowledge: The Genre and Activity of the Experimental Article in Science*. Madison: U of Wisconsin P, 1988.

——. "Systems of Genres and the Enactment of Social Intentions." *Genre and the New Rhetoric*. Ed. Aviva Freedman and Peter Medway. Bristol, PA: Taylor, 1994. 79–101.

Bazerman, Charles, and James Paradis, eds. *Textual Dynamics of the Professions: Historical and Professional Studies of Writing in Professional Communities*. Madison: U of Wisconsin P, 1991.

Belenky, Mary Field, et al. *Women's Ways of Knowing: The Development of Self, Voice, and Mind*. New York: Basic, 1986.

Bell-Metereau, Rebecca. "Breaking Boundaries, Solving Problems, Giving Gifts: Student Empowerment in Small Group Work." *Writing With: New Directions in Collaborative Teaching, Learning, and Research*. Ed. Sally Barr Reagan, Thomas Fox, and David Bleich. Albany: State U of New York P, 1994. 247–64.

Bereiter, Carl. "Implications of Postmodernism for Science, or, Science as Progressive Discourse." *Educational Psychologist* 29 (1994): 3–12.

Berkenkotter, Carol. "The Legacy of Positivism in Empirical Composition Research." *JAC* 9 (1989): 69–82.

——. "Theoretical Issues Surrounding Interdisciplinary Interpenetration." *Social Epistemology* 9 (1995): 175–87.

Berkenkotter, Carol, and Thomas N. Huckin. *Genre Knowledge in Disciplinary Communication: Cognition/Culture/Power*. Hillsdale, NJ: Erlbaum, 1995.

——. "You Are What You Cite: Novelty and Intertextuality in a Biologist's Experimental Article." *Professional Communication: The Social Perspective*. Ed. Nancy R. Blyler and Charlotte Thralls. Newbury Park, CA: Sage. 109–27.

Berkenkotter, Carol, Thomas N. Huckin, and John Ackerman. "Conventions, Conversations, and the Writer: Case Study of a Student in a Rhetoric Ph.D. Program." *Research in the Teaching of English* 22 (1988): 9–44.

——. "Social Context and Socially Constructed Texts: The Initiation of a Graduate Student into a Writing Community." *Textual Dynamics of the Professions: Historical and Contemporary Studies of Writing in Professional Communities*. Ed. Charles Bazerman and James Paradis. Madison: U of Wisconsin P, 1991. 191–215.

Berlin, James A. "Poststructuralism, Cultural Studies, and the Composition Classroom: Postmodern Theory in Practice." *Rhetoric Review* 11 (1992): 16–33.

——. *Rhetorics, Poetics, and Cultures: Refiguring College English Studies*. Urbana, IL: NCTE, 1996.

Bizzell, Patricia. *Academic Discourse and Critical Consciousness*. Pittsburgh: U of Pittsburgh P, 1992.

——. "Beyond Anti-foundationalism to Rhetorical Authority: Problems Defining 'Cultural Literacy.'" *College English* 52 (1990): 661–75.

——. "Marxist Ideas in Composition Studies." *Contending with Words: Composition and Rhetoric in a Postmodern Age*. Ed. Patricia Harkin and John Schilb. New York: MLA, 1991. 52–67.

Bizzell, Patricia, and Bruce Herzberg. *Negotiating Difference*. Boston: Bedford, 1996.

Black, Edwin. *Rhetorical Criticism: A Study in Method*. Madison: U of Wisconsin P, 1965.

Blakeslee, Ann. "Activity, Context, Interaction, and Authority: Learning to Write Scientific Papers in Situ." *Journal of Business and Technical Communication* 11 (1997): 125–69

Bleich, David. "Collaboration and the Pedagogy of Disclosure." *College English* 57.1 (1995): 43–61.

———. "Sexism in Academic Styles of Learning." *JAC* 10 (Fall 1990): 231–47.

Blyler, Nancy Roundy, Margaret Baker Graham, and Charlotte Thralls. "Scholarship, Tenure, and Promotion in Professional Communication." *Academic Advancement in Composition Studies*. Ed. Richard C. Gebhardt and Barbara Genelle Smith Gebhardt. Mahwah, NJ: Erlbaum, 1997. 71–86.

Borgmann, Albert. *Technology and the Character of Contemporary Life: A Philosophical Inquiry*. Chicago: U of Chicago P, 1984.

"Boundary Rhetorics and the Work of Interdisciplinarity." Special issue of *Social Epistemology* 9 (1995): 17–34.

Bowler, P. J. *The Eclipse of Darwinism: Anti-Darwinian Evolution Theories in the Decades Around 1900*. Baltimore: Johns Hopkins UP, 1983.

Britton, James. "Shaping at the Point of Utterance." *Reinventing the Rhetorical Tradition*. Ed. Aviva Freeman and Ian Pringle. Pembroke, ON: The Canadian Council of Teachers of English, 1980. 61–65.

Brody, Miriam. *Manly Writing: Gender, Rhetoric, and the Rise of Composition*. Carbondale: Southern Illinois UP, 1993.

Bruffee, Kenneth. "Collaborative Learning and the 'Conversation of Mankind.'" *College English* 46 (1984): 635–52.

———. *Collaborative Learning: Higher Education, Interdependence, and the Authority of Knowledge*. Baltimore: Johns Hopkins UP, 1993.

———. "The Way Out." *College English* 33 (1972): 457–70.

Burke, Kenneth. *Counter-Statement*. 2nd ed. Los Altos, CA: Hermes, 1953.

———. *A Grammar of Motives*. Berkeley: U of California P, 1969.

———. *A Rhetoric of Motives*. Berkeley: U of California P, 1969.

Burnett, Rebecca, and Helen Rothschild Ewald. *JAC* 14.1 (Winter 1994): 21–51.

Cain, J. A. "Common Programs and Cooperative Solutions: Organizational Activity in Evolutionary Studies, 1936–1947." *Isis* 84 (1993): 1–25.

Cazden, Courtney. *Classroom Discourse: The Language of Teaching and Learning*. Portsmouth, NH: Heineman, 1988.

Ceccarelli, Leah. "A Rhetoric of Interdisciplinary Scientific Discourse: Textual Criticism of Dobzhansky's Genetics and the Origin of Species." *Social Epistemology* 9 (1995): 91–111.

Charney, Davida. "Empiricism Is Not a Four-Letter Word." *College Composition and Communication* 47 (1996): 567–93.

Chernin, Kim. *Reinventing Eve: Modern Woman in Search of Herself*. New York: Harper Perennial, 1987.

Cizek, Gregory. "Crunchy Granola and the Hegemony of Narrative." *Educational Researcher* 24 (1995): 26–28.

Clifford, John. "Burke and the Tradition of Democratic Schooling." *Audits of Meaning*. Ed. L. Smith. Portsmouth, NH: Boynton, 1988. 29–40.

———. "Composing in Stages." *Research in the Teaching of English* 15 (February 1981): 37–53.

———. "The Subject of Discourse." *Contending with Words: Composition and Rhetoric in a Postmodern Age*. Ed. Patricia Harkin and John Schilb. New York: MLA, 1991. 38–51.

Code, Lorraine. *Rhetorical Spaces: Essays on Gendered Locations*. New York: Routledge, 1995.

———. *What Can She Know? Feminist Theory and the Construction of Knowledge*. Ithaca, NY: Cornell UP, 1991.

Conniff, Ruth. "Awesome Women in Sports." *Constellations: A Contextual Reader for Writers*. Ed. John Schilb, Elizabeth Flynn, and John Clifford. 2nd ed. New York: Harper Collins, 1992. 548–53.

Connors, Robert J. "The Abolition Debate in Composition: A Short History." *Composition in the Twenty-First Century: Crisis and Change*. Ed. Lynn Z. Bloom, Donald A. Daiker, and Edward M. White. Carbondale: Southern Illinois UP, 1996. 47–63.

———. "Personal Writing Assignments." *College Composition and Communication* 38 (1987): 166–83.

Cooper, Marilyn, and Michael Holzman. "Talking about Protocols." *College Composition and Communication* 34.3 (1984): 284–92.

Corbett, Edward P. J. *Classical Rhetoric for the Modern Student*. New York: Oxford, 1992.

Covino, William A. *The Art of Wondering: A Revisionist Return to the History of Rhetoric*. Portsmouth, NH: Boynton, 1988.

———. "Defining Advanced Composition: Contributions from the History of Rhetoric." *JAC* 8 (1988): 113–22.

———. *Forms of Wondering: A Dialogue on Writing, for Writers*. Portsmouth, NH: Boynton, 1990.

Crowley, Sharon. "Around 1971: Current-Traditional Rhetoric and Process Models of Composing." *Composition in the Twenty-First Century: Crisis and Change*. Ed. Lynn Z. Bloom, Donald A. Daiker, and Edward M. White. Carbondale: Southern Illinois UP, 1996. 64–74.

———. *The Methodical Memory: Invention in Current-Traditional Rhetoric*. Carbondale: Southern Illinois UP, 1990.

Danziger, Kurt. *Constructing the Subject: Historical Origins of Psychological Research*. Cambridge: Cambridge UP, 1990.

Dasenbrock, Reed Way. "Do We Write the Text We Read?" *College English* 53 (1991): 7–18.

Davidson, Donald. "A Nice Derangement of Epitaphs." *Truth and Interpretation: Perspectives on the Philosophy of Donald Davidson*. Ed. Ernest Le Pore. New York: Blackwell, 1986. 433–46.

———. "On the Very Idea of a Conceptual Scheme." *Inquiries into Truth and Interpretation*. Oxford: Clarendon, 1986. 183–98.

Davis, Kevin. "The Phenomenology of Research: The Construction of Meaning in Composition Research." *JAC* 15.1 (1995): 121–29.

Dawkins, Richard. *Climbing Mount Improbable.* New York: Norton, 1996.

Debs, Mary Beth. "Reflexive and Reflective Tensions: Considering Research Methods from Writing-Related Fields." *Writing in the Workplace: New Research Perspectives.* Ed. Rachel Spilka. Carbondale: Southern Illinois UP, 1993. 238–52.

Deetz, Stanley A., and Astrid Kersten. "Critical Models of Interpretive Research." *Communication and Organizations: An Interpretive Approach.* Ed. Linda L. Putnam and Michael E. Pacanowsky. Beverly Hills: Sage, 1983. 147–71.

DeJoy, Nancy. "Critical Discursive Practices and Literate Subjectivities: Redefining the Terms of Composition Studies Through the Work of James A. Berlin." *Mediations* 18.2: 37–52.

Devitt, Amy J. "Generalizing about Genre: New Conceptions of an Old Concept." *College Composition and Communication* 44 (1993): 573–86.

———. "Genre, Genres, and the Teaching of Genre." *College Composition and Communication* 47 (1996): 605–15.

———. "Intertextuality in Tax Accounting: Generic, Referential, and Functional. *Textual Dynamics of the Professions.* Ed. Charles Bazerman and James Paradis. Madison: U of Wisconsin P, 1991. 336–57.

Dewey, John. *School and Society. John Dewey: The Middle Works, 1899–1924.* Ed. Jo Ann Boydston. 15 vols. Carbondale: Southern Illinois UP, 1976–83.

Dias, Patrick X., and Anthony Paré. *Transitions: Writing in Academic and Workplace Settings.* Cresskill, NJ: Hampton, forthcoming.

Dias, Patrick X., et al. *Writing in Academic and Workplace Contexts: Affordances and Constraints.* Mahwah, NJ: Erlbaum, 1999.

Didion, Joan. "On Keeping a Notebook." *Slouching Towards Bethlehem.* New York: Noonday, 1990. 131–41.

Dobrin, Sidney I. *Constructing Knowledges: The Politics of Theory Building and Pedagogy in Composition.* New York: State U of New York P, 1997.

———. "The Politics of Theory-Building and Anti- Intellectualism in Composition." *Composition Forum* 6 (1995): 90–99.

Dobzhansky, Theodosius. *Genetics and the Origin of Species.* 3rd ed. New York: Columbia UP, 1951.

Doheny-Farina, Stephen. "Research as Rhetoric: Confronting the Methodological and Ethical Problems of Research on Writing in Nonacademic Settings." *Writing in the Workplace: New Research Perspectives.* Ed. Rachel Spilka. Carbondale: Southern Illinois UP, 1993. 253–67.

Donahue, Christiane. "L'Expression Ecrite des Etudiants de Premier Grade Universitaire: Essai d'une Methodologie Linguistique Comparative." Diss. Université de Paris V, 1997.

———. "The Lycée to University Transition in French Education: Forming Writers in an Exam-Driven System." In *Writing and Learning in Cross-National Perspective: Transitions from Secondary to Higher Education.* Ed. David Foster and David R. Russell. Urbana, IL: NCTE, forthcoming 2000.

Dunn, Patricia A. *Learning Re-Abled: The Learning Disability Controversy and Composition Studies.* Portsmouth, NH: Boynton, 1995.

Dyson, Anne Haas. "A Sociocultural Perspective on Symbolic Development in Primary Grade Classrooms." *New Directions for Child Development* 61 (1993): 25–39.

Edelman, Gerald. *Bright Air, Brilliant Fire: On the Matter of the Mind.* New York: Basic, 1992.

Ehrlich, Gretel. "Looking for a Lost Dog." *Islands, the Universe, Home.* New York: Viking, 1991. 3–7.

Elbow, Peter. *Embracing Contraries: Explorations in Learning and Teaching.* New York: Oxford UP, 1986.

———. *Writing Without Teachers.* New York: Oxford UP, 1973.

———. *Writing with Power: Techniques for Mastering the Writing Process.* New York: Oxford UP, 1981.

———. "The Uses of Binary Thinking: Exploring Seven Productive Oppositions." *Taking Stock: The Writing Process Movement in the '90s.* Ed. Lad Tobin and Thomas Newkirk. Portsmouth, NH: Boynton, 1994. 179–202.

Eldredge, Niles. *Macroevolutionary Dynamics: Species, Niches, and Adaptive Peaks.* New York: McGraw, 1989.

———. *Reinventing Darwin: The Great Debate at the High Table of Evolutionary Theory.* New York: Wiley, 1995.

———. *The Unfinished Synthesis: Biological Hierarchies and Modern Evolutionary Thought.* New York: Oxford UP, 1985.

Eldredge, Niles, and Joel Cracroft. *Phylogenetic Patterns and the Evolutionary Process: Method and Theory in Comparative Biology.* New York: Columbia UP, 1980.

Ellsworth, Elizabeth. "Why Doesn't This Feel Empowering? Working Through the Repressive Myths of Critical Pedagogy." *Feminisms and Critical Pedagogy.* Ed. Carmen Luke and Jennifer Gore. New York: Routledge, 1992. 90–119.

Emig, Janet. *The Composing Processes of Twelfth Graders.* Research Report No. 13. Urbana, IL: NCTE, 1971.

Fahnestock, Jeanne. Accommodating Science: The Rhetorical Life of Scientific Facts. *Written Communication* 3 (1986): 275–96.

Faigley, Lester. "Competing Theories of Process: A Critique and a Proposal." *College English* 48 (1986): 527–42.

———. *Fragments of Rationality: Postmodernity and the Subject of Composition.* Pittsburgh: U of Pittsburgh P, 1992.

Fals-Borda, Orlando. "Remaking Knowledge." *Action and Knowledge: Breaking the Monopoly with Participatory Action-Research.* Ed. Orlando Fals-Borda and Muhammad Anisur Rahman. New York: Ablex, 1991. 146–64.

———. "Some Basic Ingredients." *Action and Knowledge: Breaking the Monopoly with Participatory Action- Research.* Ed. Orlando Fals-Borda and Muhammad Anisur Rahman. New York: Ablex, 1991. 3–12.

Fals-Borda, Orlando, and Muhammad Anisur Rahman, eds. *Action and Knowledge: Breaking the Monopoly with Participatory Action-Research.* New York: Ablex, 1991.

Fisher, Walter R. *Human Communication as Narration: Toward a Philosophy of Reason, Value, and Action.* Columbia: U of South Carolina P, 1989.

Fishman, Stephen M., and Lucille Parkinson McCarthy. "Teaching for Student

Change: A Deweyan Alternative to Radical Pedagogy." *College Composition and Communication* 47 (1996): 342–66.

Fitts, Karen. "Practice/Praxis." *Keywords in Composition Studies*. Ed. Paul Heilker and Peter Vandenberg. Portsmouth, NH: Boynton, 1996. 187–91.

Flower, Linda, and John Hayes. "Problem-Solving Strategies and the Writing Process." *College English* 39 (1977): 449–61.

Fogarty, Daniel, S. J. *Roots for a New Rhetoric*. New York: Bureau of Publication, Teachers College Columbia University, 1959.

Foucault, Michel. *The Archaeology of Knowledge*. Trans. A. M. Sheridan Smith. New York: Pantheon, 1972.

France, Alan W. *Composition as a Cultural Practice*. Westport, CN: Bergin, 1994.

Fraser, Nancy. *Unruly Practices: Power, Discourse and Gender in Contemporary Social Theory*. Minneapolis: U of Minnesota P, 1989.

Freedman, Aviva, Christine Adam, and Graham Smart. "Wearing Suits to Class: Simulating Genres and Genres as Simulations. *Written Communication* 11 (1994): 193–226.

Freedman, Aviva, and Peter Medway, ed. *Genre and the New Rhetoric*. Bristol, PA: Taylor, 1994.

Freedman, Sarah Warshauer, and Alex McLeod. *Exchanging Writing, Exchanging Cultures: Lessons in School Reform from the United States and Great Britain*. Cambridge: Harvard UP, 1994.

Freire, Paulo. *Pedagogy of Hope*. Trans. Robert R. Barr. New York: Continuum, 1994.

———. *Pedagogy of the Oppressed*. Trans. Myra Bergman Ramos. Rev. 20th anniversary ed. New York: Continuum, 1995.

Fuller, Steve. *Philosophy, Rhetoric, and the End of Knowledge: The Coming of Science and Technology Studies*. Madison: U of Wisconsin P, 1993.

Gaillet, Lynée Lewis. "An Historical Perspective on Collaborative Learning." *JAC* 14.1 (1994): 93–110.

Gardner, Howard. *The Mind's New Science*. New York: Basic, 1985.

Gass, William. "Emerson and the Essay." *Habitations of the Word*. New York: Simon, 1985. 9–49.

Gaventa, John. "Toward a Knowledge Democracy: Viewpoints on Participatory Research in America." *Action and Knowledge: Breaking the Monopoly with Participatory Action-Research*. Ed. Orlando Fals-Borda and Muhammad Anisur Rahman. New York: Ablex, 1991. 121–31.

Geertz, Clifford. *Works and Lives: The Anthropologist as Author*. Stanford: Stanford UP 1988.

Geisler, Cheryl. "Toward a Sociocognitive Model of Literacy: Constructing Mental Models in a Philosophical Conversation." *Textual Dynamics of the Professions: Historical and Professional Studies of Writing in Professional Communities*. Ed. Charles Bazerman and James Paradis. Madison: U of Wisconsin P, 1991. 171–90.

Gergen, Kenneth J. "The Mechanical Self and the Rhetoric of Objectivity." *Rethinking Objectivity*. Ed. A. Megill. Durham, NC: Duke UP. (1994): 265–87.

Gergits, Julia M., and James J. Schramer. "The Collaborative Classroom as a Site of Difference." *JAC* 14.1 (Winter 1994): 187–202.

Giroux, Henry A. "Living Dangerously: Identity Politics and the New Cultural Racism." *Between Borders: Pedagogy and the Politics of Cultural Studies*. Ed. Henry A. Giroux and Peter McClaren. New York: Routledge, 1994. 29–55.

Goodburn, Amy, and Beth Ina. Collaboration, Critical Pedagogy, and Struggles over Difference." *JAC* 14.1 (Winter 1994): 131–48.

Goodlad, John I. *A Place Called School: Prospects for the Future*. New York: McGraw, 1984.

Gore, Jennifer M. *The Struggle for Pedagogies: Critical and Feminist Discourses as Regimes of Truth*. New York: Routledge, 1993.

Gould, Stephen Jay. "G. G. Simpson, Paleontology, and the Modern Synthesis." *The Evolutionary Synthesis: Perspectives on the Unification of Biology*. Ed. Ernst Mayr and William Provine. Cambridge: Harvard UP, 1980. 153–72.

———. "The Hardening of the Modern Synthesis." *Dimensions of Darwinism*. Ed. Marjorie Grene. Cambridge: Cambridge UP, 1983. 71–83.

Green, Judith L., and Carol N. Dixon. "Talking Knowledge into Being: Discursive and Social Practices in Classrooms." *Linguistics and Education* 5 (1993): 231–39.

Gregory, Marshall. "The Many-Headed Hydra of Theory vs. the Unifying Mission of Teaching." *College English* 59 (1997): 41–58.

Griesemer, James R., and William C. Wimsatt. "Picturing Weismannism: A Case Study in Conceptual Evolution." *What the Philosophy of Biology Is: Essays Dedicated to David Hull*. Ed. Michael Ruse. Boston: Kluwer, 1989. 75–137.

Grossberg, Lawrence. "Critical Theory and the Politics of Empirical Research." *Mass Communication Review Yearbook* 6. Ed. Michael Gurevitch and Mark R. Levy. Newbury Park, CA: Sage, 1987. 86–106.

———. "Introduction: Bringin' It All Back Home—Pedagogy and Cultural Studies." *Between Borders: Pedagogy and the Politics of Cultural Studies*. Ed. Henry A. Giroux and Peter McClaren. New York: Routledge, 1994. 1–25.

Haas, Christina. "Learning to Read Biology: One Student's Rhetorical Development in College." *Written Communication* 11 (1994): 43–84.

———. *Writing Technology: Studies on the Materiality of Literacy*. Mahwah, NJ: Erlbaum, 1996.

Haefner, Joel. "Democracy, Pedagogy, and the Personal Essay." *College English* 54 (1992): 127–37.

Hairston, Maxine. "Breaking Our Bonds and Reaffirming Our Connections." *College Composition and Communication* 33 (1982): 76–88.

Hallin, Annika. "A Rhetoric for Audiences: Louise Rosenblatt on Reading and Action." *The St. Martin's Handbook*. Ed. Andrea Lunsford and Robert Connors. 2nd ed. New York: St. Martin's, 1992. 285–304.

Halloran, S. Michael, and Annette Norris Bradford. "Figures of Speech in the Rhetoric of Science and Technology." *Classical Rhetoric and Modern Discourse*. Ed. Robert J. Connors, Lisa Ede, and Andrea Lunsford. Carbondale: Southern Illinois UP, 1984. 179–92, 284–86.

Haraway, Donna J. *Simians, Cyborgs, and Women: The Reinvention of Nature*. New York: Routledge, 1991.

———. "Writing, Literacy and Technology: Toward a Cyborg Writing." Interview with Gary A. Olson. *Women Writing Culture.* Ed. Gary A. Olson and Elizabeth Hirsh. Albany: State U of New York P, in press. 45–77.

Harding, Sandra. "Starting from Marginalized Lives: A Conversation with Sandra Harding." Interview with Elizabeth Hirsh and Gary A. Olson. *JAC* 15 (1995): 193–225.

Hardison, O. B., Jr. "Binding Proteus: An Essay on the Essay." *Essayists on the Essay: Redefining the Genre.* Athens: U of Georgia P, 1989. 11–28.

Harkin, Patricia, and John Schilb. *Contending with Words: Composition and Rhetoric in a Postmodern Age.* New York: MLA, 1991.

Harris, Joseph. "The Idea of Community in the Study of Writing." *College Composition and Communication* 40 (1988): 11–22.

———. *A Teaching Subject: Composition since 1966.* Upper Saddle River: Prentice, 1997.

Hart, Roderick, and Don Burks. "Rhetorical Sensitivity and Social Interaction." *Speech Monographs* 39 (1972): 75–91.

Hart, Roderick, R. E. Carlson, and W. F. Eadie. "Attitudes Toward Communication and the Assessment of Rhetorical Sensitivity." *Communication Monographs* 47 (1980): 1–22.

Hartman, Joan E., and Ellen Messer-Davidow, eds. *(En)Gendering Knowledge: Feminists in Academe.* Knoxville: U of Tennessee P, 1991.

Harwood, J. "Metaphysical Foundations of the Evolutionary Synthesis: A Historiographical Note." *Journal of the History of Biology* 27 (1994): 1–20.

Hatch, Thomas, and Howard Gardner. "Finding Cognition in the Classroom: An Expanded View of Human Intelligence." *Distributed Cognitions: Psychological and Educational Considerations.* Ed. Gabriel Salomon. Cambridge: Cambridge UP, 1993.

Hawisher, Gail E., Paul LeBlanc, Charles Moran, Cynthia L. Selfe. *Computers and the Teaching of Writing in American Higher Education, 1979–1994: A History.* Norwood, NJ: Ablex, 1996.

Heilker, Paul. *The Essay: Theory and Pedagogy for an Active Form.* Urbana: NCTE, 1996.

———. "Revision Worship and the Computer as Audience." *Computers and Composition* 9 (1992): 59–69.

Herndl, Carl G. "Teaching Discourse and Reproducing Culture: A Critique of Research and Pedagogy in Professional and Non-Academic Writing." *College Composition and Communication* 44 (1993): 349–63.

Hesse, Douglas. "Teachers as Students: Reflecting Resistance." *College Composition and Communication* 44 (1993): 224–31.

Hirsh, Elizabeth, and Gary A. Olson. "Starting from Marginalized Lives: A Conversation with Sandra Harding." *Women Writing Culture.* Ed. Elizabeth Hirsh and Gary A. Olson. New York: State U of New York P, 1995.

hooks, bell. *Killing Rage/Ending Racism.* New York: Holt, 1995.

Hourigan, Maureen M. *Literacy as Social Exchange.* Albany: State U of New York P, 1994.

Howard, Rebecca Moore. *The Bedford Guide to Teaching Writing in the Disciplines: An Instructor's Desk Reference.* Boston: Bedford of St. Martin's, 1995.

Howarth, William. "Itinerant Passages: Recent American Essays." *Sewanee Review* 96 (1988): 633–43.

Hull, Glynda, et al. "Remediation as a Social Construct: Perspectives from an Analysis of Classroom Discourse." *College Composition and Communication* 42 (1991): 399–29.

Huxley, Aldous. "Music at Night." *Collected Essays*. New York: Harper, 1959. 176–80.

Jarratt, Susan. "Feminism and Composition: The Case for Conflict." *Contending with Words: Composition and Rhetoric in a Postmodern Age*. Ed. Patricia Harkin and John Schilb. New York: MLA, 1991. 105–23.

Johnson, Mark. *The Body in the Mind: The Bodily Basis of Meaning, Imagination, and Reason*. Chicago: U of Chicago P, 1987.

Jones, Donald C. "Beyond the Postmodern Impasse of Agency: The Resounding Relevance of John Dewey's Tacit Tradition." *JAC* 16.1 (1996): 81–102.

Journet, Debra. "Boundary Rhetoric and Disciplinary Genres: Re-Drawing the Maps in Interdisciplinary Writing." *Genres of Writing: Mapping the Territories of Discourse*. Ed. Wendy Bishop and Hans Ostrom. Heinemann, forthcoming.

———. "Interdisciplinary Discourse and 'Boundary Rhetoric': The Case of S. E. Jelliffe." *Written Communication* 10 (1993): 510–41.

———. "Synthesizing Disciplinary Narratives: George Gaylord Simpson's Tempo and Mode in Evolution." *Social Epistemology* 9 (1995): 113–50.

Kaufer, David, and Dunmire, Patricia. "Integrating Cultural Reflection and Production in College Writing Curricula." *Reconceiving Writing, Rethinking Writing Instruction*. Ed. J. Petraglia. Mahwah, NJ: Erlbaum, 1995. 217–38.

Keller, Evelyn Fox, and Elisabeth A. Lloyd. Introduction. *Keywords in Evolutionary Biology*. Ed. Evelyn Fox Keller and Elisabeth A. Lloyd. Cambridge: Harvard UP, 1992. 1–6.

Kent, Thomas. "Beyond System: The Rhetoric of Paralogy." *College English* 51 (1989): 492–507.

———. "Externalism and the Production of Discourse." *JAC* 12.1 (Winter 1992): 57–74.

———. "Formalism, Social Construction, and the Problem of Interpretive Authority." *Professional Communication: The Social Perspective*. Ed. Nancy Roundy Blyler and Charlotte Thralls. Newbury Park, CA: Sage. 79–91.

———. "Genre Theory in the Area of Business Writing." *The Technical Writing Teacher* 14 (1987): 232–42.

———. "On the Very Idea of a Discourse Community." *College Composition and Communication* 42 (1991): 425–45.

———. "Paralogic Hermeneutics and the Possibilities of Rhetoric." *Rhetoric Review* 8.1 (Fall 1989): 24–42.

———. *Paralogic Rhetoric: A Theory of Communicative Interaction*. Lewisburg: Bucknell UP, 1993.

Kinneavy, James. *A Theory of Discourse*. New York: Norton, 1971.

Kinneavy, James, John Q. Cope, and J. W. Campbell. *The Basic Aims of Organization*. Dubuque, IA: Kendall, 1976.

Kirkpatrick, Mark. "Genes and Adaptation." *Adaptation*. Ed. Michael R. Rose and George V. Lauder. San Diego: Academics, 1996. 125–46.

Kirsch, Gesa. *Women Writing the Academy: Audience, Authority, and Transformation.* Carbondale: Southern Illinois UP, 1993.

Kirsch, Gesa, and Joy Ritchie. "Beyond the Personal: Theorizing a Politics of Location in Composition Research." *College Composition and Communication* 46.1 (February 1995): 7–29.

Kitzhaber, Albert R. "Death—or Transfiguration?" *College English* 21 (1960): 367–73.

Klamer, Arjo. "Textbook Presentation of Economic Discourse." *Economics Discourse*. Ed. Warren J. Samuels. Boston: Kluwer, 1990 .

Klaus, Carl H. "Excursions of the Mind: Towards a Poetics of Uncertainty in the Disjunctive Essay." *What Do I Know?: Reading, Writing, and Teaching the Essay.* Ed. Janis Forman. Portsmouth, NH: Boynton, 1996. 39–53.

Klein, Julie T. *Interdisciplinarity: History, Theory and Practice*. Detroit: Wayne State UP, 1990.

Klein, Renate Duelli. "How to Do What We Want to Do: Thoughts about Feminist Methodology." *Theories of Women's Studies*. Ed. Gloria Bowles and Renate Duelli Klein. London: Routledge, 1983. 88–104.

Knoblauch, C. H., and Lilian Brannon. *Rhetorical Traditions and the Teaching of Writing*. Upper Montclair, NJ: Boynton, 1984.

Kuriloff, Peshe C. "What Discourses Have in Common: Teaching the Transaction Between Writer and Reader." *College Composition and Communication* 47.4 (1996): 485–501.

Lakoff, George. *Women, Fire, and Dangerous Things: What Categories Reveal about the Mind*. Chicago: U of Chicago P, 1987.

Landau, Misia. *Narratives of Human Evolution*. New Haven: Yale UP, 1991.

Laporte, Leo. "George G. Simpson, Paleontology, and the Expansion of Biology." *The Expansion of American Biology*. Ed. K. R. Benson, J. Maienschein, and R. Rainger. New Brunswick, NJ: Rutgers UP, 1991. 80–106.

———. "Simpson's Tempo and Mode Revisited." *Proceedings of the American Philosophical Society* 127 (1983): 365–417.

Larson, Marion Hogan. "Patterns in Transition: A Writing Teacher's Survey of Organizational Socialization." *Journal of Business and Technical Communication* 10 (1996): 352–68.

Latour, Bruno. *Science in Action: How to Follow Scientists and Engineers Through Society*. Cambridge: Harvard UP, 1987.

Latour, Bruno, and Steve Woolgar. *Laboratory Life: The Social Construction of Scientific Facts*. Beverly Hills: Sage, 1979.

Laudan, Larry. *Beyond Positivism and Relativism: Theory, Method and Evidence*. Boulder, CO: Westview, 1996.

Lentricchia, Frank. *Criticism and Social Change*. Chicago: U of Chicago P, 1983.

Lerner, Gerda. *The Creation of Feminist Consciousness from the Middle Ages to Eighteen-seventy*. New York: Oxford UP, 1993.

Leverenz, Carrie Shively. "Peer Response in the Multicultural Composition Classroom: Dissensus—A Dream (Deferred)." *JAC* 14.1 (Winter 1994): 167–86.

Li, Xiao-Ming. "Good Writing." *Cross-Cultural Context*. Albany: State U of New York P, 1996.

Lincoln, Yvonna S., and Egon G. Guba. *Naturalistic Inquiry*. Newbury Park: Sage, 1985.

Lindemann, Erika. *A Rhetoric for Writing Teachers*. 2nd ed. New York: Oxford UP, 1987.

Lindemann, Erika, and Gary Tate. *An Introduction to Composition Studies*. New York: Oxford UP, 1991.

Loeb, Paul Rogat. *Generation at the Crossroads: Apathy and Action on the American Campus*. New Brunswick, NJ: Rutgers UP, 1994.

Lopate, Phillip. "What Happened to the Personal Essay?" *Against Joie de Vivre: Personal Essays*. New York: Simon, 1989. 75–86.

Lorde, Audre. *Sister Outsider: Essays and Speeches*. Freedom, CA: Crossing, 1984.

Lu, Min-zhan. "Redefining the Legacy of Mina Shaughnessy: A Critique of the *Politics of Linguistic Innocence*." *Journal of Basic Writing* 10 (1991): 26–40.

Lunsford, Andrea, ed. *Reclaiming Rhetorica*. Pittsburgh Series in Composition, Literacy, and Culture. Pittsburgh: U of Pittsburgh P, 1995.

Lunsford, Andrea, and Robert Connors. *The St. Martin's Handbook*. 2nd ed. New York: St. Martin's, 1992.

Lyon, Arabella. "Interdisciplinarity: Giving Up Territory." *College English* 54 (1992): 681–93.

Lyotard, Jean-François. "One Thing at Stake in Women's Struggles." *The Lyotard Reader*. Ed. Andrew Benjamin. Cambridge, MA: Blackwell, 1991. 111–21.

———. *Peregrinations: Law, Form, Event*. New York: Columbia UP, 1988.

———. *The Postmodern Condition: A Report on Knowledge*. Trans. Geoff Bennington and Brian Massumi. Minneapolis: U of Minnesota P, 1984.

———. "Resisting a Discourse of Mastery: A Conversation with Jean-Franáois Lyotard." Interview with Gary A. Olson. *Women Writing Culture*. Ed. Gary A. Olson and Elizabeth Hirsh. Albany: State U of New York P, in press. 169–92.

Macrorie, Ken. "Process, Product, and Quality." *Taking Stock: The Writing Process Movement in the '90s*. Ed. Lad Tobin and Thomas Newkirk. Portsmouth, NH: Boynton, 1994. 69–82.

Marshall, James. "Of What Does Skill in Writing Really Consist? The Political Life of the Writing Process Movement." *Taking Stock: The Writing Process Movement in the '90s*. Ed. Lad Tobin and Thomas Newkirk. Portsmouth, NH: Boynton, 1994. 45–55.

———. "Schooling and the Composing Process." *Contexts for Learning to Write: Studies of Secondary School Instruction*. Ed. Arthur N. Applebee. Norwood, NJ: Ablex, 1984. 103–19.

Mascia-Lees, Frances E., Patricia Sharpe, and Colleen Ballerino Cohen. "The Postmodernist Turn in Anthropology: Cautions from a Feminist Perspective." *Signs* 15.1 (1989): 7–33.

Mayr, Ernst. "Prologue: Some Thoughts on History of the Evolutionary Synthesis." *The Evolutionary Synthesis: Perspectives on the Unification of Biology*. Ed. Ernst Mayr and William Provine. Cambridge: Harvard UP, 1980. 1–48.

McGuire, J. E., and Trevor Melia. "The Rhetoric of the Radical Rhetoric of Science." *Rhetorica* 9 (1991): 301–16.

McLaren, Peter L. "Collision with Otherness: 'Traveling' Theory, Postcolonial Criticism, and the Politics of Ethnographic Practice—The Mission of the Wounded Ethnographer." *Critical Theory and Educational Research*. Ed. Peter L. McLaren and James M. Giarelli. Albany: State U of New York P, 1995. 271–300.

———. "Field Relations and the Discourse of the Other: Collaboration in Our Own Ruin." *Experiencing Fieldwork: An Inside View of Qualitative Research*. Ed. William B. Shaffir and Robert A. Stebbins. Newbury Park, CA: Sage, 1991. 149–63.

McLaren, Peter L., and Colin Lankshear. "Critical Literacy and the Postmodern Turn." *Critical Literacy: Politics, Power, and the Postmodern*. Ed. Colin Lankshear and Peter L. McLaren. Albany: State U of New York P, 1993. 379–419.

McLaren, Peter L., and Peter Leonard. "Editors' Introduction. Absent Discourses: Paulo Freire and the Dangerous Memories of Liberation." *Paulo Freire: A Critical Encounter*. New York: Routledge, 1993. 1–7.

Mehan, Hugh. *Learning Lessons: Social Organization in the Classroom*. Cambridge: Harvard UP, 1979.

Miller, Carolyn R. "Genre as Social Action." *Quarterly Journal of Speech* 70 (1984): 151–67.

———. "Rhetorical Community: The Cultural Basis of Genre." *Genre and the New Rhetoric*. Ed. Aviva Freedman and Peter Medway. Bristol, PA: Taylor. 67–78.

Miller, Susan. "New Discourse City: An Alternative Model for Collaboration." *Writing With: New Directions in Collaborative Teaching, Learning, and Research*. Ed. Sally Barr Reagan, Thomas Fox, and David Bleich. Albany: State U of New York P, 1994. 283–300.

———. "Rhetorical Community: The Cultural Basis of Genre." *Genre and the New Rhetoric*. Ed. Aviva Freedman and Peter Medway. Bristol, PA: Taylor. 67–78.

———. *Textual Carnivals: The Politics of Composition*. Carbondale: Southern Illinois UP, 1991.

Mittlefehldt, Pamela Klass. "'A Weaponry of Choice': Black American Women Writers and the Essay." *The Politics of the Essay: Feminist Perspectives*. Ed. Ruth-Ellen Boetcher Joeres and Elizabeth Mittman. Bloomington: Indiana UP, 1993. 196–208.

Moffett, James. *Coming on Center: English Education in Evolution*. Montclair, NJ: Boynton, 1981.

———. "Coming Out Right." *Taking Stock: The Writing Process Movement in the '90s*. Ed. Lad Tobin and Thomas Newkirk. Portsmouth, NH: Boynton, 1994. 17–30.

———. *Storm in the Mountains: A Case Study of Censorship, Conflict, and Consciousness*. Carbondale: Southern Illinois UP, 1988.

———. *Teaching the Universe of Discourse*. Boston: Houghton, 1968.

Moore, Rob. Personal electronic communication with the author, May 1995–March 1997.

Morgan, Gary, and Linda Smircich. "The Case for Qualitative Research." *Academy of Management Review* 5.4 (1980): 491–500.

Morrison. Toni. *Playing in the Dark: Whiteness and the Literary Imagination*. New York: Vintage, 1992.

Mumby, Dennis K. *Communication and Power in Organizations: Discourse, Ideology, and Domination*. Norwood, NJ: Ablex, 1988.

———. "Critical Organizational Communication Studies: The Next Ten Years." *Communication Monographs* 60 (1993): 18–25.

Muray, Leslie A. *An Introduction to the Process Understanding of Science, Society and the Self: A Philosophy for Modern Humanity*. Lewiston: Mellen P, 1988.

Murphy, Richard. "Anorexia: The Cheating Disorder." *College English* 52 (1990): 898–903.

Myers, Greg. "Stories and Styles in Two Molecular Biology Review Articles." *Textual Dynamics of the Professions: Historical and Professional Studies of Writing in Professional Communities*. Ed. Charles Bazerman and James Paradis. Madison: U of Wisconsin P, 1991. 45–75.

———. "Textbooks and the Sociology of Scientific Knowledge." *English for Specific Purposes* 11 (1992): 3–17.

———. *Writing Biology: Texts in the Social Construction of Scientific Knowledge*. Madison: U of Wisconsin P, 1989.

Nardi, Bonnie. "Some Reflections on the Application of Activity Theory." *Context and Consciousness*. Ed. B. Nardi. Cambridge: MIT P. 1996.

National Council of the Teachers of English. Fall Catalogue, 1996.

NCTE/IRA. *Standards for the English Language Arts*. Urbana, IL: NCTE and International Reading Association, 1996.

Nelson, John S., Allan Megill, and Donald N. McCloskey. *The Rhetoric of the Human Sciences: Language and Argument in Scholarship and Affairs*. Madison: U of Wisconsin P, 1987.

Newkirk, Thomas. "Direction and Misdirection in Peer Response." *College Composition and Communication* 35 (1984): 301–11.

Nystrand, Martin, and Adam Gamoran. "Instructional Discourse, Student Engagement, and Literature Achievement." *Research in the Teaching of English* 25 (1991): 261–90.

Paré, Anthony. "Discourse Regulations and the Production of Knowledge." *Writing in the Workplace: New Research Perspectives*. Ed. Rachel Spilka. Carbondale: Southern Illinois UP, 1993. 111–23.

Pauly, Edward. *The Classroom Crucible: What Really Works, What Doesn't, and Why*. New York: Basic, 1991.

Pechenick, Jan. *A Short Guide to Writing about Biology*. New York: Harper, 1993.

Perl, Sondra. "The Composing Processes of Unskilled College Writers." *Research in the Teaching of English* 13 (1979): 317–36.

———. "Understanding Composing." *College Composition and Communication* 31 (December 1980): 363–69.

Petraglia, Joseph, ed. *Reconceiving Writing, Rethinking Writing Instruction*. Mahwah, NJ: Erlbaum, 1995.

Petrosky, Anthony. "Rural Poverty and Literacy in the Mississippi Delta: Dilemmas, Paradoxes, and Conundrums." *The Right to Literacy*. Ed. Andrea A. Lunsford, Helene Moglen, and Maes Slevin. New York: MLA, 1990. 61–73.

Phillips, Donna Burns, Ruth Greenberg, and Sharon Gibson. "College Composition and Communication: Chronicling a Discipline's Genesis." *College Composition and Communication* 44 (1993): 443–65.

Polan, Dana. "The Spectacle of Intellect in a Media Age: Cultural Representations and the David Abraham, Paul de Man, and Victor Farías Cases." *Intellectuals: Aesthetics, Politics, Academics.* Ed. Bruce Robbins. Minneapolis: U of Minnesota P, 1990. 343–63.

Polanyi, Michael. *Personal Knowledge: Towards a Post-Critical Philosophy.* Chicago: U of Chicago P, 1962.

Prior, Paul. "Response, Revision, Disciplinarity: The Microhistory of a Dissertation Prospectus in Sociology." *Written Communication* 11 (1994): 483–533.

———. *Writing/Disciplinarity: A Sociohistoric Account of Literate Activity in the Academy.* Hillsdale, NJ: Erlbaum, in press.

Provine, William. "The Role of Mathematical Population Geneticists in the Evolutionary Synthesis." *Studies in the History of Biology* 2 (1978): 167–92.

———. *Sewall Wright and Evolutionary Biology.* Chicago: U of Chicago P, 1986.

Putnam, Linda L. "The Interpretive Perspective. An Alternative to Functionalism." *Communication and Organizations: An Interpretive Approach.* Ed. Linda L. Putnam and Michael Pacanowsky. Beverly Hills: Sage, 1983. 31–54.

Rainger, R. "What's the Use: William King Gregory and the Functional Morphology of Fossil Vertebrates." *Journal of the History of Biology* 22 (1989): 103–39.

Ratcliffe, Krista. *Anglo-American Feminist Challenges to the Rhetorical Traditions: Virginia Woolf, Mary Daly, Adrienne Rich.* Carbondale: Southern Illinois UP, 1996.

Reagan, Sally Barr, Thomas Fox, and David Bleich. *Writing With: New Directions in Collaborative Teaching, Learning, and Research.* Albany: State U of New York Press, 1994.

Reason, Peter, and John Rowan, eds. *Human Inquiry: A Sourcebook of New Paradigm Research.* New York: Wiley, 1981.

Reid, Stephen. *The Prentice Hall Guide for College Writers.* 2nd ed. Englewood Cliffs, NJ: Prentice, 1992.

Reither, James A. "Bridging the Gap: Scenic Motives for Collaborative Writing in Workplace and School." *Writing in the Workplace: New Research Perspectives.* Ed. Rachel Spilka. Carbondale: Southern Illinois UP, 1993. 195–206.

Rescher, Nicholas. *Process Metaphysics: An Introduction to Process Philosophy.* Albany: State U of New York P, 1996.

Resnick, Lauren. "Literacy in School and Out." *Daedalus* (Spring 1990): 160–85.

Roberts, R. H., and J. M. N. Good, eds. *The Recovery of Rhetoric: Persuasive Discourse and Disciplinarity in the Human Sciences.* Charlottesville: U of Virginia P, 1993.

Rogers, Carl. *Freedom to Learn.* Columbus, OH: Merrill, 1969.

Rorty, Richard. *Contingency, Irony, and Solidarity.* New York: Cambridge UP, 1989.

———. *Philosophy and the Mirror of Nature.* Princeton: Princeton UP, 1979.

Rose, Hilary. *Love, Power and Knowledge: Towards a Feminist Transformation of the Sciences.* Oxford: Polity, 1994.

Rosenblatt, Louise. *Literature as Exploration.* 4th ed. New York: MLA, 1983.

Russell, D. A. *Greek Declamation.* Cambridge: Cambridge UP, 1983

Russell, David R. "Activity Theory and Its Implications for Writing Instruction."

Reconceiving Writing: Rethinking Writing Instruction. Ed. Joseph Petraglia. Hillsdale, NJ: Erlbaum, 1995. 51–78.

———. "Collaborative Portfolio Assessment in the English Secondary School System." *Clearing House* 68 (March/April 1995): 244–47.

———. "Rethinking Genre in School and Society: An Activity Theory Analysis." *Written Communication* 14 (1997): 504–54.

———. "Vygotsky, Dewey, and Externalism: Beyond the Student/Disciple Dichotomy." *JAC* 13 (1993): 173–97.

Russell, David R., Starr Lewis, and Anella Riggs. "Growing Together: Curricular and Professional Development Through Collaborative Portfolio Assessment." *English Leadership Quarterly* 18 (1996): 13–18.

Rymer, Jone. "Scientific Composing Processes: How Eminent Scientists Write Journal Articles." *Advances in Writing Research.* Vol. 2: Writing in Academic Disciplines. Ed. David Jolliffe. Norwood, NJ: Ablex, 1988. 211–50.

Sack, William, Elliott Soloway, and P. Weingrad. "Activity Theory and Its Implications for Writing Instruction." *Reconceiving Writing, Rethinking Writing Instruction.* Ed. Joseph Petraglia. Mahwah, NJ: Erlbaum, 1995. 51–77.

———. "Re-writing Cartesian Student Models." *Journal of Artificial Intelligence in Education* 3 (4) (1992): 381–402.

Sánchez, Raúl. "Dialogue and Post-Process Theory in Advanced Composition." Conference on College Composition and Communication Convention, San Diego, 3 April 1993.

Schiappa, Edward. "Rhêtorikê: What's in a Name? Toward a Revised History of Early Greek Rhetorical Theory." *Quarterly Journal of Speech* 78 1 (1992): 1–15.

Schilb, John. *Between the Lines: Relating Composition Theory and Literary Theory.* Portsmouth, NH: Boynton, 1996.

———. "Men's Studies and Women's Studies." *Change: The Magazine of Higher Education* 14.3 (April 1982): 38–41.

Searle, John. *Minds, Brains, and Science.* Cambridge: Harvard UP, 1984.

Selzer, Jack, ed. *Understanding Scientific Prose.* Madison: U of Wisconsin P, 1993.

Shaughnessy, Mina. *Errors and Expectations: A Guide for the Teacher of Basic Writing.* New York: Oxford UP, 1977.

Shezi, Goodman Thamsanqa. "An Investigation into the Kinds and Amounts of Writing Tasks Assigned in Some Black South African Secondary and High Schools." Thesis. Department of English, Iowa State University, 1991.

Shor, Ira, ed. *Freire for the Classroom: A Sourcebook for Liberatory Teaching.* Portsmouth, NH: Boynton, 1987.

Simic, Charles. "Reading Philosophy at Night." *The Best American Essays 1988.* Ed. Annie Dillard. New York: Ticknor, 1988. 307–14.

Simons, Herbert W. *The Rhetorical Turn: Invention and Persuasion in the Conduct of Inquiry.* Chicago: U of Chicago P, 1990.

Simpson, George Gaylord. "The Historical Factor in Science." *This View of Life: The World of an Evolutionist.* New York: Harcourt, 1964.

———. *Tempo and Mode in Evolution.* New York: Columbia UP, 1944.

Sirc, Geoffrey. "Never Mind the Tagmemics, Where's the Sex Pistols?" *College Composition and Communication* 48 (1997): 9–29.

Smagorinsky, Peter. "Personal Growth in Social Context: A High School Senior's Search for Meaning in and Through Writing." *Written Communication* 14 (1997): 63–105.

Smart, Graham. "Genre as Community Invention: A Central Bank's Response to Its Executives' Expectations as Readers." *Writing in the Workplace: New Research Perspectives*. Ed. Rachel Spilka. Carbondale: Southern Illinois UP, 1993. 124–40.

Smith, Dorothy E. *The Everyday World as Problematic: A Feminist Sociology*. Boston: Northeastern UP, 1987.

Smith, J., R. Harré, and L. Van Langenhove, eds. *Rethinking Methods in Psychology*. Newbury Park, CA: Sage, 1995.

Smith, Louise Z. "In Search of Our Sisters' Rhetoric: Teaching Through Reception Theory." *Practicing Theory in Introductory College Literature Courses*. Ed. James M. Cahalan and David B. Downing. Urbana, IL: NCTE, 1991. 72–84.

Sommers, Nancy. "Revision Strategies of Student Writers and Experienced Adult Writers." *College Composition and Communication* 31 (1980): 378–88.

Sosnoski, James J., and David B. Downing. "A Multivalent Pedagogy for a Multicultural Time." *PRE/TEXT* 14 (1994): 307–40.

Spellmeyer, Kurt. "After Theory: From Textuality to Attunement with the World." *College English* 58 (1986): 893–913.

———. *Common Ground: Dialogue, Understanding, and the Teaching of Composition*. Englewood Cliffs, NJ: Prentice, 1993.

Spilka, Rachel. "Influencing Workplace Practice: A Challenge for Professional Writing Specialists in Academia." *Writing in the Workplace: New Research Perspectives*. Carbondale: Southern Illinois UP, 1993. 207–19.

Star, Susan Leigh, and James R. Griesemer. "Institutional Ecology, 'Translations' and Boundary Objects: Amateurs and Professionals in Berkeley's Museum of Vertebrate Zoology, 1907–1939." *Social Studies of Science* 19 (1989): 387–420.

Steinem, Gloria. "Do You Know This Woman? She Knows You—A Profile of Alice Walker." *Ms.* 10.12 (June 1982): 35+.

———. "If Men Could Menstruate." *Outrageous Acts and Everyday Rebellions*. New York: Signet, 1983. 69–87.

———. "I Was a Playboy Bunny." *Outrageous Acts and Everyday Rebellions*. New York: Signet, 1983. 1–23.

———. *Outrageous Acts and Everyday Rebellions*. New York: Signet, 1983.

———. "What If Freud Were Phyllis? or The Watergate of the Western World." *Moving Beyond Words*. New York: Simon, 1994: 19–90.

———. "Womb Envy, Testyria, and Breast Castration Anxiety." *Ms.* (March/April): 49–56.

Suchan, Jim. "Response to Mohan Limaye: The Need for Contextually Based Research." *Journal of Business Communication* 30 (1993): 473–76.

Sullivan, Patricia A., and James E. Porter. "On Theory, Practice, and Method: Toward a Heuristic Research Methodology for Professional Writing." *Writing in the Workplace: New Research Perspectives*. Ed. Rachel Spilka. Carbondale: Southern Illinois UP, 1993. 220–37.

Swales, John. *Genre Analysis: English in Academic and Research Settings*. Cambridge: Cambridge UP, 1990.

Swales, John, and H. Najjar. "The Writing of Research Articles: Where to Put the Bottom Line." *Written Communication* 4 (1987): 175–91.

Swartz, Omar. "Praxis." *Encyclopedia of Rhetoric and Composition: Communication from Ancient Times to the Information Age*. Ed. Theresa Enos. New York: Garland, 1996. 553.

Thralls, Charlotte, and Nancy Roundy Blyler. "The Social Perspective and Professional Communication: Diversity and Directions in Research." *Professional Communication: The Social Perspective*. Newbury Park, CA: Sage, 1993. 3–34.

Tobin, Lad. "Introduction: How the Writing Process Was Born— And Other Conversion Narratives." *Taking Stock: The Writing Process Movement in the '90s*. Ed. Lad Tobin and Thomas Newkirk. Portsmouth, NH: Boynton, 1994. 1–14.

Toulmin, Stephen. "Literary Theory, Philosophy of Science, and Persuasive Discourse: Thoughts from a Neo-premodernist." Interview with Gary A. Olson. *Philosophy, Rhetoric, Literary Criticism: (Inter)views*. Ed. Gary A. Olson. Carbondale: Southern Illinois UP, 1994. 194–219.

Trimbur, John. "Consensus and Difference in Collaborative Learning." *College English* 51.6 (1989): 602–16.

———. *Writing with a Purpose*. 11th edition. Boston: Houghton, 1995.

Troyka, Lynn Quitman. *Simon and Schuster Handbook for Writers*. 3rd ed. Englewood Cliffs, NJ: Prentice, 1993.

Uchmanowicz, Pauline. "The $5,000–$25,000 Exchange." *College English* 57 (April 1995): 426–47.

Vahapassi, Anneli. "The Domain of School Writing." *The IEA Study of Written Composition* I. International Studies in Educational Achievement: Vol. 5. Ed. T. P. Gorman, and Alan C. Purves. Oxford: Pergammon, 1988. 15–40.

Van Nostrand, A. D. "A Genre Map of R&D Knowledge Production for the U.S. Department of Defense." *Genre and the New Rhetoric*. Ed. Aviva Freedman and Peter Medway. Bristol, PA: Taylor, 1994. 133–45.

Voss, Ralph F. "Janet Emig's *The Composing Process of Twelfth Graders*: a Reassessment." *College Composition and Communication* 34.3: 278– 83.

Vygotsky, L. S. *Mind in Society: The Development of Higher Psychological Processes*. Ed. Michael Cole, et al. Cambridge: Cambridge UP, 1987.

———. *Thought and Language*. Cambridge: MIT P, 1962.

Walker, Alice. "Beauty: When the Other Dancer Is the Self." *Ms.* 11.11 (May 1983): 70+. Rpt. in *In Search of Our Mothers' Gardens: Womanist Prose*. New York: Harcourt, 1983. 384–93.

———. "In Search of Our Mothers' Gardens." *Ms.* 2.11 (May 1974): 64+.

Walker, Alice, and Pratibha Parmar. *Warrior Marks: Female Genital Mutilation and the Sexual Blinding of Women*. New York: Harcourt, 1993.

Wallace, David L., and Helen Rothschild Ewald. "Mutuality: Alternative Pedagogies in Rhetoric and Composition Classrooms." Manuscript under review.

Ward, Irene. *Literacy, Ideology, and Dialogue: Towards a Dialogic Pedagogy*. Albany, NY: State U of New York P, 1994.

Warnock, John. "Process/Product." *Encyclopedia of Rhetoric and Composition*. Ed. T. Enos. New York: Garland, 1966.

Welch, Kathleen. *The Contemporary Reception of Classical Rhetoric: Appropriations of Ancient Discourse*. Hillsdale, NJ: Erlbaum, 1990.

Wells, Susan. "Rogue Cops and Health Care: What Do We Want from Public Writing." *College Composition and Communication* 47 (1996): 325–41.

White, Hayden. *The Form of the Content: Narrative Discourse and Historical Representation*. Baltimore: Johns Hopkins UP, 1987.

———. *Tropics of Discourse: Essays in Cultural Criticism*. Baltimore: Johns Hopkins UP, 1978.

Whyte, William Foote. Introduction. *Participatory Action Research*. Ed. William Foote Whyte. Newbury Park, CA: Sage, 1991. 7–15.

———, ed. *Participatory Action Research*. Newbury Park, CA: Sage, 1991.

Whyte, William Foote, Davydd J. Greenwood, and Peter Lazes. "Participatory Action Research: Through Practice to Science in Social Research." *Participatory Action Research*. Ed. William Foote Whyte. Newbury Park, CA: Sage, 1991. 19–55.

Winsor, Dorothy A. *Writing Like an Engineer: A Rhetorical Education*. Mahwah, NJ: Erlbaum, 1996.

Winterowd, W. Ross. "Rediscovering the Essay." *JAC* 8 (1988): 146–57.

Witte, Stephen P. "Context, Text, Intertext: Toward a Constructivist Semiotic of Writing." *Written Communication* 9 (1992): 237–308.

Wolf, Naomi. *The Beauty Myth*. New York: Morrow, 1991.

———. *Fire with Fire: The New Female Power and How to Use It*. New York: Fawcett Columbine, 1993.

Wolf, Thia. "Conflict as Opportunity in Collaborative Praxis." *Writing With: New Directions in Collaborative Teaching, Learning, and Research*. Ed. Sally Barr Reagan, Thomas Fox, and David Bleich. Albany: State U of New York P, 1994. 91–110.

Woolf, Virginia. *A Room of One's Own*. New York: Harcourt, 1929.

Wright, Sewall. "Evolution in Mendelian Populations." *Genetics* 16 (1931): 97–159.

———. "The Roles of Mutation, Inbreeding, Crossbreeding and Selection in Evolution." *Proceedings of the Sixth International Congress of Genetics* 1 (1932): 356–66.

Young, Richard. "Arts, Crafts, Gifts and Knacks: Some Disharmonies in the New Rhetoric." *Reinventing the Rhetorical Tradition*. Ed. Aviva Freeman and Ian Pringle. Pembroke, ON: Canadian Council of Teachers of English, 1980. 53–60.

Contributors

Nancy Blyler is a professor of English in the rhetoric and professional communication program at Iowa State University. She has coedited, with Charlotte Thralls, *Professional Communication: The Social Perspective* and authored, with David Mair, *Strategies for Technical Communication*. She was the 1995 recipient of the NCTE Award for Best Article on History or Theory of Technical or Scientific Communication.

John Clifford is a dean of the College of Liberal Arts at the University of North Carolina at Wilmington, where he teaches writing, literature, and theory. He is the coeditor, with John Schilb, of *Writing Theory and Critical Theory*. His essay "Testing the Limit of Tolerance in a Democratic Classroom" appears in *Narrative as Knowledge*. *Making Literature Matter*, a textbook written with John Schilb, will appear in 1999.

Barbara Couture is a professor of English at Washington State University. She is the author of *Toward a Phenomenological Rhetoric: Writing, Profession, and Altruism*; the editor of and contributor to *Functional Approaches to Writing: Research Perspectives* and *Professional Writing: Toward a College Curriculum*; and the coauthor, with Jone Rymer Goldstein, of *Cases for Technical and Professional Writing*, which won the NCTE Excellence in Technical and Scientific Communication Award for Best Book.

Nancy C. DeJoy is an assistant professor of English at Millikin University, where she helped to develop the first-year Program in Critical Reading, Writing, and Researching. In 1994, she revived the Summer Seminar in Rhetoric and Composition, and she has received a number of teaching awards and honors, including Millikin University's Faculty Friend to Students Award for her work against sexual assault on campus. She is the editor of *Composition Chronicle*.

Sidney I. Dobrin is the director of Writing Programs at the University of Florida and coedits *JAC: A Journal of Composition Theory*. He is the author of *Constructing Knowledges: The Politics of Theory-Building and*

Pedagogy in Composition. He is currently coauthoring, with Christian Weisser, *Natural Discourse: Composition Studies and Environmental Theory* and coediting *Ecocomposition: Theoretical and Pedagogical Approaches.*

Elizabeth Ervin is an assistant professor of English at the University of North Carolina at Wilmington, where she teaches a variety of classes in writing, rhetoric, and women's studies. She has most recently published in *Composition Studies* and *Rhetoric Review* and is currently doing research on issues related to public discourse, public intellectualism, and understandings of "civic space."

Helen Rothschild Ewald is an associate professor in the Department of English at Iowa State University. She teaches courses in composition and rhetoric, especially courses dealing with pedagogy. Her research has appeared in journals such as *College Composition and Communication, JAC: A Journal of Composition Theory,* and the *Journal of Business Communication.*

David Foster is a professor in the Department of English at Drake University, where he teaches courses in composition, nineteenth- and twentieth-century British literature, and literary/discourse theory. He is particularly interested in studying how students develop as writers, and he has published articles in a variety of journals on topics such as postmodernist rhetoric, aesthetics, and pedagogical theory and practice.

Debra Journet is a professor and the chair of the Department of English at the University of Louisville, where she works in the doctoral program in rhetoric and composition. Her research focuses on narrative, genre, and the rhetoric of sciences and has appeared in journals such as *Written Communication, Social Epistemology, Mosaic,* and *Technical Communication Quarterly.*

Thomas Kent teaches rhetorical and literary theory in the Department of English at Iowa State University. He is the author of two books, *Paralogic Rhetoric: A Theory of Communicative Interaction* and *Interpretation and Genre: The Role of Generic Perception in the Study of Narrative Texts.*

Gary A. Olson is a professor of English and the coordinator of the graduate program in rhetoric and composition at the University of South Florida. His most recent book, with Lynn Worsham, is *Race, Rhetoric, and the Postcolonial.*

Joseph Petraglia is an associate professor of rhetoric and writing in the Department of English at Texas Christian University. He is the author of *Reality by Design: The Rhetoric and Technology of Authenticity in Education* and the editor of *Reconceiving Writing, Rethinking Writing Instruction.*

George Pullman is an associate professor in the Department of English at Georgia State University. He has published articles in various journals, including *Rhetoric Review, Rhetoric Society Quarterly,* and *JAC: A Journal of Composition Theory.* He is currently working with Lynée Gaillet on an interactive hypertextual edition of *The Present State of Scholarship in Historical and Contemporary Rhetoric.*

David Russell is an associate professor of English at Iowa State University. He has authored *Writing in the Academic Disciplines, 1870–1990: A Curricular History* and has coedited, with Charles Bazerman, *Landmark Essays in Writing Across the Curriculum* and *The Activity of Writing/The Writing of Activity,* a special issue of *Mind, Culture, and Activity.*

John Schilb is Culbertson Chair of Writing at Indiana University. He is the author of *Between the Lines: Relating Composition Theory and Literary Theory* and the coeditor, with Patricia Harkin, of *Contending with Words: Composition and Rhetoric in a Postmodern Age* and, with John Clifford, of *Writing Theory and Critical Theory.*

Index